Who Should Read This Book?

"Read" may be the wrong word. "Engage" would be better, because this is not so much a book as it is a classic text, and Jewish classics are not read so much as they are engaged. Included here is a classic text of Jewish prayer, spanning 2,000 years of Jewish experience with the world and with God; and nine thoughtful commentaries on that text, each one reaching back in a different way, again through 2,000 years of time. The question ought to be, "Who should engage this book in personal dialogue?"

If you like to pray, or find prayer services baffling: Whether you are Orthodox, Conservative, Reconstructionist, or Reform, you will find that *My People's Prayer Book* tells you what you need to know to pray.

- The Hebrew text here is the most authentic one we have, and the variations among the Jewish movements are described and explained. They are all treated as equally authentic.
- The translation is honest, altogether unique, and outfitted with notes comparing it to others' translations.
- Of special interest is a full description of the *Halakhah* (the "how to") of prayer and the philosophy behind it.

If you are a spiritual seeker or Jewishly curious: If you have wondered what Judaism is all about, the prayer book is the place to begin. It is the one and only book that Jews read each and every day. The commentaries explain how the prayers were born, and synopsize insights of founding Rabbis, medieval authorities, Chasidic masters, and modern theologians. The layout replicates the look of Jewish classics: a text surrounded by many marginal commentaries allowing you to skip back and forth across centuries of insight.

If you are a teacher or a student: This is a perfect book for adult studies, or for youth groups, teenagers, and camps. Any single page provides comparative insight from the length and breadth of Jewish tradition, about the texts that have mattered most in the daily life of the Jewish people.

If you are a scholar: Though written in friendly prose, this book is composed by scholars: professors of Bible, Rabbinics, Medieval Studies, Liturgy, Theology, Linguistics, Jewish Law, Mysticism, and Modern Jewish Thought. No other work summarizes current wisdom on Jewish prayer, drawn from so many disciplines.

If you are not Jewish: You need not be Jewish to understand this book. It provides access for everyone to the Jewish wisdom tradition. It chronicles the ongoing Jewish-Christian dialogue, and the roots of Christian prayer in Christianity's Jewish origins.

The *My People's Prayer Book: Traditional Prayers, Modern Commentaries* series

Prayers of Awe

My People's Passover Haggadah: *Traditional Texts, Modern Commentaries*

My People's Prayer Book

TRADITIONAL PRAYERS, MODERN COMMENTARIES

Vol. 1 — The *Sh'ma* and Its Blessings

EDITED BY RABBI LAWRENCE A. HOFFMAN

COMMENTATORS

MARC BRETTLER	ELLIOT N. DORFF
SUSAN L. EINBINDER	DAVID ELLENSON
JOEL M. HOFFMAN	LAWRENCE A. HOFFMAN
LAWRENCE KUSHNER	DANIEL LANDES
JUDITH PLASKOW	NEHEMIA POLEN

Jewish Lights Publishing
Nashville, Tennessee

My People's Prayer Book: Traditional Prayers, Modern Commentaries Vol. 1 — The Sh'ma *and Its Blessings*

2011 Hardcover Edition

Library of Congress Cataloging-in-Publication Data
My people's prayer book : traditional prayers, modern commentaries / edited and with introductions by Lawrence A. Hoffman.
p.   cm.
Includes the traditional text of the siddur, English translation, and commentaries.
Contents: vol. 1. The Sh'ma and its blessings.
ISBN-13: 978-1-879045-79-8 (hc)
ISBN-10: 1-879045-79-6 (hc)
1. Siddur.   2. Siddurim — Texts.   3. Judaism — Liturgy — Texts.
I. Hoffman, Lawrence A., 1942–.   II. Siddur. English & Hebrew.
BM674.39.M96   1997
296.4'5 — dc21   97-26836
                                        CIP
ISBN-13: 978-1-68336-209-8 (pbk)

First Edition
10 9 8 7

Manufactured in the United States of America
✿ Printed on recycled paper.
Jacket design: Glenn Suokko
Text design: Reuben Kantor

Published by Jewish Lights Publishing
A Division of LongHill Partners, Inc.
An Imprint of Turner Publishing Company
4507 Charlotte Avenue, Suite 100
Nashville, TN 37209
Tel: (615) 255-2665
www.jewishlights.com

Contents

Contents

Commentators

Marc Brettler	*Our Biblical Heritage*
Elliot N. Dorff	*Theological Reflections*
Susan L. Einbinder	*Medieval Wisdom*
David Ellenson	*How the Modern Prayer Book Evolved*
Joel M. Hoffman	*What the Prayers Really Say*
Lawrence A. Hoffman	*Origins of the Liturgy*
Lawrence Kushner and Nehemia Polen	*Chasidic and Mystical Perspectives*
Daniel Landes	*The Halakhah of Prayer*
Judith Plaskow	*Feminist Theology*

Minhag Ami

Our Diary of Prayer Across the Centuries

PRAYER AS JEWISH ART: THE EXPRESSION OF THE JEWISH SOUL

Of all the books that line the shelves of a Jewish library, it is the Siddur, not the Talmud and not even the Bible, that Jews know best. The prayer book is our Jewish diary of the centuries, a collection of prayers composed by generations of those who came before us, as they endeavored to express the meaning of their lives. To know the prayer book is to know our history from within. It is to be in touch with the soul of the Jewish people, as it has evolved in good times and in bad, through persecutions and Golden Ages. The Siddur is our encounter with 3,000 years of fate, condensed in a form available to the average Jew, who, today no less than yesterday, may have insufficient time and knowledge to dip deeply into Talmud, Midrash, philosophy and Kabbalah, but who can capture the essence of the Jewish spirit just by reading through the pages of our liturgy.

It can equally be called the spiritual "tel" of the Jewish People. A tel is an archeological term for a mound of earth that turns out to house successive layers of civilization that have been covered over by the sands of time. Archaeologists dig down deep into the dirt to retrieve secrets of the past buried in its physical detritus: clay pots, stone slabs, fragments of homes, jewelry, and even old toys. How could it be, we wonder, that whole civilizations lived and died here, one on top of the other? How could so much desert sand have accumulated, covering up centuries of life — and not just once, but over and over again, giving the lie to the vain hopes of emperors and generals that their petty conquests and peculiar distractions would prove eternal? They are all gone now, just as, perhaps, even our own civilization will be gone in a thousand years.

So too, like it or not, the material stuff of Jewish culture too is ravaged by time. What is left of our ancient synagogues, or even of the Temple? Or of King Herod's magnificent structures where he and his courtiers would go for a weekend's rest and respite? The entire city of David now lies buried below the humble huts of a simple Arab village. We look with amazement at the unearthed remnants of Hasmonean houses, once the homes of the Maccabees (no less), who thought their Jewish commonwealth would last forever. In Ashkelon, you can sit in a park and eat lunch on enormous fragments of Roman columns, toppled by time and resting around the grounds like so many giant boulders, as if no one had dedicated a lifetime to carving their magnificent marble capitals, as if no one had ever walked through portals they once guarded, as if the glory of Rome itself had never come to rest here. But it did. The material things of all cultures, including Jewish culture, come and go.

Sir Isaac Newton was right: Everything physical obeys the law of entropy; all we build turns, in the end, to chaos, a reminder of the *tohu vavohu*, the "emptiness and void" that God once saw when the world came to be.

But Newton was not altogether right. The evolutionary spiral that gave us human consciousness, and then religious quest and moral striving, is hardly a dissipation into nothingness. If anything it is the opposite: A demonstration of the long-term progress away from chaos and toward ever-more complex organisms. Perhaps for every failure of material culture, there is an irreversible step forward in our spiritual destiny. Jews, at least, who are taught by prophets to put our faith "not in might and not in power, but in God's spirit," sense that this is so. And we point, for evidence, to the spiritual tel of Jewish time, to the accumulated reservoir of Jewish hopes and dreams: to our Siddur, our prayer book.

Some years ago, a small Midwestern town was home to a quiet unassuming man who used to say, "By myself, I am a prayer book." He had been through Hitler's camps, sustained (he insisted) by Jewish liturgy. "I was stronger than the other prisoners," he explained, "so I survived, whereas they all died, or were killed, and the thought occurred to me that I alone would remain, just me, no one else — I would be the very last Jew on the face of the earth. How, I wondered, should I prepare for the ultimate possibility that the Nazis would someday come to their deserved end, and some unknown liberator would charge me with the task of perpetuating, singlehandedly, the destiny of God's chosen people? What would I teach the next generation about what it had been like to be a Jew?

"Then it came to me. I would memorize the prayers. Everything Jewish is there, after all, and I already knew lots of them anyway, so as new inmates joined me in my barracks, I would ask them, 'What comes after *Ya'aleh v'yavo?*' 'What is the last line of that prayer we say when we unwrap the Torah?' Things like that. In the field, awake at night, even in the line-up — once, while watching them hang a man — I went endlessly over the prayers, mentally noting what I still didn't know, the parts I still had to memorize; but as the years went on, I got most of it, maybe even all of it. Yes, by myself, I am a prayer book, a 'human prayer book.'"

That man was so right! Thank God, he never had to rise to the awful task he feared. He was not the last Jew. But had he been, he could very well have begun Judaism all over again with the Siddur, for nothing better captures who we were and who we are.

Prayer books fascinate me, therefore, as they should fascinate us all. As the "human prayer book" from the camps demonstrates, they are only accidentally "books."

Jewish prayer was once an oral thing. We used to think that in the beginning, there was at least a single and authentic, original and official manuscript, something some great Rabbi must have squirreled away, taking it out from time to time to let people know what words they should say. How else could they have checked to determine the proper words of prayer? How else could Rabbis in antiquity have held the line against the multitude of errors that must have crept into Jewish practice, in an age when there were no mass-produced printed texts that worshippers could follow to make sure the person leading prayer was saying the right thing?

But no such document came into being until centuries after the service was already formed. The prayer book was no book back then. It was only an oral heritage. It is hard to fathom how very different things were in the first and second centuries, when the enterprise of collective Jewish prayer was getting under way. But we will never understand our own prayer practice until we grasp the way it was, and is no more.

THE WAY IT ALL BEGAN: THE JAZZ OF WORSHIP

With no official written record to consult, there could be no mistakes, not the way we think of mistakes, that is, as a deviation from the single proper version. Every synagogue housed its own prayer practice, every *Sh'liach Tsibbur* (the "prayer leader") had his own version of the text. In fact, every single service might well feature innovative language, by design or by default, as the same prayer leader might forget what he had done yesterday, or improvise anew the theme of a prayer that captured his attention for the moment.

The Rabbis of that era lived in a time when culture, generally, depended on oral performance, something like good jazz artistry today. The great jazz players never play the same thing the same way twice, even though you can recognize the same song every time they play it. So too with public performance elsewhere in the Greco-Roman world, from the days when wandering troubadours recited Homeric epics, to the rabbinic era somewhat later when leaders of prayer recited words of worship morning, noon and night.

The Rabbis called this improvisation *kavvanah*, a word we usually translate as inner directedness of the heart, a proper balance, we believe, to the numbed rote that mumbling through the prayer book can become. It may be that for us. Indeed, it largely is. We have a book, after all. But without one, there would have been no rote, except, of course, for worship leaders who fell short of their art and were unable to improvise at all. They would just have memorized whatever they had done before, and kept on doing it. That there were such people, we know from the Rabbis' warning, "A person's blessings distinguish a sage from an ignoramus." At stake was not whether people said the *right blessing*, but whether they said it the *right way*. Only scholars improvised; everyone else made do with the same words over and over again. "People should always try to add something new in their prayers," the Rabbis warned.

But improvisation in jazz depends on a melody line to improvise. A jazz ensemble plays together even when each member plays alone because the improvisations stretch the boundaries of the opening melody that is laid down first as the ensemble plays together. Painters too require a carefully constructed norm against which they measure what they do. Every single one of Van Gogh's sunflower petals is different, but they are all recognizably sunflowers because Van Gogh practiced endlessly to get the basic structure of the flower down just right before he dared paint his endless variations on it. So too, our prayers, even in an oral age with no printed word to fall back on, were not solely a matter of whim.

To some extent, the men and women of the Bible (long before the Rabbis) had once prayed by whim. They prayed to God when they felt moved to, and in any way they felt comfortable. Moses asks for Miriam's health in five simple Hebrew words, *El na r'fa na lah* ("God, please send her healing"). When she cannot have children, Hannah frames a bargaining prayer: if God gives her a son, she will dedicate him to the priesthood. And Solomon, newly crowned as the great King David's successor, asks for wisdom. Others who want healing, progeny or statecraft do not follow suit, because prayer was still purely personal. It was a matter of individual choice, not mandated worship designed for use by everyone on certain occasions. Even Moses, Hannah and Solomon (who do pray) give their prayers only once, and according to pure invention of the moment. This is not liturgy, the way we practice it today. It is pure improvisation. There is nothing recognizably fixed about it.

The Rabbis change all that. It is hard to say exactly when, but liturgy was probably in place, at least in rabbinic circles, by the last century B.C.E. or the first century C.E. The word "liturgy" comes from the Greek, and means "public works." It is akin to the Hebrew word *avodah*, which also means "work," but refers explicitly to "the public work of the Temple cult, the sacrificial system." The Rabbis transform private prayer of the moment into a public work like the cult: the honoring of God by the offering of our lips.

First, it was set as to time. Second, there were rules about how to do it. And third, each service was structured as to a succession of themes that had to be addressed by the oral interpreters.

What the melody line is to jazz, the thematic development is to rabbinic prayer. For instance, the *Sh'ma* must come before the *Amidah*, not afterward. As a biblical quotation, it is fixed as to wording, but it is sandwiched in a structure that the Bible does not know: Blessings before and blessings after; each blessing expressing a different theme. Prayer leaders knew the themes, so that whatever words they used as improvisatory text for the day, their choice reflected the proper order of topics. People came expecting them, and they got them. That was the fixed part of liturgy. Sunflowers have single stems with lots of petals, not the other way around. And Jewish prayer has its own proper structure, played out in time, first one theme and then another, until slowly but surely the whole service is completed, like a piece of jazz that starts somewhere, goes somewhere and ends somewhere, albeit with no predictability regarding each and every note the performers choose in executing the pattern. What notes are to jazz, words are to prayer. The words, then, varied; the overall thematic sequence stayed the same.

If improvised wording was *kavvanah* (the "something new" that sages offered when they prayed), the structure of the service was called *keva*, fixity, predictability, order. Proper prayer combined them both.

FROM ORALITY TO POETRY

By the end of the second century C.E., the rules had multiplied, and were recorded in legal literature that was just coming into being — first, in a relatively small work called the Mishnah, and then, in a much larger compilation, an extensive commentary to the Mishnah called either the Gemara or the Talmud. There are two Talmuds actually, one from Babylonia (modern-day Iraq) written in about the sixth or seventh century, and another from the Land of Israel a century or two earlier. The Babylonian Talmud especially elaborated the growing body of details regarding such things as when to say "Amen": only when hearing someone else say a blessing, not after saying it yourself; or, how to frame a blessing: God should be addressed directly (*Barukh atah*, "Blessed are You . . ."), named (*Adonai eloheinu*, "Adonai our God") and titled (*melekh ha'olam*, "king of the universe"). Clearly, *keva* was growing at the expense of *kavvanah*, possibly because in the early years, worship was the domain of the Rabbis who were a small and elite group, perfectly capable of improvising prayers for each other; whereas later, services were held in synagogues far from immediate rabbinic supervision, and the rabbinic class itself was large enough that the radical freedom of the founders had to be restricted.

Even then, however, several ways of doing a single prayer were known and welcomed. Rav Papa, for instance (a fourth-century talmudic authority), regularly remarks on alternatives, without attempting to root out one and institutionalize the other. And the Rabbis of the Talmud frequently offer different views on what a particular prayer is supposed to be. What is the "Blessing of Song," they ask. One thinks it is, *Nishmat kol chai* ("Let the soul of every living being [bless You . . .])"; another thinks it is *Y'hall'lukha* ("[Let all your creatures] praise you. . . . "). Our liturgy today contains both options.

Rav Ashi (died 425 C.E.) chanced upon a town one day, where members of the local synagogue asked him to say the *Kiddusha Rabba* ("The Great *Kiddush*"), the *Kiddush* that we say still for Shabbat lunch on Saturday after services. He had never heard of it; so he made it up, saying the blessing for wine, and then pausing to see how he was doing. When one old man, presumably a native who knew what to expect, nodded, Rav Ashi breathed a sigh of relief. His blessing could not have been what people were used to hearing. But the old man nodded anyway, not because Rav Ashi had said precisely the single set of words that he had in his head from prior Shabbat afternoons; but because he knew, as everyone did, that Rav Ashi had fulfilled the requirement of *keva* (saying a blessing on the proper theme): while not the most exciting variation imaginable, his blessing had been over wine when wine was about to be drunk.

Others, however, were developing more extensive ways of doing the Great *Kiddush* and other prayers as well. They were a generation of poets, particularly in Eretz Yisrael, beginning, perhaps, in the fourth century, and reaching a golden age of classical liturgical poetry a century or two later. We know some of their names. Yose bar Yose, Yannai and Eliezer Kalir are the very best known, Kalir especially, whom later generations either loved or hated, but certainly respected as a genius with the Hebrew language. As the rules about liturgy multiplied, and as prayer became more standardized, less free, and less creative, the yearning for "something new every day" was directed into poetry that could be inserted into the fixed formulas that were developing.

Some scholars explain the rise of poetry as a response to persecution, believing that our normal liturgy was banned by Christian monarchs, and that, in response, we invented poetry to take its place. That theory, once popular, is less widely held today. It has the benefit of being substantiated by medieval documentation, but we know now that people in the Middle Ages regularly explained novelty by imagining some sort of persecution as its motivating element. Medieval writers said similar things about the *Haftarah* too: Surely prophetic readings had been added, only because the weekly reading from Torah had been banned. But all of these accounts came centuries after the events that they tried to explain. They say more about the jaundiced view of Jewish history that their authors had than they do about the real causes for poetry or the *Haftarah*. Eliezer Kalir himself, who knew precisely what he was doing, says, "With God's approval, I shall utter riddles, giving Israel pleasure." He wrote for fun. He loved the Hebrew tongue, sought new uses of biblical precedent, and composed his poems for thoughtful worshippers who would recognize the clever use he made of this word from the book of Job, which he juxtaposed to that word from the book of Ruth, or how he played with a phrase from Genesis, and then with another from Joshua or II Chronicles — all combined according to backward or forward acrostics, along with the poet's own name spelled out somewhere along the way. If he couldn't find the right word, he made it up, coining Hebrew terms the way Shakespeare put together Elizabethan English in memorable lines that we now take for granted.

Centuries later, Kalir would be pilloried by purists who hated having to decipher his linguistic inventiveness. "Even the angels cannot understand what he has to say," said Rabbi Jacob Emden (1697–1776), perhaps the most learned rabbi of his generation. But Kalir reflected the artistry of his era. He lived in what we call the Byzantine period, a time when Christianity reigned supreme, especially in Constantinople. The Pope in Rome was merely one of several regional patriarchs then, in a city that had been stormed by Visigoths in 410, threatened by Attila the Hun in 452, and systematically sacked by Vandals three years later. By contrast, the Patriarch of Constantinople directed Christian life from the city that functioned as the real capital of the empire. Together, the heads of the empire and the church launched a building campaign to glorify their city. Visitors today still marvel at their mosaics: one tiny gleaming stone from here, and another from there — millions of them, all juxtaposed to form a brilliant whole. Kalir, in Eretz Yisrael, knew full well this Byzantine artistry. Palestine (as it was then called) was still within the orbit of the eastern church. So Kalir did with words what Byzantine builders were doing with stones.

That is how the liturgy came to be: First, mostly *ad hoc* oral improvisation around a structural core, by a rabbinic elite that was well schooled in Jewish sources; then, growing regulation, as standardization became the norm; then poetry (called *piyyutim*; singular *piyyut*) by poets (*payy'tanim*; singular *payy'tan*) who adapted the artistic norms of Byzantine art to Jewish practice. Much was fixed; but much was not. Oral performance was still what mattered most. There were no books, save, perhaps, for what we must imagine prayer leaders prepared for themselves: Copies of new poetry, at least — they couldn't improvise that — and maybe also private prayer books reminding them of the increasing bulk of fixed prayer language that was customary in their synagogue, and into which the poems would somehow be embedded.

PRAYER AS POLEMIC: THE POLITICS OF PRAYER BOOKS

All that changed by the ninth century. How we pray depends on more than theological fiat or the regulations and logic that comprise the body of Jewish law known as *Halakhah*. It grows quite naturally out of the way we live. Prayer books cannot come into being without a certain social structure. There must be enough centralized authority for someone to wield the power of determining what to include and what to omit from the book's pages; and there must also be a modicum of technological competence: at least a way to write a book, no mean feat in the days when writing was done by a stylus on unwieldy scrolls made of animal hide.

In 632, Mohammed died, having launched a conquest that even now takes the breath away. By 634, Muslims had conquered all of Arabia; by 642, all of Persia; by 649, Egypt. By the end of the century, Islam had reached India in the east and was about to enter Spain. Its grasp of the Mediterranean was so complete that a Muslim geographer boasted, "The Christians cannot float a plank on it." For a long time, the Islamic empire was plagued by dynastic instability, but by 750, a new ruling class called the Abbasids built a city known as Baghdad, and established the titular head of both empire and faith, the Caliph, there.

Almost overnight, the establishment of Baghdad revived what was left of the old rabbinate in old Babylonia. Suddenly it emerged with more power, prestige and wealth than it had ever known. Academies sprung up in the surrounding age-old cities of Sura and Pumbedita, and the chief rabbis who were in residence there adopted a new title, "Gaon" — roughly equivalent to "Excellency." The Caliph was dictating details of Islamic law and custom to faithful Muslims all across the empire; so too, his Jewish equivalent, the Gaon, began writing to Jews as if he had the authority to tell them what to do. Many turned a deaf ear, especially in Eretz Yisrael, where Palestinian Jews had prayed for centuries without Babylonian interference. They more or less thanked the Gaon for sharing, telling him that local custom outranked law, especially Babylonian law which was based on the Babylonian Talmud, not the Palestinian Talmud.

About 860, a Gaon named Amram tried to change all that. When Jews in Spain wrote to him asking him to provide the proper norms for Jewish prayer, he prepared a complete list of prayers and the rules of how they were to be performed: when to say them, whether to stand or sit while reciting them, what words to use, what errors to avoid. Thanks to the strict hierarchy that characterized Islamic society, and the model of the Caliph dictating practice from on top, Amram had the requisite social environment to compose the book, send it, and claim the right to represent all of Jewish tradition in ways that no scholar of talmudic times ever would have abrogated unto himself. He also had the technological support he needed. It was becoming possible to write books, not scrolls, books that a prayer leader could quickly rifle through to find the right page, not roll or unroll endlessly as we still do, when working with a scroll such as the *m'gillah* or the Torah itself. Amram polemicized especially against the rival Palestinians, pausing regularly in his instructions to tell his Spanish colleagues not to pray the way the Palestinians did. That is how the first prayer book was born.

Amram's book was copied by scribes all over the Jewish world, and soon became the standard book of Jewish prayer. It reflected what had become Babylonian practice in Amram's academy, locked out Palestinian alternatives, and closed off the creativity that had marked Jewish prayer for centuries. From now on, in most places, people prayed the way Amram said they should. There were some rivals, mostly another prayer book written by an even greater Gaon, Saadiah, some fifty years afterward. But Saadiah wrote his instructions in Arabic, whereas Amram had used Aramaic, the language of the Babylonian Talmud. Jews in Europe knew the latter, not the former. Except in parts of Spain, where Islam held sway and Jews used Arabic freely, Saadiah was virtually ignored, while Amram's prayer book carried the day.

Palestinian Jews ignored Amram's edict as long as they could. Amram had no use for poetry, for instance; poetry was a distinctive trait of Palestine, not Babylonia. True, the golden age of Kalir was long gone, but in Eretz Yisrael, poetry was still being written. Most of all, Palestinian Jews hesitated to canonize any single version of their prayers as the only proper one. Without the model of the Caliph bent on molding universal Muslim practice to his own way of doing things, Palestinian Jewish worshippers retained their old way of balancing fixity with creativity. They too had abandoned the purely oral form of jazz-like improvisation with which rabbinic prayer had begun, but they still allowed for considerable variation here and there, whereas Amram did not. In any event, in 1099, when the Crusaders conquered Palestine, the Jews there fled. They returned a century later when Christian rule ended, but by then, they had lived in the diaspora for one hundred years or more, enough time to adopt the Amram prayer code and forget the ways of prayer that their Palestinian ancestors had preferred.

We would know little of the Palestinian alternative, were it not for an archeological discovery at the turn of the twentieth century. Scholars stumbled across a cache of documents in the old synagogue of Cairo, many of them dating to the geonic era, and representing the heritage of Jews from Palestine. Among the debris were pages and pages of liturgical poems, as well as bits and pieces of Palestinian prayer books. That find is called the Genizah, and its fragments tell the tale of the long-lost Palestinian alternative, destroyed by history, but recovered by scholars to remind us just how late in time it was that a single prayer book successfully merged Jewish practice into a relatively homogeneous whole.

PRAYER AS MARKETING: THE IMPACT OF THE PRINTING PRESS

Without mass printing, the prayer book still went through many changes, not all of them intentional. For one thing, scribes made mistakes. Then too, local poets inserted poems into their own community's practice, but not necessarily anywhere else, so that over the years, different ways of doing prayer emerged in every geographic area where sustained Jewish life was found. We call each way of prayer a *minhag* (a "Rite"): *Minhag Carpentras,* for instance, the Rite of the City of Carpentras in southern France; or, on a larger scale, *Minhag Ashkenaz* and *Minhag Sefarad,* the way of prayer for Ashkenazi (that is, Franco-German Jews) or the way of prayer for Jews in Spain.

With the discovery of moveable type in the fifteenth century, the centuries-long trend toward standardization reached its zenith. Now even the local *minhagim,* or rites, were doomed. Using scholarship, common practice, commercialism, and even sloppy research or slovenly typesetting, printers would set plates for a book, and thousands of copies would roll off the press, quickly saturating markets far away from where the printing had been done. Handwritten manuscripts could not compete. Versions of prayers that never got printed were relegated to the dusty shelves of manuscript collections in the Vatican, St. Petersburg, Cambridge, or an occasional monastery somewhere which happened to get its hands on something old and Jewish, and filed it away for one reason or another. We continue to rescue these manuscripts from oblivion, but our Siddur has by now been standardized, thanks first to Amram and the Babylonians, and thereafter to European printing presses. There are exceptions: the prayer books of Jews in China, for instance, unaffected by European presses, and copied with Hebrew and with Chinese letters either in books or in fan-like form typical of Chinese literary custom. But mostly, Jewish liturgy has never recovered from the onslaught of the printing press, and the broad reach of Europeans who colonized the world over, and transported their own prayer practice to Jews who could not withstand their more advanced technology.

But even as the printing press destroyed one kind of creativity, it enhanced another. The Gutenberg revolution coincided roughly with the demise of Jewish life in Spain, the expulsion of Jews throughout the Mediterranean, and the rise of independent Jewish thought especially in areas under the Ottoman Turks, where Jews from

Spain had settled. Among the things Spanish émigrés had carried with them was the Kabbalah, which reached its height under Isaac Luria in the town of Safed in northern Palestine. Because of printing, Jewish prayer would never again know the jazz-like quality of its early years when oral performance was everything, and verbal versatility made each service special. But printing paved the way for kabbalistic innovation to spread like wildfire, and the very fact that it could etch particular words as if in stone lent credence to the mystics' claim that every word mattered to the point where changing a single vowel might ruin the secret message of a prayer.

Lurianic Kabbalah changed the entire theory of why Jews pray, and it could never have done so without the technological support of a printing press, which produced an inflexible set of words on paper for people to focus on. Prayers were said to have secret meaning beyond the obvious. The trick was to know what that meaning was. So kabbalistic prayer books appeared, complete with meditations telling worshippers how to read each prayer.

People slowly realized that control of printing presses meant control of Jewish practice on a scale hitherto undreamed of. Once a given set of prayers existed on printers' plates, it became hard to change them; specific forms of prayer were thus soldered into the Jewish spiritual regimen, as if given to Moses on Mount Sinai. People forgot the free reign that oral society had once provided. As the late Middle Ages gave way to modernity, authorities vied with each other to control the presses. In 1617 in Poland, the first Jewish prayer book to be authorized by an official Jewish body, the governing council of Polish Jewry, almost saw the light of day, but Polish Jewry was too ideologically divided to support the project thoroughly, and in 1648, it was savaged by a Cossack revolt led by Bogdan Chmielnicki.

Modern Jewish religious movements have adapted printing to their own ideological needs. Liberal Jews — especially the founders of Reform Judaism, and ultimately of Conservative Judaism also — learned the power of the printing press in creating a *minhag*. Throughout the nineteenth century, every liberal rabbi worth his salt devised a Siddur that remained true to the age-old structure of the Rabbis, but took the liberty of altering the text where modern sentiment dictated and of creating translations or even novel prayers that could become the instant property of millions, because the books in which they were printed were shipped to synagogues all over the world.

Along with printed texts went commentary, also. It was an easy thing to add some notes, maybe an introduction, or even such modern inventions as transliterated Hebrew for people whose Hebrew competence was minimal. Orthodox books especially needed commentary — for instance, a prayer book by the students of Samson Raphael Hirsch, the nineteenth-century German founder of modern Orthodoxy. Hirsch was no reformer, but he shared the reformers' modern sensitivity to age-old ideas and practices that did not comport with modern theology, morality and aesthetics. As long as no one knew what the prayers meant in the vernacular, it had mattered little what they said. But with translation, that luxury was lost. Since moderns wanted prayer books in translation, even Hirsch had to come to terms with prayers that bothered people: the call to return to Zion and rebuild an animal cult, for instance; or *Kol Nidre*, a haunting melody, certainly, but a text suggesting Jews could easily disavow solemn oaths and promises that they made to others. Unable ideologically to alter these inherited texts, Orthodox Jews like Hirsch could at least explain them away when they seemed embarrassing. His followers thus produced a Siddur that reproduces almost all the prayers (it omits *Kol Nidre*, a statement which even they found difficult to cope with) complete with commentary below the line, explaining that the prayers do not always mean what they seem to, when read literally.

PRAYER AS SPIRITUALITY: IN AN AGE OF SPIRITUAL AWAKENING

Most recently, we have seen the proliferation of prayer books and of commentary literature on our prayers, again because of the happy coincidence of technology and of social revolution. The computer has accelerated printing output beyond what anyone could have imagined when we still worked with electric typewriters that demanded laborious rewrites every time a draft was edited, and then manual manipulation of moveable typeface by the printer. Meanwhile, a strong economy and increasing Jewish literacy for over a decade combined with a period of genuine spiritual search to make books on religion one of the fastest growing markets in the publishing industry. The spiritual search is especially worth dwelling on for a moment.

America has always been a religious country. Its ideological founders flirted with the Enlightenment's critique of religion, but had to come to terms also with the Great Awakening (as it came to be called) that was under way as early as 1740. The Great Awakening was a massive religious revival complete with itinerant preachers and evangelical conversions, and it reestablished the primacy of the religious calling on these shores. Less than a century later, a Second Awakening occurred, this one on the expanding frontier where Methodists and Baptists were bringing religion to tent meetings and backwoods towns frequented by circuit riders. By the last half of the nineteenth century, revived Christian piety fueled the growth of abolitionism, a nation-wide YMCA movement, prohibitionism, and even the Social Gospel, a liberal critique of the social evils spawned by the industrial revolution. By the century's end, Protestant pastors whom historians describe as "Princes of the Pulpit" dominated public attention, even (as in the case of William Jennings Bryan) running for president.

Jews have been part and parcel of all this. The Great Awakening made local congregational churches (and, therefore, synagogues) paramount on these shores, and the Second Awakening created religious movements—precisely at the time that German Jews were solidifying a Jewish presence here. When Isaac M. Wise founded his Reform Movement, complete with an American seminary to train his clergy, he was copying, more or less, what every Protestant denomination was doing. By the end of the century, Jews too had "Princes of the Pulpit," and the Reform Movement's accent on prophetic ethics was the Jewish equivalent of the Social Gospel.

The 1925 Scopes Trial seemed to presage the final victory of science over religion. But religious fervor went underground temporarily, emerging more forcefully than ever in the Eisenhower era, when Ike himself told every American to join a local church or synagogue, partly because he was fighting Godless communism, but partly also out of personal conviction (he heralded himself as supremely religious and numbered Billy Graham among his friends). This time, it was the Conservative Movement that benefited most, since eastern European immigrants from 1881 to 1924 had inundated the country, and their sons and daughters, who were just reaching middle adulthood, were largely Conservative.

American Jewish prayer books reflect this religious history. The two most influential early volumes were Isaac Mayer Wise's *Minhag America* ("An American Rite") and David Einhorn's *Olat Tamid* ("An Eternal Light") which vied for authority just as Reform Judaism was emerging as a movement in the 1890s. The *Union Prayer Book* (1894-1895) provided Reform Jewish identity that was perfectly in keeping with that decade's liberal Social Gospel Movement; and the sacred drama of worship that it generated underscored the centrality of the reader — that is, the rabbinic Prince of the Pulpit — who read the service to a passive congregation, as a sort of extension to his sermon. The Conservative liturgy came into being in 1946, providing a liturgical script for Americanized eastern European congregants. It emphasized tradition, but modernized it to match American aesthetics — exactly the self-image of Conservative Jews moving to the suburbs and heeding Eisenhower's call to join a synagogue there. Mordecai Kaplan had established the Reconstructionist Foundation in 1935, a matter of great concern to those who pioneered Conservative liturgy, and who were unhappy about Kaplan's identification of God as a natural force within the universe and his denial of the concept of Jews being the chosen people. The Conservative prayer book was in part a manifesto of Conservative Jewish identity, and in part a denunciation of the alternative that Kaplan, who taught at the Conservative Movement's Jewish Theological Seminary, had provided.

As for the Orthodox, various groups and degrees of Orthodoxy had been present all along. They used different prayer books, since Orthodoxy never crystallized into a single movement the way Reform, Conservative and Reconstructionism did. But Orthodoxy has prospered, especially amid the current surge of religion that has resulted from the widespread spiritual yearning of our time. It is not too much to say that we are living through the Third Great Awakening in American history.

Since the 1970s, then, technological competence and spiritual awakening have generated a remarkable spurt of liturgical activity. And again, it is best to see Jews riding a social wave that carries all of us along, Jew and non-Jew alike. In 1963, a sweeping reform of Catholic liturgy promulgated by an international council at the Vatican (known as Vatican II) brought liturgy to the forefront of Catholic consciousness, and Protestant churches quickly followed suit. Every major Christian denomination convened liturgy committees at precisely the time that the Reform, Conservative and Reconstructionist Movements did. The most thoroughgoing liturgical project, meanwhile, has been Orthodoxy's Artscroll series, which has systematically produced a Jewish liturgical commentary, but only from a single, very traditionalistic perspective.

MINHAG AMI: MY PEOPLE'S PRAYER BOOK

Minhag Ami is part of the religious revival of our times. It seeks to satisfy the spiritual yearning of millions of modern men and women who know there is wisdom and solace in Jewish prayer but find the prayer book inaccessible or even baffling. It provides a traditional Hebrew text; a new and accurate translation (designed to let people know what the prayers actually say); and commentaries written by authors from across the spectrum of Jewish life. Jewish wisdom knows no denominational boundaries, after all; the Torah was given to all Jews at Mount Sinai, not just those identified with one movement rather than another.

What God could give in an instant, alas, takes mere mortals years to prepare. This first volume supplies "The *Sh'ma* and Its Blessings," the first of two central sections in the daily morning service. The next volume will supply the *Amidah*, the second such section, and subsequent volumes will eventually cover the rest of the Siddur. But cover it we will, for we are but the latest link in the chain going back to Amram, the Gaon who began it all.

Written in imperial Baghdad, Amram's prayer book is short on humility. Its author simply assumes he has the single right tradition, which every Jew ought to follow. Saadiah, however, who wrote the second Jewish prayer book of all time, had been born in Egypt, and lived for many years in the Land of Israel, before moving to Babylon and attaining the gaonate. Not naturally given to excessive humility, he had at least experienced the diversity of practice common to Eretz Yisrael, so that when he composed his prayer book, he appended an introduction to it — the first introduction ever used in any Jewish book — in which he sums up the situation that makes a new prayer book necessary. His words form a fitting conclusion here as well. "Of the traditions of our people, regarding prayers and blessings, there are things whose usage has so degenerated that they have been completely forgotten, utterly erased, except among select individuals." The prayer book was becoming a closed book to many, as it has again in our own time. So Saadiah provided the basic text, but aesthetically and scientifically prepared, carefully edited for proper grammar, and outfitted with enlightening commentary, and even translation, here and there, for Jews who knew the vernacular, but little Hebrew.

Such is our goal too. In the end, Saadiah says, "I seek God's help in all the matters that will occupy me here, as I do for the readers who will learn from my work." All of us engaged in *Minhag Ami* pray that the Siddur will once again be open to all Jews, and that we may each share in the richness of the Jewish soul that lies hidden in its pages.

Introduction to the Liturgy
What to Look for in the Service

Liturgy can seem confusing, more like a shapeless mass of verbiage than a carefully constructed whole; a jumble of noise, not a symphony; a blotch of random colors, hardly a masterpiece of art. But prayer *is* an art form, and like the other arts, the first step to appreciation is to recognize the pattern at work within it.

There are three daily services: morning (*Shacharit*), afternoon (*Minchah*), and evening (*Ma'ariv* or *Arvit*). For the sake of convenience, the latter two are usually recited in tandem, one just before dark, and the other immediately after the sun sets. All three follow the same basic structure, but the morning service is the most complete. It is composed of seven consecutive units that build upon each other to create a definitive pattern. Though the words of each unit remained fluid for centuries, the structural integrity of the service has remained sacrosanct since the beginning.

Services are made of prayers, but not all prayers are alike. Some are biblical quotations, ranging in size from a single line to entire chapters, usually psalms. There are rabbinic citations also, chunks of Mishnah or Talmud that serve as a sort of Torah study within the service. Medieval poetry occurs here too, familiar things like *Adon Olam* or older staples marked less by rhyme and rhythm than by clever word plays and alphabetic acrostics. And there are long passages of prose, the work again of medieval spiritual masters, but couched in standard rabbinic style without regard for poetic rules.

Most of all, however, the Siddur is filled with blessings, a uniquely rabbinic vehicle for addressing God, and the primary liturgical expression of Jewish spirituality.

Blessings (known also as *benedictions*, or, in Hebrew, *b'rakhot* — sing., *b'rakhah*) are so familiar that Jewish worshippers take them for granted. We are mostly aware of "short blessings," the one-line formulas that are customarily recited before eating, for instance, or prior to performing a commandment. But there are "long blessings" too, generally whole paragraphs or even sets of paragraphs on a given theme. These are best thought of as small theological essays on such topics as deliverance, the sanctity of time, the rebuilding of Jerusalem, and the like. They sometimes start with the words *Barukh atah Adonai . . .* ("Blessed are You, Adonai . . ."), and then they are easily spotted. But more frequently, they begin with no particular verbal formula, and are hard to identify until their last line, which invariably does say, *Barukh atah Adonai . . .* ("Blessed are You, Adonai . . .") followed by a short synopsis of the blessing's theme (". . . who sanctifies the Sabbath," ". . . who hears prayer," ". . . who redeems Israel," and so forth). This final summarizing sentence is called a *chatimah*, meaning a "seal," like the seal made from a signet ring that seals an envelope.

The bulk of the service as it was laid down in antiquity consists of strings of blessings, one after the other, or of biblical quotations bracketed by blessings that introduce and conclude them. By the tenth century, the creation of blessings largely ceased, and eventually, Jewish law actually opposed the coining of new ones, on the grounds that post-talmudic Judaism was too spiritually unworthy to try to emulate the literary work of the giants of the Jewish past. Not all Jews agree with that assessment today, but the traditional liturgy that forms our text here contains no blessings dated later than the tenth century.

The word we use to refer to all the literary units in the prayer book, without regard to whether they are blessings, psalms, poems, or something else, is *rubric*. A rubric is any discrete building block of the service, sometimes a single prayer (this blessing rather than that, or this quotation, but not that poem), and sometimes a whole set of prayers that stands out in contrast to other sets: The *Sh'ma and Its Blessings,* for instance, the topic of this entire volume, is a large rubric relative to the *Amidah* (the topic of Volume Two). But considered independently, we can say that the *Sh'ma and Its Blessings* subsumes smaller rubrics: the *Sh'ma* itself, for instance (a set of biblical readings); some blessings that bracket it; and the *Bar'khu,* or official call to prayer, that introduces the entire thing.

At the liturgy's core are three large rubrics, not only the two already mentioned (the *Sh'ma* and Its Blessings and the *Amidah* — known also as the *T'fillah* or *Sh'moneh Esreh*), but also the public reading of Torah. The *Sh'ma and Its Blessings* and the *Amidah* were recited every day; Torah is read on Monday and Thursday (market days in antiquity), when crowds were likely to gather in the cities, and on Shabbat and holidays, of course. The *Sh'ma and Its Blessings* is essentially the Jewish creed, a statement of what Jews have traditionally affirmed about God, the cosmos and our human relationship to God and to history. The *Amidah* is largely petitionary. The Torah reading is a recapitulation of Sinai, an attempt to discover the will of God through sacred scripture. Since the *Sh'ma and Its Blessings* begins the official service, it features a communal call to prayer at the beginning: our familiar *Bar'khu.* We should picture these units building upon each other in a crescendo-like manner, as follows:

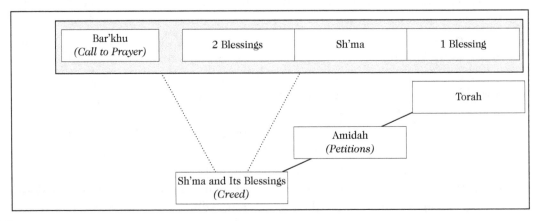

It is, however, hard for individuals who are normally distracted by everyday concerns to constitute a community given over wholeheartedly to prayer. Already in the second century, therefore, we hear of some Rabbis who assembled prior to the actual Call to Prayer in order to sing psalms of praise known as a *Hallel*; and even before that — at home, not the synagogue — it was customary to begin the day immediately upon awakening by reciting a series of daily blessings along with some study texts. By the ninth century, if not earlier, these two units too had become mandatory, and the home ritual for awakening had moved to the synagogue, which is where we have it today. The warm-up section of psalms is called *P'sukei D'zimrah* — meaning "Verses of Song" — and the prior recital of daily blessings and study texts is called *Birkhot Hashachar* — "Morning Blessings." Since they now precede the main body of the service, gradually building up to it, the larger diagram can be charted like this:

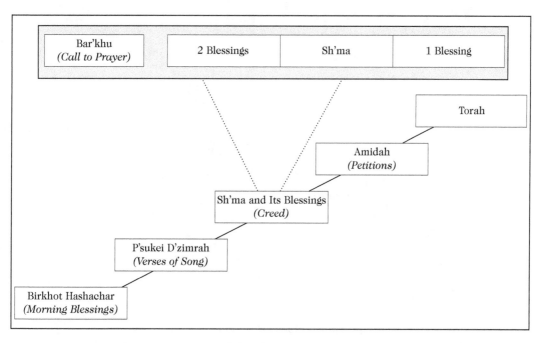

Two other expansions of this basic structure probably occurred in the first two centuries C.E., although our evidence for their being that early is less certain.

First, a Conclusion was added. It featured a final prayer called the *Kaddish* which as yet had nothing to do with mourning, but merely followed the Torah reading, and therefore closed the service, by looking ahead to the coming of God's ultimate reign of justice. Eventually other prayers were added to the Conclusion, including the *Alenu*, which had originally been composed as an introduction to the blowing of the Shofar on Rosh Hashanah, but was moved here in the Middle Ages.

Second, the Rabbis, who were keenly aware of the limits to human mortality, advised all Jews to come to terms daily with their frailty and ethical imperfection. To do so, they provided an opportunity for a silent confession following the *Amidah*, but before the Torah reading. In time, this evolved into silent prayer in general, an opportunity for individuals to assemble their most private thoughts before God; and later still, sometime in the Middle Ages, it expanded on average weekdays into an entire set of supplicatory prayers called the *Tachanun*.

The daily service was thus passed down to us with shape and design. Beginning with daily blessings that celebrate the new day and emphasize the study of sacred texts (*Birkhot Hashachar*) it continues with songs and psalms (*P'sukei D'zimrah*) designed to create a sense of community. There then follows the core of the liturgy: an official call to prayer (our *Bar'khu*), the recital of Jewish belief (the *Sh'ma and Its Blessings*) and communal petitions (the *Amidah*). Individuals then pause to speak privately to God in silent prayer (later expanded into the *Tachanun*), and then, on select days, they read from Torah. The whole concludes with a final *Kaddish* to which other prayers, most notably the *Alenu*, were added eventually.

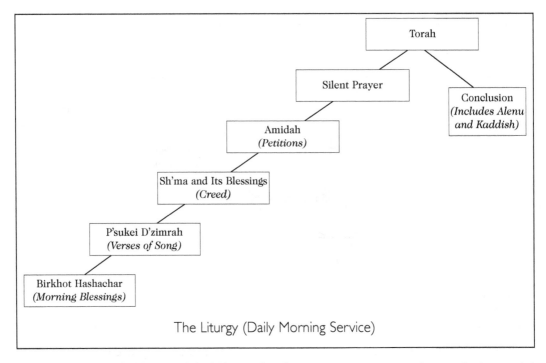

The Liturgy (Daily Morning Service)

On Shabbat and holidays, this basic structure expands to admit special material relevant to the day in question, and contracts to omit prayers that are inappropriate for the occasion. On Shabbat, for instance, the petitions of the *Amidah* are excluded, as Shabbat is felt to be so perfect in itself as to make petitioning unnecessary. But an entire service is added, a service called *Musaf* (literally, "Addition"), to correspond to the extra sacrifice that once characterized Shabbat worship in the Temple. Similarly, a prophetic reading called the *Haftarah* joins the Torah reading, and extra psalms and readings for the Sabbath are inserted here and there. The same is true for holidays when, in addition, numerous *piyyutim* (liturgical poems) get said, especially for the High Holy Days, when the sheer size of the liturgy seems to get out of hand. But even there, the basic structure remains intact, so that those who know its intrinsic shape can get beyond what looks like random verbiage to find the genius behind the liturgy's design.

THE SH'MA AND ITS BLESSINGS: WHAT DO JEWS BELIEVE?

This volume deals in detail with the *Sh'ma and Its Blessings*, which can further be divided into three units:

1. Three biblical citations that make up the *Sh'ma* itself;
2. The Call to Prayer with which the unit starts;
3. Three blessings that surround the *Sh'ma*, giving it its full name, *Sh'ma and Its Blessings*.

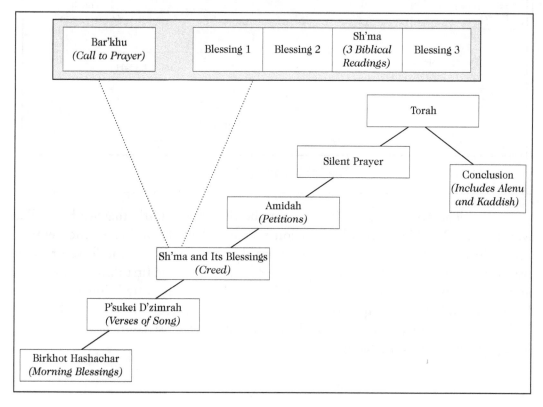

This liturgical statement of Jewish faith is recited in the service for morning and evening (but not afternoon). A later volume handles the evening recitation. Here, we concentrate on the morning version, which features three accompanying blessings, known as the *Yotser* (literally, ". . . who creates," and thus, colloquially, "Creation"), *Birkat Hatorah* ("The Blessing over Torah," literally, but generally just called "Revelation") and *G'ullah* ("Redemption"). Taken together with the *Sh'ma*, which is a set of biblical citations highlighting the absolute singularity of God, the rubric affirms our faith in one and only one God, who created the universe, revealed the Torah to Israel, and will someday redeem the world from injustice and strife.

The *Sh'ma* is interrupted by a final addition: a single congregational response, *Barukh shem . . .* ("Blessed is the One, the glory of whose kingdom is renowned forever"). It affirms the promise that God alone rules the universe, thereby highlighting the final tenet of the creed, the ultimate redemption that Jews hold out as the hope of history.

The full chart for the *Sh'ma and Its Blessings* thus looks like this:

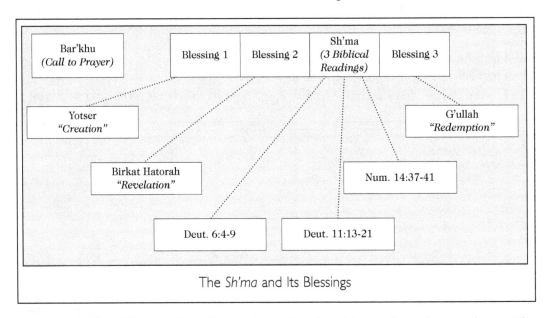

The *Sh'ma* and Its Blessings

The *Sh'ma and Its Blessings* may be the oldest rubric that we have. The Mishnah (c. 200 C.E.) records a version that may have been said in the Temple. Jewish historian Josephus (c. 37–95) knows that the *Sh'ma* in some form or other was recited twice daily. The first line of the *Sh'ma* is often the first thing memorized, and the first prayer recited regularly by Jewish children. It is traditionally also the last prayer said upon a deathbed. In a sense, then, it brackets each day as it brackets each individual's life, and can be said to constitute the most familiar and the most loving entryway into the Siddur.

Introduction to the Commentaries

How to Look for Meaning in the Prayers

THE ART OF JEWISH READING

I remember the day I looked at a manuscript of a prayer book that no one could identify. It had been smuggled out of Russia, then the Soviet Union, and was obviously the liturgy for Rosh Hashanah, but who had written it, and when? It was handwritten, so the style told us much, but in addition, someone had written marginal notes in another handwriting, and yet a third person had written comments to the comments — a third unknown scholar of years gone by whose name we wanted to rescue from oblivion.

Standing before the massive volume, I reflected on the sheer joy of studying a traditional Jewish text. I had seen printed versions before, but never a handwritten instance. What a wonderful habit we Jews developed once upon a time: writing a text in the middle of the page and then filling up the margins with commentaries. Every page becomes a crosscut through Jewish history. Jewish Bibles come that way; so does the Talmud; and the Mishnah; and the codes. We never read just the text. We always read it with the way other people have read it.

To be a Jewish reader, then, is to join the ranks of the millions of readers who came before us, and who left their comments in the margins, the way animals leave tracks in the woods. Go deep into the forest, and you will come across deer runs, for example: paths to water sources, carved out by hundreds of thousands of deer over time. The deer do not just inhabit the forest, they are *part* of the forest; they change the forest's contours as they live there, just as the forest changes them, by offering shelter, food and water. There is no virgin forest, really; it is an ecosystem, a balance between the vegetation and the animals who live there.

So too, there are no virgin texts. They too are ecosystems, sustaining millions of readers over time. When we read our classic texts, we tread the paths of prior readers, in search of spiritual nourishment. *My People's Prayer Book* is therefore not just the Siddur text; it is the text as read by prominent readers from among the people. You are invited to share our path, and even to break new ground yourself, passing on to others your own marginal notes, should you wish.

For the Hebrew text, we have chosen the Ashkenazi edition favored by the renowned historian of the liturgy, the late E.D. Goldschmidt, perhaps the greatest master of liturgical text who ever lived. Born in Germany, later a refugee from the Nazis, Goldschmidt moved to Israel where he assiduously collected and compared thousands of manuscripts for the Siddur, to arrive at an authoritative version as free of scribal and printing error as possible.

The Goldschmidt text is here translated by Joel Hoffman so as to reproduce not only the content of the original Hebrew, but also its tone, register and style, and so to bring to modern readers the same experience (to the greatest extent possible) that the original authors would have conveyed with their words. In terms of content, we assume that by and large, words have meaning only to the extent that they contribute to sentences and concepts — as, for example, "by and large" which has nothing to do with "by" or "large."

We try to reproduce a tone and register similar to the original text: formal, but not archaic; prose or poetry, depending on the Hebrew. Where the Hebrew uses obscure words we try to do the same, and where it uses common idiom, we try to use equally common idiom. Parallel structure and other similar literary devices found in the Hebrew are replicated in the English translation. We have not doctored the text to make it more palatable to modern consciousness. Blatant sexisms are retained, for instance, wherever we think the author intended them. We depend upon our commentaries to bridge the gap between the translation of the original and our modern sensibilities.

The heart and soul of *My People's Prayer Book* is its choice of commentaries that surround the prayerbook text. Translator Joel M. Hoffman explains his choice of words, provides alternatives, and compares his own translation with a selection of the most popularly used prayer books in the English-speaking world. Marc Brettler comments particularly on the way the Bible is embedded in the *Siddur*. Judith Plaskow and Elliot N. Dorff provide theological reflections on what the prayers might mean, should mean, could mean, cannot mean, or have to mean (even if we wish they didn't). Susan L. Einbinder adds medieval insight: the world of prayer for Jews recovering from the Crusades or celebrating a golden age in Spain. Daniel Landes gives us the Halakhah of prayer, the rules and traditions by which this sacred liturgical drama has traditionally been carried out (how the *Sh'ma* is said, for instance) and insight into the spiritual values behind the Halakhah, like the nature of *kavvanah* ("prayerful intentionality"). Nehemia Polen and Lawrence Kushner supply a Kabbalistic commentary, adding wisdom from the world of Chasidic masters, and David Ellenson surveys liberal prayer books of the last 200 years to see how their writers agonized over attempts to update this book of Jewish books for modern times. My own contribution is a summary of what we know about the historical development of the liturgy: when prayers were written, and what they meant in the context of their day.

Some of the commentaries require greater elaboration here, however. They cite a specific body of literature, or had to make some choices that readers should know about in advance.

Translator Joel Hoffman had to make a judicious selection of translations to compare with his own. For an Orthodox version, he relied on Philip Birnbaum's classic (1949) *Daily Prayer Book: Hasiddur Hashalem* ("Birnbaum"), but looked also at *Siddur Kol Ya'akov* ("Artscroll," 1984). American Reform was represented by the *Gates of Prayer* ("GOP," 1975) and revisions since; Conservative Jews will find their *Siddur Sim Shalom* ("SSS," 1985) and Reconstructionists will see their *Kol Han'shamah* ("KH," 1994) cited. He compared British liturgy too: *Forms of Prayer* ("FOP," 1977) from the Reform Synagogues of Great Britain; and both *Service of the Heart* ("SOH," 1967) and *Siddur Lev Chadash* ("SLC," 1995) from the Union of Liberal and Progressive Synagogues. For biblical citations, including the *Sh'ma,* he consulted the Jewish Publication Society Bible ("JPS"), but compared it with the New Revised Standard Version of 1989 ("NRSV"), and *The Five Books of Moses,* by Everett Fox ("Fox," 1995).

My own historical commentary had to deal with the fact that the Goldschmidt translation is only for Ashkenazi Jews, more specifically, the Ashkenazi version common in eastern Europe, often under the influence of Elijah ben Solomon of Vilna, known as the Vilna Gaon (1720–1797). To balance the picture, I cite Sefardi practice also.

But the word Sefardi has two distinct meanings.

Nowadays, it usually describes Jews whose liturgy was influenced by Chasidism and the specific brand of Kabbalah initiated by Isaac Luria (the "Ari"), in six-teenth-century Palestine. Goldschmidt compiled a scientific edition of this variant too, and I used that to represent "Sefardi practice." But "Sefardi" can also mean the old Spanish-Portuguese custom carried by Jews from Spain in 1492, and then brought to the Netherlands; from where it moved to England (among other places) and eventually to America as well. When I want to draw attention to this Spanish-Portuguese custom, I call it that, using as my guide the standard work published in England at the turn of the century by Moses Gaster, *The Book of Prayer and Order of Service According to the Custom of the Spanish and Portuguese Jews.* I try also to cite *Seder Rav Amram* and *Siddur Saadiah,* the first two Jewish prayer books of which we are aware, from ninth and tenth-century Babylon. And from the same era, roughly, I use the Genizah Fragments, manuscripts telling us how Jews prayed in Eretz Yisrael prior to the Crusades.

David Ellenson was asked to fill in the gap caused by the fact that even the standard Ashkenazi and Sefardi versions hardly represent the majority of Jews today. As Jews have evolved, so have our modern movements, each with its own version of what our forebears once considered normative. The last two hundred years have witnessed the composition of countless Jewish prayer books, and Ellenson surveys the most prominent of these for instances where the traditional text evoked debate.

For historical reasons, many of these prayer books are Reform, beginning with the *Hamburg Temple Prayer Book*s of 1819 and 1841, the very first efforts to make the content of the classical liturgy comport with modern ideas. His survey of the nineteenth century also included *Seder T'filah D'var Yom B'Yomo* (1854; republished, 1870) by Rabbi Abraham Geiger, the preeminent leader of German Reform.

For early American liturgies, he turned to Rabbis Isaac Mayer Wise and David Einhorn. Wise's *Minhag America* (1857) was the most popular prayer book of its day, and Einhorn's *Olath Tamid* (1856) became the prototype for the *Union Prayer Book*, which was adopted in 1895 as the official liturgy for North American Reform Jews. In 1975, *Gates of Prayer* replaced the *UPB*, and in 1996 the latest in a series of gender-inclusive editions of *GOP* appeared. All three of these official movement books are cited here.

Among the non-American prayer books of the late 1900s, he made extensive use of *Ha'avodah Shebalev*, adopted by the Israeli Progressive Movement in 1982, and *Siddur Lev Chadash*, published by the Union of Progressive and Liberal Synagogues in London in 1995.

These Reform and Liberal prayer books are supplemented by Conservative and Reconstructionist volumes. The former include various prayer books produced since 1958 by the Rabbinical Assembly of the Conservative Movement, but especially the 1985 *Siddur Sim Shalom*. Since Conservative worship is in Hebrew, however, and since the Hebrew is generally unchanged while the vernacular equivalent is usually a literal translation of it, he has less to say about Conservative books than he does about Reform volumes, where both Hebrew and English tend to vary widely. The Reconstructionist Movement, which, like Reform, has tended toward considerable liturgical creativity, is represented primarily by *Kol Han'shamah*, published in 1996, but from time to time he discusses earlier work, especially by Mordecai Kaplan, the founder of the movement.

He gives priority to denominationally-associated prayer books because they have been most widely disseminated, but does include some others, notably, *The Book of Blessings*, authored in 1996 by Jewish feminist Marcia Falk. He uses more liberal prayer books than Orthodox ones, because liberal books were changed more, as their authors tried to remain true to their liturgical heritage, without doing an injustice to modern ideas about God, the universe and human nature. Orthodox volumes are cited here, but references to them are limited.

The halakhic commentary was included not just to explain how prayers should be said. Even without that abiding practical concern, it would have found its way here because Halakhah (Jewish law) is essential to Judaism. Frequently misunderstood as mere legalism, it is actually more akin to Jewish poetry, in that it is the height of Jewish writing, the pinnacle of Jewish concern, sheer joy to create or to ponder. It describes, explains and debates Jewish responsibility, yet is saturated with spiritual importance. Jewish movements can be differentiated by their approach to Halakhah, but Halakhah matters to them all.

A short overview of its history and some of its vocabulary will be helpful in advance.

The topic of Halakhah is the proper performance of the commandments, said to number 613, and divided into positive and negative ones, numbering 248 and 365 respectively. Strictly speaking, commandments derived directly from Torah (*mid'ora'ita*) are of a higher order than those rooted only in rabbinic ordinance (called *mid'rabbanan*), but all are binding.

The earliest stratum of Halakhah is found primarily in the *Mishnah,* a code of Jewish practice promulgated about 200 C.E. The Mishnah is the foundation for further rabbinic discussion in Palestine and Babylonia, which culminated in the two talmuds, one from each center, called the Palestinian Talmud (or the *Yerushalmi*) and the Babylonian Talmud (or the *Babli*). While dates for both are uncertain, the former is customarily dated to about 400 C.E., and the latter between 550 and 650.

With the canonization of the Babli, Jewish law developed largely from commentary to the talmuds and from responsa, applications of talmudic and other precedents to actual cases. These are still the norm today, but they were initiated by authorities in Babylonia called *Geonim* (sing. *Gaon*) from about 750 to shortly after 1000. By the turn of the millennium, other schools had developed in North Africa particularly, but also in western Europe. Authorities in these centers are usually called *Rishonim* ("first" or "early" [ones]) until the sixteenth century, when they become known as *Acharonim* ("last" or "later" [ones]).

The first law code was initiated by the Geonim (from about 750), but it was the Rishonim who really inaugurated the trend toward codifying, giving us many works, including three major ones that are widely cited here: The *Mishneh Torah,* by Maimonides (Moses ben Maimon, 1035–1104), born in Spain, but active most of his life in Egypt; the *Tur* by Jacob ben Asher (1275–1340), son of another giant, Asher ben Yechiel, who had moved to Spain from Germany, allowing Ashkenazi and Sefardi practice to intertwine in his son's *magnum opus*; and the *Shulchan Arukh* by Joseph Caro (1488–1575), who is technically the first generation of the Acharonim, but who wrote influential commentaries on both the *Mishneh Torah* and the *Tur* before composing what would become the most widely used legal corpus ever.

This halakhic commentary draws on all of the above, as well as numerous other authorities, including especially the following: Jacob Emden (1697–1776), a German rabbi, kabbalist, and halakhic authority who bequeathed us his own Siddur and commentary; Elijah ben Solomon of Vilna (1720–1797), better known as the *G'ra* or the Vilna Gaon, the most outstanding halakhic authority in eighteenth-century Lithuania, and an intellectual leader who pioneered the modern, but traditional, study of classical texts; *Mishnah B'rurah,* a decisive commentary on part of the *Shulchan Arukh,* composed by Israel Meir Hakohen Kagan (1838–1933) of Poland; *Arukh Hashulchan,* a summary of halakhic opinion that spans the various codes and their interpreters, published in parts from 1883 to 1907 by Yechiel Michael Epstein (1829–1098) of Belorussia and Lithuania; Avraham Karelitz (1878–1953), better known as the *Chazon Ish,* a modern master of Halakhah who began as an authority in Vilna, but who moved to Israel, and advised the early Israeli government on halakhic matters; and Rabbi Joseph Soloveitchik (1903–1993), who moved from Lithuania to Berlin and then to Boston, where he became known as *"the" Rov* ("the" Rabbi), leaving a lasting impression on today's generation of halakhists.

Other commentators too tend to favor some sources over others — Judith Plaskow makes frequent use of Marcia Falk's *Book of Blessings* as well as *Birkat Shalom,* a prayer book published by Chavurat Shalom of Somerset, Massachusetts. But by and large their comments require no detailed introduction here.

We have gone out of our way to provide a panoply of scholars, all students of the prayerbook text, and all committed to a life of prayer, but representative of left, right and center in the Jewish world. They represent all of us, all of *Am Yisrael*, all of those God had in mind when God said to Ezekiel (34:30) "They shall know that I, Adonai their God, am with them, and they, the House of Israel, are My people." Unabashedly scholarly and religious at one and the same time, *My People's Prayer Book — Minhag Ami*, "A Way of Prayer for My People" — will be deemed a success if it provides the spiritual insight required to fulfill yet another prophecy (Isaiah 52:6), that through our prayers,

> My people (*ami*) may know my name
> That they may know, therefore, in that day,
> That I, the One who speaks,
> Behold! Here I am.

1 | *Bar'khu*
בָּרְכוּ
Call to Prayer

<table>
<tr><td>

[All rise]

[Prayer leader]

¹ Bless Adonai who is to be blessed.

[Congregation, then Prayer leader]

² Blessed be Adonai, who is to be blessed for ever and ever.

[Congregation, quietly]

³ Blessed, praised, glorified, exalted and extolled be the name of the king over the kings of kings, the holy one, blessed is He. ⁴ He is the first and He is the last, and other than Him there are no gods. ⁵ Pave the way for the one who rides where the sun sets — his name being Yah — and rejoice before Him. ⁶ His name is exalted beyond all blessing and praise. ⁷ Blessed is the one the glory of whose kingdom is renowned forever. ⁸ May Adonai's name be blessed from now until eternity.

[All are seated]

</td><td>

[All rise]

[Prayer leader]

¹ בָּרְכוּ אֶת-יְיָ הַמְבֹרָךְ.

[Congregation, then Prayer leader]

² בָּרוּךְ יְיָ הַמְבֹרָךְ לְעוֹלָם וָעֶד.

[Congregation, quietly]

³ יִתְבָּרַךְ וְיִשְׁתַּבַּח, וְיִתְפָּאַר וְיִתְרוֹמַם וְיִתְנַשֵּׂא שְׁמוֹ שֶׁל מֶלֶךְ מַלְכֵי הַמְּלָכִים, הַקָּדוֹשׁ בָּרוּךְ הוּא, ⁴ שֶׁהוּא רִאשׁוֹן וְהוּא אַחֲרוֹן, וּמִבַּלְעָדָיו אֵין אֱלֹהִים. ⁵ סֹלּוּ לָרֹכֵב בָּעֲרָבוֹת, בְּיָהּ שְׁמוֹ, וְעִלְזוּ לְפָנָיו. ⁶ וּשְׁמוֹ מְרוֹמָם עַל כָּל בְּרָכָה וּתְהִלָּה. ⁷ בָּרוּךְ שֵׁם כְּבוֹד מַלְכוּתוֹ לְעוֹלָם וָעֶד. ⁸ יְהִי שֵׁם יְיָ מְבֹרָךְ מֵעַתָּה וְעַד עוֹלָם.

[All are seated]

</td></tr>
</table>

MARC BRETTLER

"Bless Adonai who is to be blessed" How can human beings bless God, who is the source of all blessings, and blesses all created beings, including humanity (Gen. 1:22, 28)? Blessing God was a common biblical pattern, however. The conclusion to *(p. 30)*

LAWRENCE A. HOFFMAN

THE SH'MA AND ITS BLESSINGS BEGINS WITH A FORMAL CALL TO PRAYER, KNOWN COLLOQUIALLY AS "THE BAR'KHU."

"Bless Adonai who is to be blessed" The *Bar'khu* goes back at least to the second century, but not *(p. 32)*

ELLIOT N. DORFF

"Bless Adonai who is to be blessed" We bless other people by wishing them well, but how can we bless God, who is the source of all blessing? Since we can praise God, some prayer books *(p. 30)*

LAWRENCE KUSHNER
NEHEMIA POLEN

"Bless Adonai" The core rubric of all Jewish liturgy is the *b'rakhah*, the blessing. The worship service itself is an elaborate sequence of blessings, one *(p. 33)*

בָּרְכוּ אֶת-יְיָ הַמְבֹרָךְ. ¹

בָּרוּךְ יְיָ הַמְבֹרָךְ לְעוֹלָם וָעֶד. ²

SUSAN L. EINBINDER

"Bless Adonai who is to be blessed. Blessed be . . . forever and ever" Along with the statutory liturgy, the Jews of medieval Ashkenaz and Sefarad had inherited a vast corpus of liturgical poems called *piyyutim* *(p. 31)*

¹ Bless Adonai who is to be blessed. ² Blessed be Adonai, who is to be blessed for ever and ever.

DANIEL LANDES

*T*he proper time for reciting *Sh'ma* — "when you rise up" — is subjectively experienced as beginning when one can recognize a slight acquaintance from the distance of four *amot* (1 *amah* = 18.9 or 22.7 inches; 4 *(p. 34)*

DAVID ELLENSON

"Bless Adonai who is to be blessed. Blessed be . . . forever and ever" These lines, which mark the traditional call to worship, have been retained in virtually all Liberal liturgies of the past two centuries. The one notable exception to this *(p. 32)*

JUDITH PLASKOW

"Adonai" How is it best to render the mysterious, unpronounceable four-consonant name of God, the name so sacred that it was uttered only by the high priest when he entered the holy of holies on Yom Kippur? Adonai is not that name, but a *(p. 36)*

JOEL M. HOFFMAN

"Bless Adonai who is to be blessed. Blessed be . . . who is to be blessed" We use "bless" twice, though some others prefer "praise." GOP and SLC end the first line with "to whom our praise is due," and STH provides "to whom all praise is *(p. 32)*

MARC BRETTLER

Ps. 135 (19–21), now part of the Shabbat morning liturgy too, reads, "House of Israel, bless Adonai, House of Aaron, bless Adonai, House of Levi, bless Adonai." Similar ideas occur in Ps. 134:1, "Now bless Adonai, all the servants of Adonai" and in Neh. 9:5, "The Levites . . . said, 'Rise and bless Adonai your God for ever and ever.'" The call to prayer here is so similar, that it may deliberately be patterned after Nehemiah, the context of which ("Rise") indicates that even the custom of standing during the *Bar'khu* ("Bless Adonai . . .") has ancient roots; it likely reflects the practice of standing before someone of a higher social status.

The fact that biblical people "blessed" God, even knowing that God was the source of all blessings, reflects what Moshe Greenberg calls "the social analogy" in religious traditions. God is typically understood by analogy with human familial, social, and political institutions. Various attributes typical of those institutions are then projected onto God, even when they are inappropriate. So here, since members of families can bless each other, and subjects can bless a king, we end up with a call to bless the One who cannot benefit from blessings given by humans.

The inappropriateness of this call to bless Adonai is implicitly recognized here through the addition of *hamvorakh*, which has no biblical precedent, and most likely should be understood in the sense of "(already) blessed."

"For ever and ever" The superlative nature of God is clarified through the response which includes "for ever and ever," following the pattern of the opening and conclusion of the central Ps. 145, which appears in the morning and afternoon liturgy as *Ashre:* "I will extol You, my God and king, and bless your name for ever and ever" (v. 1) and "My mouth shall utter the praise of Adonai, and all creatures shall bless his holy name for ever and ever" (v. 21). This notice of the eternality of God raises a central theme, so that it is probably no accident that the entire rubric of the *Sh'ma* and Its Blessings opens with it and then closes with it too (end of the third blessing, the *G'ullah*), by quoting Exod. 15:18, "Adonai will reign for ever and ever."

—◆—

ELLIOT N. DORFF

(e.g., the Conservative Movement's *Sim Shalom*) translate *Bar'khu* and *Barukh* as "praise" rather than "bless." The usual Hebrew word for praise, however, is not from the root *b.r.kh*, but from *h.l.l*, as in the prayers called *Hallel*. More than just "praise," then, *Bar'khu* is an invitation to *acknowledge* or *recognize* God, derived originally, perhaps, from *berekh*, "knee," since people in antiquity would drop to their knees before a monarch to acknowledge his or her sovereignty. Jewish sources also describe worship gestures like bowing (*kor'im*) and fully prostrating oneself (*mishtachavim*), but these are restricted to a few prayers to avoid the mistaken impression that we are bowing down to the ark, or to the Torah within it, as an idol. We fully prostrate ourselves only on the High Holy Days when we reenact the ancient Temple rite that emphasizes God's transcendent sovereignty; we bend the knee (*kor'im*) and bow (*umishtachavim*) at limited occasions in the daily service.

But the root *b.r.kh* still means acknowledging God, placed here (at the very beginning of the *Sh'ma*, the first formal rubric of the public service) to ask us to transcend our self-centered view of the world and our self-congratulatory stance within it. The Torah, in fact, defines idolatry as the view that "my strength and the power of my hand accomplished all these things" (Deut. 8:17). By opening prayer with *Bar'khu* and by repeating it, as *Barukh,* throughout the Siddur's many "blessings," the liturgy reenforces the importance of recognizing our creatureliness before our creator.

Adopting that appropriately humble attitude prompts us to confront the frightening fact that we are not in full control of our lives. Depending on God for many things means God can deprive us of those things at will. *Bar'khu* evokes a certain awe, therefore, and even fear. But simultaneously, recognizing our dependence upon God as sovereign moves us to praise and thanksgiving for what we do in fact have.

Each time we "bless" God, then, we have in mind the root meaning of acknowledging God's sovereignty, and the corollary meanings of respecting and fearing, while also praising and thanking God for the many ways in which God has used divine power to benefit us.

——◆——

SUSAN L. EINBINDER

(singular: *piyyut*). This corpus, whose earliest pieces go back to Palestine of the first centuries C.E., had its own very interesting history; while scholars disagree over whether *piyyut* was always a supplement to an established liturgy or whether it initially comprised the liturgy, its traces in early Eretz Yisrael mark it as the first and most enduring truly national Jewish literature. When the official liturgy of the service was established by Amram and Saadiah Gaon in ninth- and tenth-century Babylonia, *piyyutim* did not disappear. On the contrary, over the centuries, new liturgical poets (*payy'tanim*) continued to compose sacred poetry for use in the daily and holiday liturgies.

Poetry mattered especially to the upper class Jews of medieval Spain: sophisticated, cultured and acculturated to Andalusian court life, elegance and beauty were supremely important to them. This was as true in matters of the spirit as it was in daily life, and in both realms the influence of Arab aesthetics and learning made an impact. A heightened sensitivity to the pleasures of the aesthetic life, to the delights of wine and landscape and love, was reflected first in the birth of secular poetry, and then in the transfer of many of the secular world's motifs to the domain of the sacred. The medieval Andalusian Jew's treatment of the liturgy reflects a new value on the place of private emotion and private life.

Spanish Jewish poets particularly loved to embellish the section preceding the *Bar'khu*. The official call to prayer was often preceded by a short but lovely poem emphasizing the transition from private to public worship. These were composed by some of the greatest writers of Hebrew poetry's "Golden Age" — poets like Solomon ibn Gabirol (c. 1020–c. 1057), the first Hebrew poet to write sacred verse in the forms and music of Arabic secular poetry, and by Judah Halevi (before 1075–1141). Their little compositions preceding the *Bar'khu* catch the tension between the private and public aspects of Jewish prayer. They had no precedent in Hebrew liturgical writing for speaking in a personal voice, however, so their innovations in this regard are daring. The poet generally speaks as an "I" who awakens and is brought by private meditations on his relationship to God to worship among fellow Jews. As Ibn Gabirol muses here, for instance, contemplation of the vast physical world leads him to the mystery of human existence, and then to God:

Three things there are, together in my eye
  That keep the thought of Thee forever nigh.
I think about thy great and holy name
  Whenever I look up and see the sky.
My thoughts are roused to know how I was made,
  Seeing the earth's expanse where I abide.
The musings of my mind when I look inside —
  At all times, O my soul, "Bless Adonai!"

> (Translation by Raymond Scheindlin, *The Gazelle: Medieval Hebrew Poems on God, Israel and the Soul*)

———◆———

DAVID ELLENSON

pattern is found in *The Book of Blessings* by Marcia Falk. In light of her own naturalistic, non-hierarchical, and non-personal view of the Divine, Falk has amended this prayer to read, "Let us bless the source of life," and has changed the congregational response to, "As we bless the source of life, so we are blessed." In so doing, she has championed a theological position that elevates the position of humanity in a way that is unprecedented in the entire history of Jewish prayer.

———◆———

JOEL M. HOFFMAN

due." Though more poetic options, there is little to support them as accurate translations. Birnbaum offers the more literal "who is blessed," while KH gives us "the blessed One." In FOP we find "whom we are called to bless." SSS suggests another poetic but less literal translation: "Source of blessing." *Bar'khu* is the plural imperative calling on the congregation to "bless God." As for *m'vorakh*, the crucial decision is between "who is to be blessed" and "who is blessed." The Hebrew can mean either.

———◆———

LAWRENCE A. HOFFMAN

necessarily as a call to prayer introducing the *Sh'ma* and Its Blessings. Originally, it may have been associated with the *Kaddish*, and it was said not just here but after the *Amidah* also. Genizah fragments show us that some Jews in *Eretz Yisrael* prior to the Crusades may not have said the *Bar'khu* at all; instead, they introduced the *Sh'ma* with a benediction that we no longer have: "Blessed are You, Adonai our God, ruler of the universe, who has sanctified us with his commandments and commanded us about the commandment of reading the *Sh'ma*: to declare his royalty with full intention and to declare his unity with good intent and to serve him with willing body. Amen."

בא"י אמ"ה וּבָרוּךְ אַתָּה יְיָ, אֱלֹהֵינוּ מֶלֶךְ הָעוֹלָם, אֲשֶׁר קִדְּשָׁנוּ בְּמִצְוֹתָיו וְצִוָּנוּ עַל מִצְוַת קְרִיַּת שְׁמַע לְהַמְלִיכוֹ בְּלֵבָב שָׁלֵם וּלְיַחֲדוֹ בְּלֵב טוֹב וּלְעָבְדוֹ בְּנֶפֶשׁ חֲפֵיצָה. אָמֵן.

"Blessed be Adonai, who is to be blessed forever and ever" The congregational response to the *Bar'khu* is called a "Doxology," from the Greek word *doxa* meaning "glory." Each of the five sections that comprise the biblical book of Psalms contains a final doxological conclusion, simply an unbridled praise of God and a reference to "forever." Books One and Four, for instance, end, "Blessed is Adonai, the God of Israel, from everlasting to everlasting" (Pss. 41:14, 106:48), and Book Three concludes, "Blessed is Adonai forevermore" (Ps. 89:55). So too, Jewish liturgy features congregational responses to invitations to pray, modeled after the Psalms. This is only one of several. The *Kaddish* features *Y'hei sh'meih rabba m'vorakh, l'olam ul'olmei ulmaya* ("May his great name be praised forever and ever"), and the *Birkat Hamazon* (the Grace after Meals) has, *Yehi shem Adonai m'vorakh mei'atah v'ad olam* ("May the name Adonai be praised from now until eternity"). The congregational response to the first line of the *Sh'ma* is likewise a doxology, *Barukh shem k'vod malkhuto l'olam va'ed*. Though it adds the idea of God's ultimate rule, it too emphasizes the three features of a liturgical doxology in Judaism: 1) praise for God without stipulating any specific reason for the praise; 2) an emphasis on God's name, either given as Adonai or just referred to as "the great name" or just "the name"; and 3) a temporal phrase promising such praise eternally (see below, "Blessed be the name").

———◆———

LAWRENCE KUSHNER
NEHEMIA POLEN

after another. It is only fitting therefore that the first words of the service summon us to blessing: *"Bar'khu et Adonai,* Let us bless God." But the word "blessing," perhaps as much in English as in Hebrew, is over-determined, overused, desensitized, hollow. It sounds solicitous and connotes manipulation: "You're so nice. Please do us a favor." But according to Chaim of Volozhyn (1749–1821), a Kabbalist and possibly even a crypto-Chasid, "blessing" has a different primary meaning. In his *Nefesh Hachayim*, the Volozhyner cites the Talmud (Ber. 7a) where Rabbi Ishmael is invited actually to pray *for* God:

> Rabbi Ishmael ben Elisha said: I once entered into the innermost part [of the Sanctuary] to offer incense and I saw *Akathriel Yah*, the Lord of Hosts, seated upon a high and exalted throne. God said to me: "Ishmael, my son, bless Me!" I replied, "May it be your will that your mercy may suppress your anger and your mercy prevail over your other attributes, so that You

may deal with your children according to the attribute of mercy, and may, on their behalf, stop short of the limit of strict justice!" And God nodded to me. . . .

But how can a person actually bless God! Through speech, suggests Chaim of Volozhyn, people "can call forth the Divine flow of blessing." We can evoke what would otherwise have remained only latent, unrealized, unfulfilled. We cannot, to be sure, put something there that was not already there, but we can bring something into reality that was only hitherto a possibility. Thus the one who blesses becomes an agent of self-realization and fulfillment for the one who receives the blessing. We "conjure" a blessing. Even for God. And when we "bless" God, since God is the source of all life, we effectively enable the Holy One to bless us. In blessing God, we are blessing ourselves!

The one who offers a blessing is like a coach whispering to an athlete before the competition, "You can do it!" More than encouragement, positive spin, or sincere wish, the words of blessing literally bring forth, reify an otherwise unrealizable force.

In this way, blessing is not supplication but symbiosis. God needs us to summon blessings, just as we could not live without them. And so the service begins: *Bar'khu et Adonai,* "Bless God."

——◆——

DANIEL LANDES

amot = either 6.3 feet or 7.5 feet, approximately); or when one can distinguish between the white and royal blue of one's *tallit* and *tsitsit.* Objectively, this is understood as starting either from the actual appearance of the sun on the horizon, or (the predominant view) after the *amud hashachar,* literally, the "pillar of light" that precedes the sun, that is (in practice), the lightening of the eastern sky. From this starting point, the time extends up to three halakhic hours (1 halakhic hour = $^1/_{12}$ of daylight for any particular day), that is, a fourth of the day.

Since the *Sh'ma* is coupled with the *Amidah* (see below, "Blessed are You . . . who redeemed Israel"), Halakhah prefers that it be said as early as possible, allowing sunrise to occur just as the *Amidah* begins. The ideal time for the *Amidah* thus determines the timing of the *Sh'ma.*

Saying *Sh'ma* early is preferred for another reason too: in order to say it with the presumed majority of risers.

How early can one begin? The halakhic consensus is that the entire *Sh'ma* and Its Blessings may infrequently be said at *amud hashachar,* but ideally, the first blessing (which celebrates the creation of light) demands that some actual light be visible.

The *Shulchan Arukh* rules that one may say the *Sh'ma* as late as the fourth halakhic hour of the day, "although one does not thereby attain the reward of reciting it in its proper time." The point arises from a double meaning inherent in the word *t'fillah.* The Talmud counts the fourth hour as a time when *T'fillah* is appropriate. In this context, *T'fillah* is a proper noun meaning the *Amidah* specifically. But *t'fillah* can also mean "prayer" in general. By extension, then, the blessings of the *Sh'ma* (which are considered a form of *t'fillah* in the latter sense) may still be recited then; and since the *Sh'ma* is embedded in the blessings, it follows that it too may be said that late. Communities should therefore not schedule services so late that the *Sh'ma* cannot be said prior to the third or fourth hour.

Only in a true emergency can the *Sh'ma* and Its Blessings be said as late as midday (the outer limits of the time for morning prayer). Thereafter it is too late no matter what, since that is surely past the time of "rising." Nonetheless, the *Shulchan Arukh* permits "the recitation of the *Sh'ma* without its blessings all day." The blessings must be omitted lest they be "blessings said in vain," but the *Sh'ma* alone is like reading Torah, so is always permissible, especially as it fulfills a further commandment, to remember the Exodus, which also holds all day long. *Mishnah B'rurah* (by Israel Meir Hakohen Kagan, 1838–1933) explains further, "It is a good thing to recite it [even late and without the blessings] since one thereby accepts the yoke of heaven." The affirmation of God's unity, a *mitzvah* that is never time-bound, may be carried out even when the obligation or opportunity for a full liturgical recital of the *Sh'ma* has ended.

The perpetual need for this affirmation explains why women, who are halakhically exempted from all time-bound *mitzvot* and thus from the recital of *Sh'ma* and Its Blessings, are nonetheless encouraged to include the *Sh'ma* in their daily prayers. Children too should do so, if they have reached the age of understanding. It was halakhically unthinkable that Jews would begin their daily business without affirming God's unity, even if they were exempt from the formal liturgical manner of doing so.

Regardless of where individual worshippers may be in the service, even if they have already personally said the *Sh'ma*, when the congregation as a whole arrives at "Hear O Israel . . ." they must join the community in its public and vocal recitation.

Conversation, including body language like winking or gesturing, is forbidden during *Sh'ma* and Its Blessings. Reciting the *Sh'ma* requires the right place too: a clean, non-odorous environment. God's unity must be affirmed with full consciousness, no distraction and deep intent.

These and other halakhic details derive from certain philosophical considerations, including: 1) dual *mitzvot* regarding the *Sh'ma*: a) to affirm the doctrine of God's unity, and b) to do so liturgically; 2) A twofold need for *kavvanah*: a) *kavvanat halev* (inner intentionality regarding what is being said), and b) *kavvanah la'tseit* (having the intention to fulfill the requisite *mitzvah*); 3) the implications of the liturgical *Sh'ma* being embedded in a blessing structure; 4) a difference between *ex post facto* (known in Hebrew as *b'di'avad*) and *ab initio* (known as *l'chatchilah*) — the latter is the ideal, but the former may be acceptable retroactively; 5) the intrinsic connection of the *Sh'ma* to the following prayer, the *Amidah*; and 6) the need for community. These and other concerns are the basis for the comments below.

"Bless . . . who is to be blessed" As the call to formal prayer, the *Bar'khu* requires a *minyan*, and is said standing. If there is no *minyan* it is omitted. The prayer leader (*sh'liach tsibbur*) bows at *Bar'khu* and stands erect again at God's name.

"Blessed be . . . who is blessed for ever and ever" The congregation responds to the call to prayer, bowing at the first word and rising again at God's name. The prayer leader

repeats the line almost immediately behind the congregation. No *amen* is recited. The congregation sits only when the repetition by the prayer leader is over. From this point on, until the *Amidah* ends, one must not interrupt one's prayer. Each blessing preceding or following the *Sh'ma*, and each biblical section of the *Sh'ma* is considered an integral unit, known as a *perek* (pl.: *p'rakim*). One may interrupt within a *perek* only to give the proper responses to the *Kaddish*, the *Bar'khu* and the *K'dushah*.

As this is the beginning of communal prayer latecomers must join in with the community here, even if they have not had the opportunity yet to catch up on the earlier prayers. Between the *p'rakim* one can additionally say *amen* if one hears other blessings being recited.

The rest of the *Sh'ma* and its blessings, all the way to the *Amidah*, should be said sitting down.

———◆———

JUDITH PLASKOW

circumlocution so firmly fixed as the name of God that many observant Jews avoid it, substituting *Hashem* ("the name"), except during prayer. Most prayer books translate Adonai as "Lord," substituting an English circumlocution for the Hebrew one.

But Adonai, as God's most familiar and intimate name, raises problems that are not present in the tetragrammaton. From the title *Adon* ("Lord") we get *Adoni* ("my Lord") in the Bible to indicate authority or superordinate/subordinate relationships, and God's "name," Adonai, is the plural of *Adoni*, literally, "My Lords," but taken to be singular because God is One. The name is thus hierarchical in a way that is not true of the tetragrammaton יהוה which seems to be related to the verb "to be." When God introduces Godself to Moses out of the burning bush (Exod. 3:13), God says, "I am who I am," or as Buber and others translate, "I will be who I will be." To this, God adds, "Say to the people of Israel, 'I am has sent me to you'" (Exod. 3:15). This elliptical, mysterious, and fluid image of a God who is and who will be is very different from the fixed hierarchy of Adonai, especially as Adonai comes to be seen as God's one, unalterable, and proper name.

The decision to leave Adonai untranslated admits the possibility of a variety of renderings, but reinforces the notion that Adonai is actually God's name. Some contemporary prayer books with a feminist sensibility (*Birkat Shalom*, for example, a project of Chavurat Shalom in Somerville, Mass.) simply translate Adonai as "God." *V'taher Libenu*, the Siddur of Congregation Beth-El in Sudbury, Mass., tries to dismantle the metaphor of God as hierarch by rendering *Adonai* as "Holy One of Blessing." Perhaps the most interesting solution is offered by the Reconstructionist *Kol Han'shamah*. Whenever the tetragrammaton appears, it is interpreted with a different metaphor for God appropriate to the context of the particular blessing — "The Infinite," "The Eternal," "The Redeeming One," "The Creator," "The Precious One," and so forth — so as to convey the fluidity and ineffability of יהוה and invite the worshipper to contribute to the continuing process of naming.

———————◆◆◆———————

JOEL M. HOFFMAN

"*Blessed, praised, glorified . . .*" As often in the liturgy, we have a series of adjectives. More important than their individual meanings is the affect of their being piled up together.

"*King over the kings of kings*" Translated more or less literally. Other emperors may have been the "kings of kings," and so God was King over them. "King of kings of kings" would be more accurate, but harder to read.

"*Other than Him there are no gods*" Or " . . . is no god."

"*Pave the way*" From the root *s.l.l,* to cast a highway. Birnbaum's "extol" reflects the common view that the word means "praise," an opinion dating back to the Targum's translation of Ps. 68:5, the source of this phrase. Rashi accepts the Targum's understanding, but Ibn Ezra prefers linking it to Isaiah   *(p. 38)*

JUDITH PLASKOW

"*The king over the kings of kings*" The Bar'khu introduces a series of images of a masculine, hierarchical and wholly Other God that many feminist (and nonfeminist) Jews find profoundly alienating. The pronouns that point to God are male — God is "Him," and "the Holy One, blessed is He" — and so are "his" roles and characteristics. God is "King over the kings of kings," "master of war," and "merciful Father." Far from fostering connection with God, for some worshippers, these images constitute an actual block to relationship.

"*May Adonai's name be blessed . . .*" The liturgy abounds with overwhelmingly one-sided images that evoke the omnipotence of God and the insufficiency and dependence of human power and knowledge. Here, however, we find at least a hint of an image   *(p. 39)*

³יִתְבָּרַךְ וְיִשְׁתַּבַּח, וְיִתְפָּאַר וְיִתְרוֹמַם וְיִתְנַשֵּׂא שְׁמוֹ שֶׁל מֶלֶךְ מַלְכֵי הַמְּלָכִים, הַקָּדוֹשׁ בָּרוּךְ הוּא, ⁴שֶׁהוּא רִאשׁוֹן וְהוּא אַחֲרוֹן, וּמִבַּלְעָדָיו אֵין אֱלֹהִים. ⁵סֹלּוּ לָרֹכֵב בָּעֲרָבוֹת, בְּיָהּ שְׁמוֹ, וְעִלְזוּ לְפָנָיו. ⁶וּשְׁמוֹ מְרוֹמָם עַל

³ Blessed, praised, glorified, exalted and extolled be the name of the king over the kings of kings, the holy one, blessed is He. ⁴ He is the first and He is the last, and other than Him there are no gods. ⁵ Pave the way for the one who rides where the sun sets — his name being Yah — and   *(p. 38)*

LAWRENCE A. HOFFMAN

"*Blessed, praised, glorified, exalted and extolled*" In traditional practice, 1) the prayer leader recites the call to prayer, 2) the congregation responds with the doxology ("Blessed be Adonai" — see above), which 3) the prayer leader then repeats while the congregation says this meditation quietly. It seems to be composed of several doxologies. Since the choice of doxology for any particular part of the service was not fixed at first, it may be that we have a remnant of many alternative responses that were once common here, some of which have since been assigned elsewhere in the liturgy. On the other hand, the custom appears first only in eleventh-century France. It was an innovation, possibly connected with a medieval Jewish belief in purgatory, punishment after death. Ashkenazi Jews held that our children can release us from such punishment if they lead the congregation in the *Bar'khu* or say the response to the *Kaddish* (*Yehei shmeih rabba . . .*). At first minor children were allowed to lead services for that   *(p. 38)* rejoice before Him. [6] His name is exalted beyond all blessing and praise. [7] Blessed is the one the glory of whose kingdom is renowned forever. [8] May Adonai's name be blessed from now until eternity.

כָּל בְּרָכָה וּתְהִלָּה. ⁷בָּרוּךְ שֵׁם כְּבוֹד מַלְכוּתוֹ לְעוֹלָם וָעֶד. ⁸יְהִי שֵׁם יְיָ מְבֹרָךְ מֵעַתָּה וְעַד עוֹלָם.

JOEL M. HOFFMAN

62:11, where the meaning is certainly to clear a highway, akin to the modern idiomatic sense of "paving the way." Especially in light of the following "the one who rides," our translation of "pave the way" seems much more likely. NRSV translates, "lift up a song," but adds a footnote, "Or, 'Cast up a highway.'"

"Where the sun sets" Hebrew, *aravot*, a technical term for the last, or sometimes the second to last, of the seven concentric circular rings thought to constitute the heavens. God was pictured as residing there in a throne-like chariot that moved across the sky drawing the sun in its wake. From their expression invoking the sun, we translate, "where the sun sets." (Our similar expression "rides off into the sunset" does not mean the same thing at all.) NRSV suggests, "rides among the clouds."

"His name being Yah" A dubious translation, but one that attempts to understand the Hebrew, *b'yah sh'mo*. The problem is the introductory *bet*, which seems literally to mean, "In/with/by Yah, his name." The Targum to Psalm 62:11, where the phrase first occurs, omits the *bet*, and its appearance in the biblical texts puzzled medieval grammarians (Ibn Ezra, e.g.). With the *bet*, the Hebrew does not mean "Yah is his name." Artscroll suggests, "Extoll him . . . with His name, YAH."

"May Adonai's name . . ." Or, "Let Adonai's name . . ."

———◆———

LAWRENCE A. HOFFMAN

purpose, but when people objected to their doing so, they were given this passage to say during the *Bar'khu*. Eventually it became a general congregational response. Reform liturgies usually omit it.

"His name being Yah" The first two letters of the tetragrammaton, which the Midrash on Psalms associates with the two attributes of God with which the cosmos was created: "a father to orphans, and a judge who hears the pleas of widows." The Rabbis used "orphans and widows" to stand for all of society's poor and disinherited classes. The universe will remain intact only if it is governed justly.

———◆———

JUDITH PLASKOW

of reciprocity. "Rejoice before [God]. . . . May Adonai's name be blessed." The God who is "beyond all blessing and praise" nonetheless needs the praise and blessing of human beings. In the words of the Rabbis, when we are God's witnesses, God is God, and when we are not God's witnesses, God is, so to speak, not God (*Midrash to Psalms*, 123:1). Marcia Falk expresses the idea of the importance of human agency by beginning a number of her blessings, "Let us bless the source of life." As she puts it, finding and naming what is holy is a fundamentally human act. In a covenantal context, God is not alone and self-sufficient, indifferent to human praise and rejoicing. God needs a community in order to witness and give meaning to God's sovereignty.

2 | *Yotser*
יוֹצֵר

Blessing on Creation

[1] Blessed are You, Adonai our God, ruler of the world, who forms light and creates darkness, makes peace and creates everything, illumining the earth and those who dwell there in mercy, in his goodness forever renewing daily the work of creation. [2] How numerous are your works, Adonai! [3] You made all of them in wisdom. [4] The earth was filled with your creatures. [5] The exalted ruler ever since, lauded, glorified and extolled for days immemorial, God immemorial, in your great mercy have mercy on us: lord, acting as our strength; rock, acting as our protector; defender, acting as our salvation; protector, acting on our behalf.

[6] Almighty *Blessed Great Diviner*

The sun's lights' maker and designer:
The Good One made his name divine
And 'round his might set lights to shine.
[7] In holiness his hosts ascend
Exalting God, telling without end
Of the holiness of God sublime.

[1] בָּרוּךְ אַתָּה, יְיָ אֱלֹהֵינוּ, מֶלֶךְ
הָעוֹלָם, יוֹצֵר אוֹר וּבוֹרֵא חֹשֶׁךְ,
עֹשֶׂה שָׁלוֹם וּבוֹרֵא אֶת הַכֹּל.

הַמֵּאִיר לָאָרֶץ וְלַדָּרִים עָלֶיהָ בְּרַחֲ־
מִים, וּבְטוּבוֹ מְחַדֵּשׁ בְּכָל־יוֹם תָּמִיד
מַעֲשֵׂה בְרֵאשִׁית. [2] מָה רַבּוּ מַעֲשֶׂיךָ,
יְיָ. [3] כֻּלָּם בְּחָכְמָה עָשִׂיתָ. [4] מָלְאָה
הָאָרֶץ קִנְיָנֶךָ. [5] הַמֶּלֶךְ הַמְרוֹמָם לְבַדּוֹ
מֵאָז, הַמְשֻׁבָּח וְהַמְפֹאָר וְהַמִּתְנַשֵּׂא
מִימוֹת עוֹלָם. אֱלֹהֵי עוֹלָם, בְּרַחֲמֶיךָ
הָרַבִּים רַחֵם עָלֵינוּ, אֲדוֹן עֻזֵּנוּ, צוּר
מִשְׂגַּבֵּנוּ, מָגֵן יִשְׁעֵנוּ, מִשְׂגָּב בַּעֲדֵנוּ.

[6] אֵל בָּרוּךְ גְּדוֹל דֵּעָה

הֵכִין וּפָעַל זָהֳרֵי חַמָּה.

טוֹב יָצַר כָּבוֹד לִשְׁמוֹ,

מְאוֹרוֹת נָתַן סְבִיבוֹת עֻזּוֹ.

[7] פִּנּוֹת צְבָאָיו קְדוֹשִׁים,

רוֹמְמֵי שַׁדַּי תָּמִיד מְסַפְּרִים

כְּבוֹד אֵל וּקְדֻשָּׁתוֹ.

41

⁸ Be blessed, Adonai our God, for the excellent work of your hands, and for the glowing lights that You created, they will glorify You. ⁹ Be blessed our rock, our ruler and redeemer, creator of holy beings, your name be praised forever, our ruler, who formed his servants, the servants who all stand high above the world, reverently and with one voice reciting the words of the living God, the eternal ruler. ¹⁰ They are all beloved; they are all pure; they are all mighty; and they all carry out their creator's will with awe and reverence. ¹¹ They all open their mouths with holiness and purity, with poetry and song, and bless, praise, glorify and adore, sanctify and exalt the name of God, great mighty and awesome ruler, the Holy One. ¹² And from each other they all take the rule of the kingdom of heaven upon themselves, and give permission to each other to sanctify their creator. ¹³ With calm spirit, with pure speech and with holy melody, they all answer as one, reverently:

Holy, holy, holy is the Lord of hosts.

⁸ תִּתְבָּרַךְ, יְיָ אֱלֹהֵינוּ, עַל-שֶׁבַח מַעֲשֵׂה יָדֶיךָ, וְעַל-מְאוֹרֵי-אוֹר שֶׁעָשִׂיתָ, יְפָאֲרוּךָ. סֶלָה. ⁹ תִּתְבָּרַךְ צוּרֵנוּ, מַלְכֵּנוּ וְגוֹאֲלֵנוּ, בּוֹרֵא קְדוֹשִׁים. יִשְׁתַּבַּח שִׁמְךָ לָעַד מַלְכֵּנוּ, יוֹצֵר מְשָׁרְתִים, וַאֲשֶׁר מְשָׁרְתָיו כֻּלָּם עוֹמְדִים בְּרוּם עוֹלָם, וּמַשְׁמִיעִים בְּיִרְאָה, יַחַד בְּקוֹל, דִּבְרֵי אֱלֹהִים חַיִּים וּמֶלֶךְ עוֹלָם. ¹⁰ כֻּלָּם אֲהוּבִים, כֻּלָּם בְּרוּרִים, כֻּלָּם גִּבּוֹרִים, וְכֻלָּם עֹשִׂים בְּאֵימָה וּבְיִרְאָה רְצוֹן קוֹנָם. ¹¹ וְכֻלָּם פּוֹתְחִים אֶת פִּיהֶם בִּקְדֻשָּׁה וּבְטָהֳרָה, בְּשִׁירָה וּבְזִמְרָה, וּמְבָרְכִים וּמְשַׁבְּחִים, וּמְפָאֲרִים וּמַעֲרִיצִים, וּמַקְדִּישִׁים וּמַמְלִיכִים-

אֶת שֵׁם הָאֵל הַמֶּלֶךְ הַגָּדוֹל, הַגִּבּוֹר וְהַנּוֹרָא, קָדוֹשׁ הוּא. ¹² וְכֻלָּם מְקַבְּלִים עֲלֵיהֶם עֹל מַלְכוּת שָׁמַיִם זֶה מִזֶּה, וְנוֹתְנִים רְשׁוּת זֶה לָזֶה לְהַקְדִּישׁ לְיוֹצְרָם. ¹³ בְּנַחַת רוּחַ, בְּשָׂפָה בְרוּרָה, וּבִנְעִימָה קְדֹשָׁה, כֻּלָּם כְּאֶחָד עוֹנִים וְאוֹמְרִים בְּיִרְאָה.

קָדוֹשׁ קָדוֹשׁ קָדוֹשׁ יְיָ צְבָאוֹת.

42

¹⁴ The whole earth is full of his glory.

¹⁵ The ofanim and the holy creatures rise dramatically toward the serafim. ¹⁶ Before them they praise God:

The glory of Adonai is blessed from his place.

¹⁷ To the blessed God they shall render songs, to the ruler, the living and eternal God, they shall sing hymns and proclaim praise, for He alone is a worker of wonder, a creator of innovation, a master of war, a sower of righteousness, a grower of salvation, a creator of healing, awesome in splendor, a lord of wonder, in his goodness forever renewing daily the work of creation. ¹⁸ As it is said: "... to the maker of the great lights, whose mercy is everlasting." ¹⁹ Shine a new light on Zion, that we all might soon merit its light. ²⁰ Blessed are You, Adonai, creator of the lights.

¹⁴מְלֹא כָל הָאָרֶץ כְּבוֹדוֹ.

¹⁵וְהָאוֹפַנִּים וְחַיּוֹת הַקֹּדֶשׁ, בְּרַעַשׁ גָּדוֹל מִתְנַשְּׂאִים לְעֻמַּת שְׂרָפִים. ¹⁶לְעֻמָּתָם מְשַׁבְּחִים וְאוֹמְרִים.

בָּרוּךְ כְּבוֹד יְיָ מִמְּקוֹמוֹ.

¹⁷לָאֵל בָּרוּךְ נְעִימוֹת יִתֵּנוּ. לַמֶּלֶךְ, אֵל חַי וְקַיָּם, זְמִרוֹת יֹאמֵרוּ, וְתִשְׁבָּחוֹת יַשְׁמִיעוּ. כִּי הוּא לְבַדּוֹ פּוֹעֵל גְּבוּרוֹת, עֹשֶׂה חֲדָשׁוֹת, בַּעַל מִלְחָמוֹת, זוֹרֵעַ צְדָקוֹת, מַצְמִיחַ יְשׁוּעוֹת, בּוֹרֵא רְפוּאוֹת, נוֹרָא תְהִלּוֹת, אֲדוֹן הַנִּפְלָאוֹת, הַמְחַדֵּשׁ בְּטוּבוֹ בְּכָל יוֹם תָּמִיד מַעֲשֵׂה בְרֵאשִׁית, ¹⁸כָּאָמוּר לְעֹשֵׂה אוֹרִים גְּדֹלִים, כִּי לְעוֹלָם חַסְדּוֹ. ¹⁹אוֹר חָדָשׁ עַל צִיּוֹן תָּאִיר, וְנִזְכֶּה כֻלָּנוּ מְהֵרָה לְאוֹרוֹ. ²⁰בָּרוּךְ אַתָּה, יְיָ, יוֹצֵר הַמְּאוֹרוֹת.

MARC BRETTLER

"*Makes peace and creates everything*" Except for the last word, this is a quotation from Isa. 45:7, which reads *hara*, "trouble," not *hakol*, "everything." The biblical context makes "trouble" a better translation then the usual word, "evil," because it is juxtaposed with *shalom*, "peace" in the sense of "tranquility." The "Isaiah" passage is really by an anonymous prophet whose work is appended to Isaiah, and more properly called *(p. 46)*

LAWRENCE A. HOFFMAN

THE SERVICE MOVES DIRECTLY TO THE FIRST OF THE THREE BLESSINGS THAT SURROUND THE SH'MA, THE "BLESSING OF CREATION" (YOTSER) WHICH AFFIRMS GOD'S FORMATIVE ROLE IN ALL EXISTENCE. *(p. 50)*

בָּרוּךְ אַתָּה, יְיָ אֱלֹהֵינוּ, מֶלֶךְ¹
הָעוֹלָם, יוֹצֵר אוֹר וּבוֹרֵא חְשֶׁךְ,
עֹשֶׂה שָׁלוֹם וּבוֹרֵא אֶת הַכֹּל.

הַמֵּאִיר לָאָרֶץ וְלַדָּרִים עָלֶיהָ
בְּרַחֲמִים, וּבְטוּבוֹ מְחַדֵּשׁ בְּכָל־
יוֹם תָּמִיד מַעֲשֵׂה בְרֵאשִׁית.

LAWRENCE KUSHNER
NEHEMIA POLEN

"*Who forms light and creates darkness*" If God created the sun and moon and all the heavenly luminaries on the fourth day of *(p. 51)*

SUSAN L. EINBINDER

"*Blessed are You . . . creates everything*" The fate of the *Yotser* is indicative of the cultural differences between medieval Ashkenaz and Sefarad. The *(p. 47)*

¹ Blessed are You, Adonai our God, ruler of the world, who forms light and creates darkness, makes peace and creates everything, illumining the earth and those who dwell there in mercy, in his goodness forever renewing daily the work of creation. ² How numerous *(p. 46)*

DANIEL LANDES

"*Blessed are You . . . ruler of the world, who forms light*" To be said seated. The blessing is recited out loud by the prayer leader and in an *(p. 52)*

DAVID ELLENSON

"*Renewing daily the work of creation*" All liberal prayer books of the last two centuries have retained the theme of creation, but they have expressed this blessing's version of it in different ways. In consonance with their tendency to abbreviate *(p. 48)*

JUDITH PLASKOW

"*Makes peace and creates everything*" The blessings surrounding the *Sh'ma* are replete with images of divine power. But here, the liturgy sidesteps the ultimate expression of that power: God's responsibility for evil. In rendering Isaiah *(p. 53)*

JOEL M. HOFFMAN

"*Forms light*" As in many other instances, the Hebrew is ambiguous between present tense verbs and nouns, so that "Former of light" would serve equally. There is little difference in meaning even in the English. We choose *(p. 49)* are your works, Adonai! [3] You made all of them in wisdom. [4] The earth was filled with your creatures. [5] The exalted ruler ever since, lauded, glorified and extolled for days immemorial, God immemorial, in your great mercy have mercy on us: lord, acting as our strength; rock, acting as our protector; defender, acting as our salvation; protector, acting on our behalf.

²מָה רַבּוּ מַעֲשֶׂיךָ, יְיָ. ³כֻּלָּם בְּחָכְמָה עָשִׂיתָ. ⁴מָלְאָה הָאָרֶץ קִנְיָנֶךָ. ⁵הַמֶּלֶךְ הַמְרוֹמָם לְבַדּוֹ מֵאָז, הַמְשֻׁבָּח וְהַמְפֹאָר וְהַמִּתְנַשֵּׂא מִימוֹת עוֹלָם. אֱלֹהֵי עוֹלָם, בְּרַחֲמֶיךָ הָרַבִּים רַחֵם עָלֵינוּ, אֲדוֹן עֻזֵּנוּ, צוּר מִשְׂגַּבֵּנוּ, מָגֵן יִשְׁעֵנוּ, מִשְׂגָּב בַּעֲדֵנוּ.

MARC BRETTLER

Second- or Deutero-Isaiah. He was active in the Babylonian exile (586–538 B.C.E.), when various forms of Persian dualism, including Zoroastrianism, became the norm. Our verse is thus polemical, emphasizing Judaism's monotheistic faith, according to which a single deity must be responsible for the opposites of light and darkness, peace and trouble. This polemic served little function in later periods, where, if anything, it was problematic, since it explicitly attributes the creation of trouble to God, and for this reason, was revised in the liturgy. Though deeply indebted to biblical precedents, the liturgy is not enslaved to the Bible, which it regularly revises to fit the changed needs of worshippers.

"You made all of them in wisdom. The earth was filled with your creatures. The exalted ruler . . ." Two themes converge here: God the wise creator and God the king. The first is a direct quotation from Ps. 104:24, "How numerous are your works, Adonai! You made all of them in wisdom. The earth was filled with Your creatures." The whole psalm is recited in the Rosh Chodesh (New Moon) liturgy. The quotation of this single verse may recall by extension the psalm as a whole and the vast range of God's beneficence: the earth, for instance (v. 5), which produces abundant vegetation, including the grape "which makes the heart of people rejoice" (vv. 13–16), and the vast ocean (vv. 25–26). This psalm rather than the creation stories from Genesis is chosen because it connects creation and wisdom, and emphasizes God's continuing role in the universe.

The other attribute, God's kingship, arises most prominently in Pss. 95–99, in the *Kabbalat Shabbat* service. But it is everywhere in the liturgy, and presented here in superlative terms, particularly within time: "The exalted ruler ever since (*me'az*) . . . extolled for days immemorial." The emphasis here is on the past, recollecting Ps. 93:3 ("Your throne is firm ever since [*me'az*], You have existed from eternity") because this paragraph's theme is creation; other instances (biblical and liturgical) prefer God's current or future kingship.

These two notions of God as creator and as king go back to ancient Semitic traditions of the king as a wise constructor of public buildings, as seen in Solomon, who built a palace and Temple (1 Kgs. 6–7). As the supremely wise king, God too is a "master builder," and the world is God's handiwork — as in Ps. 96:10, "Declare among the nations, 'God has become king'; He has indeed established the world so it shall not totter."

———◆———

SUSAN L. EINBINDER

Jews of medieval Ashkenaz extended their conservative attitudes towards the liturgy towards the *piyyutim* as well, and outfitted the *Sh'ma* and Its Blessings with as little poetic change as possible. By contrast, for Spanish Jewry, a more cosmopolitan and urbane elite, seeking ways to express itself liturgically, the *Yotser* seemed especially suited to the types of individualistic and humanistic composition that the Sefardi poets so excelled in writing.

From early times through the medieval period, the *Sh'ma* and Its Blessings had been one of many favorite sites for inserting liturgical poetry (*piyyutim*). The *piyyutim* designated for this part of the liturgy were a composite arrangement of several poetic parts, linked to different parts of the various benedictions surrounding the *Sh'ma*, and known collectively as a *Yotser*, after the theme word of the first benediction — "Blessed are You, Adonai, creator (*Yotser*) of the lights." A full set of inserts would occur only on Sabbaths and holidays, and would number seven; weekday prayers might use only a few of the standard seven parts, which were sufficiently independent as to able to appear independently of each other.

1. *Guf Hayotser* ("the body of the *Yotser*"): The first and major component, which draws on the theme of creation in a series of poetic tercets and choral verses, and concludes with a reference to the *K'dushah*. It appears right here, at the section of the first blessing which praises God as the source of light and creator of the heavenly bodies.
2. *Ofan*: The second part, which is devoted to an elaborate description of the angelic host, and takes its name from the *ofanim*, one of the angelic bands mentioned here.
3. *M'orah*: The third poem, inserted before the conclusion of the *Yotser* benediction, and used frequently to extend the light imagery in metaphorical ways.
4. *Ahavah*: The fourth unit, an elaboration of the second benediction before the *Sh'ma*, and illustrated especially beautifully in Spain.
5. *Zulat*: The fifth segment, placed in the benediction following the *Sh'ma*, and receiving its name from the liturgical statement there to which it is attached, "There is no God like You" (*ein elohim zulatekha*).
6. *Mi kamokha*: The sixth unit, given a name for its function, the linkage of the two verse sections of the *Mi kamokha*.
7. *G'ullah*: The final poem, which comes just before the conclusion (*chatimah*) of the final *Sh'ma* benediction; in Spain, this poetic insert also received special attention.

Discussion and examples of all seven will follow in the commentary below.

———◆———

DAVID ELLENSON

the traditional service by deleting repetitious passages and phrases, Reform versions have usually included only the bare bones of the blessing, omitting, for instance, the description of the angels ("Holy, holy, holy . . .") and the lengthy sections of praise, which seemed to be extraneous to the theme. In so doing, they followed the prayer book of Saadiah Gaon (882–942), who had prescribed such a shortened version for individuals worshipping alone. They also followed the theories of the preeminent academic scholar of the nineteenth century, Leopold Zunz (1794–1886), who had identified this as the original and pristine version of the prayer, to which the other material has been later appended. His theory turned out to be incorrect, but the Reformers could hardly have known it at the time, and by following the most scientific hypothesis on prayer that they had available, they were able to remain faithful to the traditional idea and text of the prayer book (based on precedents drawn from the Tradition itself), while shortening the service as well.

One of the first Reform prayer books to display this tendency was David Einhorn's *Olath Tamid* (1856), a forerunner of the North American *Union Prayer Book*. Einhorn deleted the rhymes, alphabetical acrostics, and other elements that Zunz had considered relatively late in origin. His text read, "We praise Thee, O Lord our God, King of the Universe. At Thy word the light shineth forth, and by Thy command darkness spreadeth its folds. Peace Thou establishest for all that Thou hast called into being. In Thy mercy Thou sendest light to the earth and to them that dwell thereon and renewest daily and without ceasing the face of Thy creation. Thy handiwork proclaimeth Thy glory and the lights which Thou hast fashioned sing of Thy greatness. And we, too, would extoll and praise Thee, at whose command the light shineth forth."

The major American Reform prayer books of the 1900s — the *Union Prayer Book* (1895) and *Gates of Prayer* (1975) — and the British *Siddur Lev Chadash* (1995) still mostly follow Einhorn's text for this prayer, although *Gates of Prayer* offers an alternative Shabbat version which restores the alphabetical acrostic, among other things.

The tendency to abbreviate this part of the service has not been confined to the Reform Movement alone. In keeping with the philosophy of its founder, Mordecai Kaplan, by which God is seen as a natural force inherent in the universe, the 1958 Reconstructionist *Festival Prayer Book* entitles this section of the service, "God of Nature," and offers only a slightly lengthier version of this prayer than is found in other liberal liturgies. In *The Book of Blessings* (1996), feminist liturgist Marcia Falk offers the following succinct prayer as an expression of her own somewhat similar theological views: "Let us bless the source of life, source of darkness and light, heart of harmony and chaos, creativity and creation."

Most European Reform liturgists, however, elected not to reduce the service at this point — as in, for instance, the first Reform prayer books ever written, those produced by the German Hamburg Temple in 1819 and 1841. The foremost Reformers of the nineteenth century, Rabbis Abraham Geiger (of Germany) and Isaac Mayer Wise (in Cincinnati), were also exponents of this position. By maintaining the traditional blessing, they successfully portrayed Reform Judaism as a general trend for all "enlightened" Jews, as opposed to a denominationally distinct Jewish movement. They hoped this moderate stance would attract Jews who were modern, but who still retained emotional attachment to the familiar service.

———◆———

JOEL M. HOFFMAN

"forms," not "creates," because we reserve "creates" for *borei*, which appears next. Birnbaum and FOP agree. The point is not so much the nuances of meaning that *yotser* and *borei* convey, but rather that three verbs are used with four objects, and we need to assign English equivalents consistently.

"Illumining" Others, "giving light" and variations thereon. ("Enlighten" is tempting, but wrong.) The more common "illuminate" would be appropriate, but is ambiguous, suggesting both spiritual and physical light. "Illumine" is properly limited to the physical light of creation of which our blessing speaks.

"Who dwell there" "Dwell," not "live," because "live" is ambiguous in that it also contrasts with "die" in a way that the Hebrew *darim* does not.

"In mercy" "With mercy" might be nice here, but "in mercy" creates a proper parallel with "in goodness" that follows.

"Forever renewing daily the work of creation" At first glance redundant, as in Birnbaum's "every day, constantly," GOP and SLC's "continually, day by day," or Artscroll's "daily, perpetually," but more likely a daily process that never ceases: every day, God renews creation, and the process goes on forever.

"How numerous are your works" The Hebrew *rabu* can mean "many" or "great," but in the current context, the former is more likely, since the next phrase is, "You made all of them in wisdom." (Birnbaum and Artscroll disagree, offering "great.") GOP, SLC, STH and SSS all use "manifold," a poetic word from a much higher register than the Hebrew *rabu*, which many worshippers today may not even understand. "Your works" is the Hebrew *ma'asekha*, from the root *ma'aseh*, rendered "the work [of creation]," immediately prior, so we use the same English equivalent here.

"The earth was filled . . ." Hebrew *mal'ah*. Most translations read, "The earth is full," or "abounds with" (present tense). But the next sentence refers to God's role *me'az*, "ever since," so that we are left wondering, "since what?" The meaning of this phrase seems intertwined with those around it. God "made" the many works of creation, so that the earth "*was* filled" with creatures, all of whom "ever since" praised their creator.

"Your creatures" From the root *k.n.h*, "buy," not "create." Words from the root *k.n.h* are often used for the world's creatures relative to God. In the *Avot*, God is *koneh hakol*

"'creator' of everything," and the ancient Palestinian version from the Genizah, as well as our Friday night liturgy, say *koneh shamayim va'arets*, "God 'creates' heaven and earth." *K.n.h* may originally have implied "having control over," or "being legal master of," the way a shepherd is master of livestock. The usual way of attaining legal control was purchase, so the word gradually grew to mean "to buy," but God could make us, thereby acquiring us without buying us.

"For days immemorial, God immemorial" From the Hebrew *mimot olam, elohei olam.* Repeating "immemorial" captures the deliberate repetition of the Hebrew. *Mimot olam,* literally, is "days eternal," in the sense of forever in the past, up to now. "The dawn of days" would be especially nice here, but would make it impossible to capture the Hebrew word play in which *olam* appears twice.

"Acting as . . . acting on" A deliberate attempt to capture the Hebrew parallelism: four attributes of God set in apposition, each comprising two words.

◆

LAWRENCE A. HOFFMAN

"Who forms light and creates darkness" Each of the *Sh'ma's* blessings responds to a specific philosophic topic that exercised thinkers in late antiquity, thereby commenting implicitly on how Jewish belief differed from that of others at the time. Our benediction on creation emphasizes light, in particular, because the ancients saw the universe divided into light and darkness, two realms that they identified further with good and bad, or sometimes, spirit and matter. An extreme form of this dualism led to the notion that there must be two gods, or at least, an all-powerful god and a lesser power called a demiurge. The demiurge, or second deity, was regarded as the source of darkness, materiality and evil. While Jews too associated God primarily with the light of the universe, they stopped short of the radical dualism that would have compromised the principle of monotheism. They therefore attributed not just light but darkness also to God. But they were ambivalent about God's role in "creating darkness," so in the final line of the blessing, the *chatimah*, they mention only, "Blessed are You, Adonai, creator of the lights."

"Makes peace and creates everything" The midrash says, "Great is peace; it is equal to everything." Some commentators conclude that we therefore mean, "By making peace, God implicitly created everything."

"The exalted ruler" The *Yotser* is sewn together from fragments of many different prayers. There must originally have been an unlimited number of ways in which the oral artist who led the prayer service might have rendered the theme of creation. Only eventually did some unknown editor combine bits and pieces of some of them into the form we now have. From here to the end of the paragraph, for instance, we see a composition that emphasizes God's praise but has little to say about creation, the supposed topic of the blessing to begin with. It also introduces poetic features like rhyme (see the

last line in Hebrew, *adon uzeinu, tsur misgabeinu . . .*) and the emphatic use of sound from the letter "M" (*hamelekh ham'romam . . .*).

It is probable that early liturgy functioned not only cognitively, but affectively as well, that is, it gave a message of content, but it also evoked trance-like behavior on the part of worshippers, who used the affect of the language to have what we would call an out-of-body experience. Living in a pre-Copernican universe, Jews believed that the earth was the center of a cosmos that expanded outward in concentric rings of astral bodies swirling endlessly around them, and producing what was called "the music of the spheres." The outermost spheres were the seven heavens, and in the final one, God sat enthroned in a chariot. The angels lived endlessly in the light of God's chariot, praising God by saying "Holy, Holy, Holy," just as Isaiah had seen. The goal of worship was to free one's spiritual self, so to speak, and then to "trip" to the outer reaches of the cosmos, there to behold God and to join momentarily in the angelic praise. Toward that end, language as a virtual mantra was introduced: Hence, our paragraph (from "The exalted ruler" to "acting on our behalf") which omits cognitive content almost entirely, substituting instead rhyme and redundant praise of God.

The blessing therefore culminates later in Isaiah's vision (see below, "Holy, holy, holy"). Inducing an out-of-body experience, it was hoped, would transport worshippers to the final heaven where they could join the angels in their praise of God — a state of bliss still reflected in our expression, "Being in seventh heaven!"

———◆———

LAWRENCE KUSHNER
NEHEMIA POLEN

creation, then where did the light that God created on the first day come from? The Talmud (Chag. 12a) offers a daring solution, one with far-reaching implications for Jewish spirituality. It suggests that the first light of creation was not optical but spiritual, a light so dazzling that in it Adam and Eve were able to see from one end of space to the other end of time:

> Was the light really created on the first day [as we find in Genesis 1:3, "God said let there be light, and there was light"]? It is written [further on]: "God set them [the sun and the moon] in the firmament of heaven" (Gen. 1:17), about which it says, "There was evening and there was morning, a *fourth* day" (Gen. 1:19). This discrepancy is to be explained according to Rabbi Eleazar. For Rabbi Eleazar said: In the light that the Holy One created on the first day, one could see from one end of the world to the other; but as soon as the Holy One beheld the generation of the flood and the generation of the tower of Babel, and saw that their actions were corrupt, God arose and hid it from them, for it is said, "Light is withheld from the wicked" (Job 38:15). Then, for whom did God reserve it? For the righteous in the time to come (cf. Avot 2.16), for it is said, "God saw that the light was good" (Gen. 1:4). "Good" is an allusion not to the light but to the righteous for whom it is reserved, as it is said, "Say of the righteous that they are good" (Isa. 3:10). As soon as God saw the light that was reserved for the righteous, God rejoiced, for it is said, "The light of the righteous rejoices" (Prov. 13:9).

The Zohar amplifies the legend.

> Rabbi Isaac said: "The light created by God in the act of creation flared from one end of the universe to the other and was hidden away, reserved for the righteous in the world to come, as it is written, 'Light is sown for the righteous' (Psalm 97:11). Then the worlds will be fragrant, and all will be one. But until the world to come arrives, it is stored and hidden away."

> Rabbi Judah responded: "If the light were completely hidden, the world would not exist for even a moment! Rather, it is hidden and sown like a seed that gives birth to other seeds and fruit. Thereby the world is sustained. Every single day, a ray of that light shines into the world, keeping everything alive; with that ray God feeds the world. And everywhere that Torah is studied at night one thread-thin ray appears from that hidden light and flows down upon those absorbed in it. Since the first day, the light has never been fully revealed, but it is vital to the world, renewing each day the act of Creation."

> (Translation, Daniel Matt, *The Essential Kabbalah*)

If the light of the first day of creation, that light of ultimate awareness, in other words, were to fall into the hands of the wicked, they would use it to destroy the world. (It's true. If we ourselves could see into the future, we'd make a terrible mess of things!) Yet, if God were to withdraw the light from creation entirely, deprive it of even the possibility of ultimate awareness, the universe would collapse, implode. So how did the Holy One solve the problem? God hid the light, but only for the righteous in the time to come.

Now if that be so, asks Elimelekh of Lizhensk (1717–1787) in his *No'am Elimelekh*, why do we say here, in the present tense, "Who *forms* light and *creates* darkness"? We would expect the blessing to use the past tense, "Who *formed* light and *created* darkness." The explanation, he suggests, is that God — in an act of grace — is *continually* creating light. And thus, to the righteous the hidden light of creation, ultimate awareness, is revealed each and every day. It appears to them that even as they are discovering light, God is continuously creating it for them. They feel as if they are actually growing into newly fashioned levels of awareness, each brighter than the one before.

As in so much of Chasidism, the vision here is not eschatological but psychological, deeply personal and interior. The light is not a thing made in the past and hidden for the future but continuously created with each act of righteousness. In this way, the holy ones in each generation ascend into this hidden light and the *Yotser* blessing here invites us to join them.

———◆———

DANIEL LANDES

undertone by the congregation. One should carefully enunciate the words *yotser or*, being careful to separate them from each other.

———◆———

JUDITH PLASKOW

45:7, "I form light and create darkness, I make peace and create evil" as "who forms light and creates darkness, makes peace and creates everything," the Rabbis introduce a euphemism that avoids attributing evil to God. Of course, it is true that "everything" includes woe and evil, but the word conjures — and is probably meant to conjure — the plenitude of creation, rather than its destructive or negative aspects.

This alteration of Isaiah raises the question of truth in liturgy. Do we want a liturgy that names the truths of our lives, however painful or difficult they may be, or do we want a liturgy that elevates and empowers, that focuses on the wondrous aspects of creation alone? Are these goals in conflict, or can hearing truth itself be empowering? In *The Book of Blessings,* Marcia Falk comes down on the side of truth. If God is all in all, she argues, then the divine domain must include the "bad," and the bad ought to be named. Her blessing here says, "Let us bless the source of life / source of darkness and light / heart of harmony and chaos, / creativity and creation."

What does it mean, however, to pray to a God who is "heart of chaos"? The naming of this truth — that if one God is responsible for the universe, then that God must be responsible for evil — surely elicits feelings of protest as much as reverence. "Shall not the judge of all the earth do right?" Abraham asks God, arguing over the intended destruction of Sodom and Gemorrah (Gen. 18:25). We might pose analogous questions in the context of and in relation to the liturgy as a whole. Shall not the king leave room for his subjects? Shall not the father honor the independence of his children? Is it not our obligation to struggle against the "bad" in the universe, whatever its origins? Thus our prayer might need to be expanded in the direction of protest. The masculine and hierarchical images of the prayer book in many ways capture the truth of our social and religious structures. We can seek to change those images as a step toward change in the structures, or we can name them as evil and woe and, in the context of a covenantal relationship, protest against them.

"Our protector . . ." More than just male, God is portrayed as utterly exalted beyond all human power to know, approach, or even speak his glory. This liturgical picture of God is difficult to reconcile with the reciprocal notion of covenant, for all creation and power are in God's hands. Like the parent who resists the child's necessary steps toward independence, the "Lord act[s] as our strength . . . our protector . . . our salvation"; a "protector acting on our behalf." Such divine omnipotence leaves little sphere for human action, and metaphors of sovereignty, lordship, kingship, and judicial and military power convey an impression of arbitrary and autocratic rule that is quite at odds with our notions of just government, and thus with a concept of God as just governor.

Feminist objections to such images stem from the sense that there is a reciprocal relationship between the symbols that a community uses for God and its social and institutional structures. Because the reality of God is ultimately so mysterious as to be unknowable, we must attempt to express our experiences of encounter with God in the vocabulary available to us. We draw our metaphors from what we value, and they reinforce that value. In a community in which women are excluded from public religious life, imagining the ultimate power in the universe as male supports the notion that maleness is the norm of Jewish humanity and that women are of lesser value.

Moreover, God as Lord and ruler or king is the pinnacle of a vast hierarchy that extends from God "himself" to angels/men/women/children/animals, and finally the earth. As hierarchical ruler, God becomes a model and authority for the many schemes of dominance human beings create for themselves.

◆ ◆ ◆

MARC BRETTLER

"**A**lmighty **B**lessed **G**reat **D**iviner" This acrostic begins and ends with reference to the luminaries, which (line 2) are God's creation, and later on (lines 6 and 7) praise God in return. This style of concluding by returning full-circle to the beginning is a perpetuation of a common biblical device, which may be seen for example in Ps. 8, which opens and concludes "Adonai . . . how majestic is your name in the whole world," or the Tower of Babel story, which is framed by the words "the whole world" (Gen. 11:1, 9). This envelope or *inclusio* structure (as it is called) hints at the ancient belief in the cyclical character of the natural world.

───

LAWRENCE A. HOFFMAN

"**A**lmighty **B**lessed **G**reat **D**iviner" An alphabetic acrostic in which the master metaphor of light emerges no longer in the primary sense of the lights of creation, but as a reference to angels, who are imagined as being without bodies, and, therefore, as consisting only of pure light, and able to exist in the seventh heaven along with God, the former of all light from the beginning of time. The acrostic is also a poem, of the aabbccb variety:

El barukh g'dol de'AH (a)

Heikhin ufa'al zohorei chaMAH (a)

Tov yatsar k'vod liSHMO (b)

M'orot natan s'vivot uZO (b)

Pinot tz'va'av k'doSHIM (c)

Rom'mei shaddai tamid m'sapRIM (c)

K'vod el uk'dushaTO (b)

◆ ◆ ◆

⁶אֵל בָּרוּךְ גְּדוֹל דֵּעָה

הֵכִין וּפָעַל זָהֲרֵי חַמָּה.

טוֹב יָצַר כָּבוֹד לִשְׁמוֹ,

מְאוֹרוֹת נָתַן סְבִיבוֹת עֻזּוֹ.

⁷פִּנּוֹת צְבָאָיו קְדוֹשִׁים,

רוֹמְמֵי שַׁדַּי תָּמִיד מְסַפְּרִים

כְּבוֹד אֵל וּקְדֻשָּׁתוֹ.

⁶Almighty Blessed Great Diviner

The sun's lights' maker and designer:

The Good One made his name divine

And 'round his might set lights to shine.

⁷In holiness his hosts ascend

Exalting God, telling without end

Of the holiness of God sublime.

JOEL M. HOFFMAN

"**A**lmighty **B**lessed **G**reat **D**iviner" Thus begins an acrostic poem in Hebrew. English by chance lets us use the same initial letters as in the Hebrew for the first four English words. But were we to continue in a similar vein, trying to find four words starting with "h, u, z, h," we would have to resort to such nonsense as, "hurling upward zodiacs higher." And so we abandon the acrostic in the English, providing only a sense of it in the first line. But we keep the Hebrew rhyme intact (aabbccb) along with the meter, at the cost of missing some of the nuances of the individual words. Literally, they mean: "[The] blessed God of great knowledge prepared and activated the lights of the sun. The good One [God] created honor for his name, putting lights around his strength. His chief hosts are holy, exalting the Almighty, always telling of God's glory and of his holiness." But the meaning of the individual words here was never the point. They were chosen for their meter and their initial letter.

───

MARC BRETTLER

*B*e blessed . . . they will glorify You" The concluding notion of the luminaries blessing God is expanded and serves stylistically as a transition to the next sentence, "Be blessed our rock."

"His servants" Following an ancient near eastern tradition in which stars and planets are also seen as deities, the biblical *(p. 58)*

ELLIOT N. DORFF

*B*e blessed our rock . . . creator of holy beings" From its primary topic of creating the morning light, the liturgy moves to the ofanim and serafim, mythic heavenly servants of God *(p. 59)*

SUSAN L. EINBINDER

*H*oly, holy, holy . . . The ofanim and holy creatures . . . praise God" This section of the liturgy attracted the *piyyut* known as the *ofan*. Technically, the *ofan* served to connect *(p. 60)*

LAWRENCE A. HOFFMAN

*T*hey are all beloved" Again (see above, "Almighty Blessed Great Diviner") an acrostic, but only a partial one that may once have extended throughout the alphabet. We have left only the *alef*, *bet*, and *gimel* phrases: *kulam ahuvim* (*alef*); *kulam b'rurim* (*bet*); *kulam giborim* (*gimel*), but some prayer books deriving from ancient Greece and Turkey have a more or less complete acrostic, composed of synonyms for the angels.

"They all carry out their creator's will" (*kulam osim b'eimah . . . kulam pot'chim et pihem*) Again (see above, *(p. 63)*

8 תִּתְבָּרַךְ, יְיָ אֱלֹהֵינוּ, עַל־שֶׁבַח
מַעֲשֵׂה יָדֶיךָ, וְעַל־מְאוֹרֵי־אוֹר
שֶׁעָשִׂיתָ, יְפָאֲרוּךָ. סֶלָה. 9 תִּתְ־
בָּרַךְ צוּרֵנוּ, מַלְכֵּנוּ וְגוֹאֲלֵנוּ,
בּוֹרֵא קְדוֹשִׁים. יִשְׁתַּבַּח שִׁמְךָ
לָעַד מַלְכֵּנוּ, יוֹצֵר מְשָׁרְתִים,
וַאֲשֶׁר מְשָׁרְתָיו כֻּלָּם עוֹמְדִים

8 Be blessed, Adonai our God, for the excellent work of your hands, and for the glowing lights that You created, they will glorify You. 9 Be blessed our rock, our ruler and redeemer, creator of holy beings, your name be praised forever, our ruler, who formed his *(p. 57)*

DANIEL LANDES

*H*oly, holy, holy" The first blessing of the *Sh'ma* contains a *K'dushah*, the prayer that declares God's sanctity. The *K'dushah* occurs also in the *Amidah* where it is considered the *(p. 64)*

DAVID ELLENSON

*C*reator of holy beings . . . his servants" This paragraph introduces a mystical theme which virtually all Reform liturgists have found objectionable. The words "Creator of holy beings" and "his servants," as well as the verbose and repetitive character of the text which follows, were believed to have originated in circles of *(p. 60)*

JUDITH PLASKOW

*H*igh above the world . . ." While the feminist critique of the liturgy — articulated not only by me, but also by Marcia Falk, Ellen Umansky, and others — focuses on images of God as male hierarch, other Jews find these prayers disturbing because they assume a dichotomy between the natural *(p. 64)*

JOEL M. HOFFMAN

*T*hey will glorify You" It is not clear who "they" is. Perhaps the hosts from the previous paragraph? Another possible reading gives us "You will be glorified." The Hebrew might mean either.

(p. 62)

servants, the servants who all stand high above the world, reverently and with one voice reciting the words of the living God, the eternal ruler. [10] They are all beloved; they are all pure; they are all mighty; and they all carry out their creator's will with awe and reverence.[11] They all open their mouths with holiness and purity, with poetry and song, and bless, praise, glorify and adore, sanctify and exalt the name of God, great mighty and awesome ruler, the Holy One. [12] And from each other they all take the rule of the kingdom of heaven upon themselves, and give permission to each other to sanctify their creator. [13] With calm spirit, with pure speech and with holy melody, they all answer as one, reverently:

Holy, holy, holy is the Lord of hosts. [14] The whole earth is full of his glory.

[15] The ofanim and the holy creatures rise dramatically toward the serafim. [16] Before them they praise God:

The glory of Adonai is blessed from his place.

[17] To the blessed God they shall render songs, to the ruler, the living and eternal God, they shall sing hymns and proclaim praise, for He alone is a worker of wonder, a creator of innovation, a master of war, a sower of righteousness, a grower of salvation, a creator of healing, awesome in splendor, a lord of wonder, in his goodness forever renewing daily the work of creation.

בְּרוּם עוֹלָם, וּמַשְׁמִיעִים בְּיִרְאָה, יַחַד בְּקוֹל, דִּבְרֵי אֱלֹהִים חַיִּים וּמֶלֶךְ עוֹלָם. [10] כֻּלָּם אֲהוּבִים, כֻּלָּם בְּרוּרִים, כֻּלָּם גִּבּוֹרִים, וְכֻלָּם עֹשִׂים בְּאֵימָה וּבְיִרְאָה רְצוֹן קוֹנָם. [11] וְכֻלָּם פּוֹתְחִים אֶת פִּיהֶם בִּקְדֻשָּׁה וּבְטָהֳרָה, בְּשִׁירָה וּבְזִמְרָה, וּמְבָרְכִים וּמְשַׁבְּחִים, וּמְפָאֲרִים וּמַעֲרִי־צִים, וּמַקְדִּישִׁים וּמַמְלִיכִים־

אֶת שֵׁם הָאֵל הַמֶּלֶךְ הַגָּדוֹל, הַגִּבּוֹר וְהַנּוֹרָא, קָדוֹשׁ הוּא. [12] וְכֻלָּם מְקַבְּלִים עֲלֵיהֶם עֹל מַלְכוּת שָׁמַיִם זֶה מִזֶּה, וְנוֹתְנִים רְשׁוּת זֶה לָזֶה לְהַקְדִּישׁ לְיוֹצְ־רָם. [13] בְּנַחַת רוּחַ, בְּשָׂפָה בְרוּרָה, וּבִנְעִימָה קְדֻשָּׁה, כֻּלָּם כְּאֶחָד עוֹנִים וְאוֹמְרִים בְּיִרְאָה.

קָדוֹשׁ קָדוֹשׁ קָדוֹשׁ יְיָ צְבָאוֹת.

[14] מְלֹא כָל הָאָרֶץ כְּבוֹדוֹ.

[15] וְהָאוֹפַנִּים וְחַיּוֹת הַקֹּדֶשׁ, בְּרַעַשׁ גָּדוֹל מִתְנַשְּׂאִים לְעֻמַּת שְׂרָפִים. [16] לְעֻמָּתָם מְשַׁבְּחִים וְאוֹמְרִים.

בָּרוּךְ כְּבוֹד יְיָ מִמְּקוֹמוֹ.

[17] לָאֵל בָּרוּךְ נְעִימוֹת יִתֵּנוּ. לְמֶלֶךְ, אֵל חַי וְקַיָּם, זְמִרוֹת יֹאמֵרוּ, וְתִשְׁבָּחוֹת יַשְׁמִיעוּ. כִּי הוּא לְבַדּוֹ פּוֹעֵל גְּבוּרוֹת, עֹשֶׂה חֲדָשׁוֹת, בַּעַל מִלְחָמוֹת, זוֹרֵעַ צְדָקוֹת, מַצְמִיחַ יְשׁוּעוֹת, בּוֹרֵא רְפוּא־וֹת, נוֹרָא תְהִלּוֹת, אֲדוֹן הַנִּפְלָאוֹת, הַמְחַדֵּשׁ בְּטוּבוֹ בְּכָל יוֹם תָּמִיד מַעֲשֵׂה

18 As it is said: ". . . to the maker of the great lights, whose mercy is everlasting." 19 Shine a new light on Zion, that we all might soon merit its light. 20 Blessed are You, Adonai, creator of the lights.

בְּרֵאשִׁית, 18כָּאָמוּר לְעֹשֵׂה אוֹרִים גְּדֹלִים, כִּי לְעוֹלָם חַסְדּוֹ. 19אוֹר חָדָשׁ עַל צִיּוֹן תָּאִיר, וְנִזְכֶּה כֻלָּנוּ מְהֵרָה לְאוֹרוֹ. 20בָּרוּךְ אַתָּה, יְיָ, יוֹצֵר הַמְּאוֹרוֹת.

MARC BRETTLER

authors personified the luminaries as "the host of heaven," namely, angels, whose central biblical role was praising God. Several biblical texts are used to depict this function.

The word "angel" is somewhat misleading, however, since the Hebrew *malakh* is better translated as messenger. The word is regularly used of human messengers also, especially royal messengers (e.g. 1 Sam. 16:19), and from human usage it expands to include divine ones, like the *malakh* from God who halts the sacrifice of Isaac (Gen. 22:15).

The "servants" mentioned here (the *m'shartim*) are similarly found in the Bible as human messengers of kings (e.g. Esth. 1:10) and as angelic messengers of God (Ps. 103:21; 104:4). God's heavenly royal entourage mirrors the royal earthly one. The story of Job (chaps. 1–2) hinges on the role of *hasatan* (best translated as the adversary, rather than Satan), a member of God's retinue. The whole host of heaven is described as surrounding God on his throne (1 Kgs. 22:19–23), a vision shared by Isaiah (chap. 6) and Ezekiel (first few chaps.) in their initiation as prophets.

Above all, these angels praise God, like royal court singers, who played a similar role on earth. The most explicit description is Isaiah 6:3 (quoted here) where angels called serafim recite to each other "Holy, holy, holy is the Lord of hosts. The whole earth is full of his glory." But the elaboration of precisely how these words are said has no biblical precedent. That is the product of the Rabbis' own creative reading of their sacred sources.

"They all carry out . . . with awe and reverence" Another section with clear biblical precedence is the notion that "they all carry out their creator's will with awe and reverence." In the story of Job, for instance, *hasatan* ("the adversary" — see above, "His servants") has no independent power, so needs God's permission to carry out his plan.

"The ofanim and the holy creatures" The liturgy combines models from Isaiah and Ezekiel. Beginning with the trishagion ("Holy, holy, holy"), from Isaiah 6:3, it blends the serafim, the heavenly beings from Isaiah 6:2 with "ofanim and the holy creatures," found in the opening chapters of Ezekiel. In Ezekiel, these ofanim are just wheels on the divine chariot, but post-biblical literature redefined them as angels. Ezekiel's vision also included four unnamed "creatures" (Ezek. 1:5) who reappear in rabbinic imagination as "holy creatures," again, angelic types, who populate the divine entourage, and find their way into this montage of heavenly worship that we call the *K'dushah*.

"The glory of Adonai is blessed from his place" From Ezekiel 3:12, an immensely difficult text to translate, and possibly textually corrupt. Many scholars amend the first

word *barukh* to *b'rum*, so that it reads, "When the glory of Adonai lifted up from its place," in which case these words in their original context do not refer to heavenly praises. The liturgy, however, accepts the word *Barukh* as it is found, and identifies it with angelic discourse, akin to the unambiguous "Holy, holy, holy" of Isaiah.

"To the blessed God . . . to the maker of the great lights, whose mercy is everlasting." The liturgy continues the theme of divine praise by piling up divine attributes for which praise is due. Then it returns to the overall theme of the luminaries who represent God's heavenly court, by citing Ps. 136:7 ("To the maker of great lights . . ."). The liturgy assumes that the reader knows how the psalm begins: "Praise Adonai for He is good, whose mercy is everlasting"; and how it ends: "Praise the God of heavens, whose mercy is everlasting." Both phrases are imagined to be part of angelic praise, and therefore fitting allusions here. Psalm 136:7 is also a fitting contrast to Ps. 104:24 with which the blessing began (see above, "How numerous are your works, Adonai! You made all of them in wisdom"), in that Ps. 104 treats the universalistic theme of creation, whereas Ps. 136 focuses also on the Exodus, a particularistic theme which anticipates the blessing on God's special love of Israel ("Revelation") that is about to follow.

"Shine a new light on Zion" The theme of light is transformed into a petition, to which the entire part of the blessing may be seen as a prelude, explaining why the petition should be answered. This movement from prelude to petition is common to biblical prayer as well. The prose prayer of Moses in Deut. 3:23–24 explains first, "O Lord God, you have begun to show your servant your greatness and your strong arm; is there any [other] god in heaven or on earth who can do your mighty deeds?" Then it states the request: "May I cross over and see the good land which is across the Jordan?" (For a poetic example, see Ps. 18 and its parallel, 2 Sam. 22.) God is like a powerful patron, who may be swayed by hearing petitioners recount his great accomplishments. Here, the request for redemption is couched in the metaphor of light, following a biblical tradition that a new light will usher in the eschatological age (e.g. Isa. 60:19; Zech. 14:7). The earlier discussion of God as a creator of light thus explains the expectation that God will be able to grant the request, which is, after all, just for one more light.

———◆———

ELLIOT N. DORFF

described by Isaiah (6:1–13) and Ezekiel (1; 3:10–15). The eloquent descriptions of the heavenly host reflect conditions in antiquity when any sovereign worthy of the name had a large retinue as a visible sign of his or her greatness. Our author elaborates upon God's majestic retinue to indicate how impressive God's sovereignty is. Moreover, if sun, moon, stars, and even angels continually sing praises to God, acknowledging "that He alone is a worker of wonder, a creator of innovation," we certainly must praise God for God's many gifts — including each day's morning.

———◆———

Susan L. Einbinder

the two verses of the *K'dushah* and point them towards the biblical verse which concludes them. While the form of the *ofan* varies greatly, its theme is usually the same — a description of the angelic host and its song of praise. Like worshippers of other ages, the medievals were fascinated by angels, and some of the earlier *ofanim* are detailed descriptions of these beautiful, terrifying creatures, wrought of fire (or fire and water), winged and radiant, carrying torches and wearing crowns, surrounding and bearing the throne of God and singing to his glory.

"Blessed are You, Adonai, creator of the lights" The *piyyut* composition known as the *M'orah* would be inserted here, in order to focus on its imagery of light. Increasingly the poets used the *M'orah* as a way of talking about the symbolic or metaphoric interpretations of God as a creator of "light," for instance, God as the author of Torah, which "illumines" the people.

———◆———

David Ellenson

eighth-century mystics who used them to achieve a trance-like state. The belief in angelology, and the attempt to comprehend God in this ecstatic way ran completely counter to the rational sensibilities and beliefs of the early Reformers. Indeed, the manifest content of these prayers has generally been viewed as too "problematic" to allow for reinterpretation. Reform prayer books such as David Einhorn's *Olath Tamid* (1856), the 1895 *Union Prayer Book*, the 1975 *Gates of Prayer*, the 1982 Israeli *Ha'avodah Shebalev*, and the 1995 British *Siddur Lev Chadash*, as well as all Reconstructionist prayer books between 1945 and 1963, eliminated these sections altogether. Given the Enlightenment heritage which spawned liberal Judaism, giving it a rationalistic non-mystical commitment to truth, such removal is hardly surprising.

Far more interesting are those non-Orthodox prayer books which have retained elements of these texts in their liturgies. For example, the *Hamburg Temple Prayer Books* of both 1819 and 1841 maintained them in their entirety. As the first Reform liturgies composed during the modern era, these Hamburg Temple services were written so as not to alienate members of the community who were still tied viscerally to the traditional prayer service.

Isaac Mayer Wise too officially condemned angelology as superstition, but as in Hamburg, he wanted to attract traditional Jews, so he went out of his way to temper his liturgical reform by leaving the Hebrew of these prayers largely intact.

In recent times, some liberal liturgies, such as the Reconstructionist *Kol Han'shamah* (1994), have restored angelology to the service. They do so, however, because of their renewed appreciation of the wisdom and spiritual depth contained in the mystical, non-rational elements of religious tradition, not in order to avoid communal schism.

Retaining or restoring these texts in Hebrew is one thing; reproducing them in English is another. Facing the need to say what the prayers mean, liberal liturgists have offered interesting and varied translations, as well as commentaries justifying what they did. For example, instead of "Creator of holy beings," Wise says, "Creator of all that is pure." He was careful also to avoid any suggestion that "his servants" are "angels," though that is undoubtedly the original intent of the prayer. Unlike Philip Birnbaum's influential modern Orthodox prayer book which explicitly says, "ministering angels," Wise obviated any mystical or angel-like connotation by rendering "his servants" as "his ministering orbs," an idea he received from the rationalistic and anti-mystical tradition of medieval Jewish philosophy. In so doing, Wise, like countless liberal liturgists of the modern period, employed translation as a tool which allowed him to leave the Hebrew text intact while simultaneously removing or muting those meanings he found objectionable.

In contrast to *Minhag America*, the contemporary Reconstructionist *Kol Han'shamah* (1994) acknowledges the angelology inherent in this section of the service and boldly calls God "Creator of the holy beings," adding, "Let your name be praised eternally, majestic one, the fashioner of ministering angels." However, the commentary of Rabbi David Teutsch, President of the Reconstructionist Rabbinical College, allows for multiple meanings of these words so as to mute any necessary supernaturalistic meaning. "The tradition," he says, "leaves ample room for each generation to understand angels as it will, whether as natural forces or as revealing moments in our lives, the divine in people we meet, or manifestations of the goodness in our world or in the inner workings of the human heart."

"The ofanim and the holy creatures rise dramatically toward the serafim" For reasons cited above (see "Creator of holy beings"), the *Hamburg Temple Prayer Book* of 1841 retained these lines, but it translated "holy creatures" as *Lichtgestalten,* "figures of light," and in a commentary, denied any mystical interpretation by asserting that all the "beings" identified here are metaphors for the "powers of nature." Typically, it set the norm for many liberal books thereafter, by preserving the Hebrew text while utilizing translation and commentary to reject meanings it found troublesome. On the other hand, Isaac Mayer Wise found the angelology in this passage too blatant to allow for a naturalistic interpretation, and deleted it altogether from his *Minhag America*.

"Shine a new light on Zion, that we all might soon merit its light" This prayer for messianic redemption, with its Zionistic overtones, was highly problematic for scores of early Reform liturgists who were eager to demonstrate loyalty to their country of residence by purging Judaism of all its nationalistic dimensions. The very first Reform rite, the 1819 *Hamburg Temple Reform Prayer Book*, removed it completely. By 1841, the next *Hamburg Temple Prayer Book* restored it, but reduced the size of its letters, placed it in brackets, and left it untranslated. Abraham Geiger's 1854 prayer book removed the brackets and published this line in normal-sized print, but left it untranslated.

In America, both Isaac M. Wise and David Einhorn followed the example set by the 1819 *Hamburg Temple Prayer Book* and removed this line altogether. Their precedents have guided Reform liturgy until the present day, and while all progressive movements in Judaism have become fervent supporters of the Zionist enterprise and the State of Israel, this line has not been reinserted in either the American *Gates of Prayer* or the British *Siddur Lev Chadash*. The one notable exception to this trend in modern Reform Jewish liturgy is the Israeli Progressive Prayer Book, *Ha'avodah Shebalev*, which has restored this line to the Israeli Reform rite.

◆

JOEL M. HOFFMAN

"Holy beings" Or, "holy ones."

"His servants" Birnbaum, KH and Artscroll: "ministering angels."

"High above the world" Birnbaum: "the heights of the universe." Artscroll's ". . . stand at the summit of the universe" is a nice poetic adaptation.

"With one voice" Hebrew, *yachad b'kol.* Birnbaum has, "in unison, aloud." But the verb *mashmi'im* clearly indicates "aloud," and so more likely "*kol*" is part of the entailment of *yachad.* KH beautifully suggests, "giving voice in awestruck unison," a poetic rendition which, however, strays too far from our goals of translation.

"Eternal ruler" Or "Ruler of the world."

"Beloved" Or, "loved."

"Their creator's will (konam)" From the root *k.n.h,* "to buy" (see above, "Your creatures").

"Purity" Hebrew, *tahor*: not the rarer word we saw above for purity (*barur*).

"Poetry and song" *Shirah* and *zimrah.* The former denotes either song or poetry, while the latter is more clearly song. Birnbaum gives us "song and melody."

"Take the rule . . . and give permission" Birnbaum has "accept" not "take," but thereby misses the contrast between *m'kablim* and *not'nim* in the Hebrew. We use "rule of the kingdom of heaven" not "yoke of the kingdom of heaven" (even though *ol* is usually rendered "yoke") because few readers today know what a yoke is.

"Upon themselves" Relating back to "from each other," and translated literally. The meaning is unclear.

"Holy melody" Hebrew, *n'imah,* probably unrelated to the common Hebrew word *na'im* ("nice, pleasant"). Syriac and Arabic have similar roots meaning "to sing."

"Lord of hosts" Artscroll suggests that the Hebrew *ts'va'ot* is actually a name for God, and offers ". . . holy is Hashem, Master of Legions."

"The whole earth is full of his glory" "His glory fills the whole earth" might seem more natural, but would not convey the same emphasis as the Hebrew, which deliberately makes "the whole earth" (*m'lo khol ha'arets*) the subject of the sentence. GOP suggests the more literal, "the fullness of the whole earth is his glory," according to which the glory comes from the fact that the whole earth is full — an interesting idea, supported by the Hebrew, and possibly related to the blessing's introductory emphasis on "How numerous are your works" (see above), but seemingly out of context here.

"Ofanim" KH: "angels of the chariot," in accord with the chariot imagery earlier in the blessing (see above, "Where the sun sets").

"Holy creatures" Perhaps, "other holy creatures" is the point.

"Dramatically" Lit., "with great noise." Cf. "with beat of drum" or, "with flourish of trumpet."

"Living and eternal" As in Birnbaum, but perhaps "eternal" merely emphasizes "living." Artscroll: "living and enduring."

"A worker of wonder . . ." The Hebrew now provides eight attributes, each listed as either a noun or a verb followed by a plural ending in "*ot*." We strive to maintain similar parallelism of form in English.

"Forever renewing daily" As above.

"As it is said: '. . . to the maker'" Psalm 136:7, but the quotation is out of context. The actual verse reads, "Give thanks to God, whose mercy is everlasting . . . , to the maker of the great lights, whose mercy is everlasting." As it stands, we have an ungrammatical fragment, so we have added ellipses and quotation marks.

◆

LAWRENCE A. HOFFMAN

"They are all beloved"), a partial acrostic, this time with *ayin* (*kulam osim*) and *peh* (*kulam pot'chim*). Originally, this too may have employed all the letters.

"With holiness and purity, with poetry and song, they bless, praise, glorify, adore, sanctify and exalt" The theme of angels continues, this time with two strings of roughly identical words ("holiness and purity, poetry and song" and "bless, praise, glorify, adore, sanctify, exalt") set in apposition, not because the meaning is enhanced by using them all, but because the Rabbis used language for affect, not just content. In oral cultures (such as they inhabited), ritual leaders have no books. But they do not memorize single correct versions of texts either. Instead, they commit to memory huge repertoires of stock phrases that they string together randomly for verbal impact. Our text represents just one of many possible verbal selections, preserved by time, but originally, the words on any given day would have varied with the mood and recall of the prayer leader. The closest similarity today is a sermon by an African American preacher, the late Martin Luther King, Jr., for instance, who did not write out his speeches word for word, but improvised them as he went along, by drawing on his bank of stock expressions, many of them biblical, all of them resonant with oral impact.

"Take the rule of the kingdom of heaven upon themselves" The blessing anticipates the *Sh'ma* which the Rabbis called, "Taking the yoke [or rule] of the kingdom of heaven upon ourselves." *K'riyat Sh'ma*, the "recitation of the *Sh'ma*" which humans do on earth thus parallels the angelic *k'riyat K'dushah*, so to speak, a "recitation of the *K'dushah*" in heaven. Humans, who experience earthly dominion, conceptualize God as supreme king; angels, who are holy beings, think of God as "most holy." Each species, humans and angels, accepts God's rule from its own perspective.

"Holy, holy, holy" Technically a *K'dushah*, or more properly, a *K'dushat Hashem* ("Sanctification of the name [of God]"), a human repetition of the paradigmatic praise of God assumed to characterize the worship of the heavenly hosts, and recorded in the vision

of Isaiah ("Holy, holy, holy"). It occurs most prominently in the third blessing of the *Amidah*, but also here, and in a blessing that introduces the conclusion of the morning service, called *K'dushah D'sidra*. All three were probably in existence by the second century.

"Shine a new light on Zion" In a famous rejection of tradition, Saadiah Gaon (882–942) banned this petition, holding it to be out of place in a blessing that deals with creation, not deliverance. Sefardim follow Saadiah. Sherira Gaon (d. 998) ruled in its favor, however, and Ashkenazim follow him, possibly because of heightened messianic hope in northern Europe.

Rabbi Eleazer ben Nathan of Mayence (known as the RaBaN, c. 1090–c. 1170) harmonized Ashkenazi practice with Saadiah's objection by holding that the light in question is indeed messianic, but was part of creation too, since God brought it into being with the universe, and then stored it away for the end of time.

In Ashkenazi practice, the metaphor of light is thus extended from 1) its initial sense, the lights of creation, to 2) angels (see above, "*A*lmighty *B*lessed *G*reat *D*iviner") and finally, 3) the restorative light for Zion at the end of time.

———◆———

DANIEL LANDES

most holy of all prayers. This *K'dushah* is of lesser status, so is said sitting down, and is sometimes called *K'dushah D'y'shivah,* "the Seated *K'dushah.*" Nonetheless, it too requires a *minyan*, in which the congregation responds loudly at *Kadosh kadosh kadosh* and at *Barukh k'vod.* Many authorities (e.g., the Vilna Gaon, 1720–1797) rule that without a *minyan* one actually skips these two verses, since the Talmud holds that "all matters of holiness require the presence of ten." The dominant opinion, however, permits their private recitation, and some allow that private recitation to be said aloud, on the grounds that this is only a report of the angels sanctifying God, not our own attempt to do so. Some would require that such a private but aloud recitation be chanted with cantillation, to show that one is only reciting verses (*Mishnah B'rurah*).

"Creator of the lights" The congregation should finish the blessing before the prayer leader repeats it, so that worshippers may say *amen* after hearing the prayer leader finish.

———◆———

JUDITH PLASKOW

and supernatural realms. The exalted Lord dwells "high above the world," in a parallel universe up in the heavens. There he is surrounded by a fabulous court of ofanim, serafim and other "holy creatures" who serve him. As Mordecai Kaplan pointed out long ago, such "supernaturalism" is thoroughly at odds with the modern temper, which, rather than imagining the deity as occupying a separate universe, tends to enlarge the concept of the natural so as to include the sacred.

"A worker of wonder, a creator of innovation, a master of war, a sower of righteousness, a grower of salvation, a creator of healing, awesome in splendor, a lord of wonder . . ."
The language of the liturgy raises a fundamental question about prayer: Can we pray with words we do not believe, or words that have destructive social and religious consequences? The question of truth in relation to religious language is complex. Religious symbols are properly described as being "multivocal" — that is, they have many, sometimes colliding, layers of meaning. Just as some people embrace the liturgy with literalistic piety, others criticize its metaphors from a perspective on religious symbols that is every bit as naive. Calling God "Lord" or "king," or using other images evoking divine power, need not mean that God actually sits enthroned in heaven with a crown on his head. It can be a way of expressing a sense of finitude, limit, and frailty, a dependence on forces beyond human power to understand and control. Nor is there an absolute and rigid relationship between religious symbols and their political uses. The notion of God as king can authorize human hierarchies, but it can also express the conviction that no human being should be king over another. Images of God as warrior, savior, and protector can disparage human agency and foster passivity, but — as both the history of Israel and the recent record of liberation theologies in the third world indicate — they can also bring hope to the oppressed and encourage engagement in the struggle for liberation.

A more nuanced way of thinking about liturgical images of God is to ask whether the range of metaphors found in the prayer book is sufficiently broad that it makes clear the symbolic character of any individual image. Can most worshippers find at least some images that speak the truth of their own experiences? In this context, the piling up of imagery, such as we have here, can be read as an invitation to create even more metaphors — and not necessarily those that are synonyms for what is already present. Yet some worshippers may find that expanding the imagery is not enough; they must also discard those traditional and well-worn metaphors that, for them, make prayer impossible.

A number of recent prayer books exemplify either or both of these strategies of adding to or stripping down the liturgy. *Birkat Shalom*, for example, changes the Hebrew from feminine to masculine when it moves from *Bar'khu* to *Yotser*. In this way, it breaks down the hegemony of the traditional male language without simply substituting a female God for a male one. Addressing God as both female and male, it communicates the idea that God incorporates qualities associated with both genders, while also transcending them. *The Book of Blessings* too introduces a host of new images of God, all of them, however, as immanent source of life. Interestingly, both prayer books also leave out much of the language in the blessings around the *Sh'ma*, as if to say that it is possible neither to use all the traditional hierarchical metaphors right now, nor to find substitute language for them, so it is better to focus on what is essential and to allow new images to emerge in their time.

◆ ◆ ◆

3 | *Birkat Hatorah*
בִּרְכַת הַתּוֹרָה
Blessing on Revelation

¹ **Y**ou have loved us most lovingly, Adonai our God, cared for us greatly, even exceedingly caringly. ² Our father, our ruler, for the sake of our ancestors who trusted in You and whom You therefore taught the laws of life, so be gracious to us and teach them to us. ³ Our father, merciful father, show us mercy and inspire us to understand and to consider, to listen, learn and teach, to keep and do and perpetuate all the teachings of your Torah in love. ⁴ Enlighten our eyes with your Torah and draw our minds near to You with your commandments and unite our hearts to love and revere your name, that we will never be shamed. ⁵ Because we have trusted your great and awesome name, we will rejoice and celebrate with your salvation.

⁶ **B**ring us to peace from the four corners of the earth and lead us upright to our land. ⁷ It is You who are the God who effects salvation. ⁸ You have chosen us from among all peoples and nations and brought us closer to your great name with truth, to acknowledge You and declare your unity with love. ⁹ Blessed are You, Adonai, who chooses his People Israel with love.

אַ¹הֲבָה רַבָּה אֲהַבְתָּנוּ, יְיָ אֱלֹהֵי- נוּ, חֶמְלָה גְדוֹלָה וִיתֵרָה חָמַלְתָּ עָלֵינוּ. ²אָבִינוּ מַלְכֵּנוּ, בַּעֲבוּר אֲבוֹתֵינוּ שֶׁבָּטְחוּ בְךָ וַתְּלַמְּדֵם חֻקֵּי חַיִּים, כֵּן תְּחָנֵנוּ וּתְלַמְּדֵנוּ. ³אָבִינוּ, הָאָב הָרַחֲמָן, הַמְרַחֵם, רַחֵם עָלֵינוּ, וְתֵן בְּלִבֵּנוּ לְהָבִין וּלְהַשְׂכִּיל, לִשְׁמֹעַ לִלְמֹד וּלְלַמֵּד, לִשְׁמֹר וְלַעֲשׂוֹת וּלְקַיֵּם אֶת-כָּל-דִּבְרֵי תַלְמוּד תּוֹרָתֶךָ בְּאַהֲבָה. ⁴וְהָאֵר עֵינֵינוּ בְּתוֹרָתֶךָ, וְדַבֵּק לִבֵּנוּ בְּמִצְוֹתֶיךָ, וְיַחֵד לְבָבֵנוּ לְאַהֲבָה וּלְיִרְאָה אֶת-שְׁמֶךָ. וְלֹא-נֵבוֹשׁ לְעוֹלָם וָעֶד, ⁵כִּי בְשֵׁם קָד-שְׁךָ הַגָּדוֹל וְהַנּוֹרָא בָּטָחְנוּ. נָגִילָה וְנִשְׂמְחָה בִּישׁוּעָתֶךָ.

וַ⁶הֲבִיאֵנוּ לְשָׁלוֹם מֵאַרְבַּע כַּנְפוֹת הָאָרֶץ, וְתוֹלִיכֵנוּ קוֹמְמִיּוּת לְאַר-צֵנוּ. ⁷כִּי אֵל פּוֹעֵל יְשׁוּעוֹת אָתָּה. ⁸וּבָנוּ בָחַרְתָּ מִכָּל-עַם וְלָשׁוֹן וְקֵרַבְתָּנוּ לְשִׁמְךָ הַגָּדוֹל סֶלָה בֶּאֱמֶת, לְהוֹדוֹת לְךָ וּלְיַחֶדְךָ בְּאַהֲבָה. ⁹בָּרוּךְ אַתָּה, יְיָ, הַבּוֹחֵר בְּעַמּוֹ יִשְׂרָאֵל בְּאַהֲבָה.

MARC BRETTLER

"*You have loved us most lovingly*" This, the second blessing, bridges the gap between the last blessing's final request for deliverance, to the *Sh'ma*, which accents love of God. The deliverance theme recurs in the request to "Bring us to peace *(p. 70)*

ELLIOT N. DORFF

"*You have loved us most lovingly*" The second blessing moves from God as awesome creator of all being to God as compassionate lover of Israel, from a God concerned with the universal to a God who cares specially for a particular people, from an impressively transcendent God to a warmly immanent one. That is a *(p. 70)*

¹אַהֲבָה רַבָּה אֲהַבְתָּנוּ, יְיָ אֱלֹהֵי־
נוּ, חֶמְלָה גְדוֹלָה וִיתֵרָה חָמַלְתָּ
עָלֵינוּ. ²אָבִינוּ מַלְכֵּנוּ, בַּעֲבוּר
אֲבוֹתֵינוּ שֶׁבָּטְחוּ בְךָ וַתְּלַמְּדֵם
חֻקֵּי חַיִּים, כֵּן תְּחָנֵּנוּ וּתְלַמְּדֵנוּ.
³אָבִינוּ, הָאָב הָרַחֲמָן, הַמְרַחֵם,
רַחֵם עָלֵינוּ, וְתֵן בְּלִבֵּנוּ לְהָבִין

¹ You have loved us most lovingly, Adonai our God, cared for us greatly, even exceedingly caringly. ² Our father, our ruler, for the sake of our ancestors who trusted in You and whom You therefore taught the laws of life, so be gracious to us and teach them to us. ³ Our father, merciful *(p. 70)*

DAVID ELLENSON

"*For the sake of our ancestors who trusted in You*" While all liberal liturgies have affirmed our gratitude for the gift of revelation, Isaac Mayer Wise found this particular phrase so problematic that he omitted the Hebrew word *ba'avur*, "for the *(p. 71)*

LAWRENCE A. HOFFMAN

*THE BLESSING OF CREATION (*YOTSER*) IS FOLLOWED BY THE BLESSING OF REVELATION (*BIRKAT HATORAH*) WHICH AFFIRMS GOD'S GIFT OF TORAH TO ISRAEL.*

"*You have loved us most lovingly*" The two Talmuds maintain that originally, the Ten Commandments were recited here, but were dropped when heretics charged that they alone (not the entire Torah) were given at Sinai. We are unsure of the identity of these *(p. 72)*

LAWRENCE KUSHNER
NEHEMIA POLEN

"*Enlighten our eyes with your Torah and draw our minds near to You with your commandments*" Literally, "Enlighten our eyes with your Torah and cause our heart to cleave (*dabek*) to your commandments." The second blessing commences with *ahavah rabbah,* "great love." The primary symbol in Judaism for this love is, of course, our study of and devotion to God's Torah, the way of all creation. This *(p. 73)*

JOEL M. HOFFMAN

"*You have loved us most lovingly*" It is difficult to capture the beauty of the opening, *ahavah rabbah ahavtanu*. Others: "With a great love hast thou loved us" (Birnbaum), "Deep is your love for us" (GOP; SSS), and "With an abounding love You love us" (KH). *(p. 72)* father, show us mercy and inspire us to understand and to consider, to listen, learn and teach, to keep and do and perpetuate all the teachings of your Torah in love. [4] Enlighten our eyes with your Torah and draw our minds near to You with your commandments and unite our hearts to love and revere your name, that we will never be shamed. [5] Because we have trusted your great and awesome name, we will rejoice and celebrate with your salvation.

וּלְהַשְׂכִּיל, לִשְׁמֹעַ לִלְמֹד וּלְלַמֵּד, לִשְׁמֹר וְלַעֲשׂוֹת וּלְקַיֵּם אֶת־כָּל־דִּבְרֵי תַל־מוּד תּוֹרָתֶךָ בְּאַהֲבָה. [4] וְהָאֵר עֵינֵינוּ בְּתוֹרָתֶךָ, וְדַבֵּק לִבֵּנוּ בְּמִצְוֹתֶיךָ, וְיַחֵד לְבָבֵנוּ לְאַהֲבָה וּלְיִרְאָה אֶת־שְׁמֶךָ. וְלֹא־נֵבוֹשׁ לְעוֹלָם וָעֶד, [5] כִּי בְשֵׁם קָדְשְׁךָ הַגָּדוֹל וְהַנּוֹרָא בָּטָחְנוּ. נָגִילָה וְנִשְׂמְחָה בִּישׁוּעָתֶךָ.

MARC BRETTLER

from the four corners of the earth" — which is itself based partly on the description of restoration in Isa. 11:12. But the new theme (love) brackets the old one here, first, in the initial phrase, "You have loved us," and second, in the conclusion, "who chooses his people with love." God's love for us will evoke, in the *Sh'ma*, our obligation to love God in return. The love is reciprocal.

But how does God love Israel? As a husband loves a wife? Or a parent a child (e.g. Prov. 3:12)? Evoking God here as "our father" and "our father, merciful father" makes it quite clear that parental love is intended. More specifically, fatherly love is what the writer has in mind, a theme that is underscored by the oral play on words between the similar sounding *av* ("father") and *ahav* ("loves").

But the image of fatherly love is complex. One strand likens it simply to natural fatherly compassion, following Ps. 103:13, "Just as a father has compassion upon his children, so Adonai has compassion upon those who fear him." Another model is educational, evoking imagery of "father (and mother) as teacher," as in Prov. 1:8, "Heed, my son, the instruction of your father and do not abandon the teaching of your mother." Yet a third tier of meaning presumes a natural link between God as heavenly Father and Israel's earthly fathers, whom God by nature is expected to remember sympathetically. The last-named idea arises especially in Moses' pleas to God in the wilderness, when God considers destroying his people, or in Exod. 32:13, where God the father is expressly asked to recall Israel's ancestral fathers.

ELLIOT N. DORFF

hard philosophical jump, for experience leads us to think it improbable that an overpowering being who inspires awe and even fear can also be so loving as to care deeply for human beings, and for a particular group of them at that.

The Rabbis, however, insist that God is both transcendent and immanent, awesome and caring. Their way of thinking typically prefers truth to consistency, describing experience in all its fullness even if the facts do not fit neatly together. They thus deliberately juxtapose two blessings that force the worshipper to go without warning from the transcendent, powerful creator to the immanent, compassionate lover. God is both for us, and no view of God that ignores either one is adequate to our experience of, or to Jewish belief about, the Holy One.

"Our father, merciful father, show us mercy and inspire us to understand and to consider . . ." Another reading of this sentence is: "Our father, merciful father, show us mercy *by* enabling us to understand and consider. . . ." That is, one of the ways God manifests love for us is just by giving us the Torah in the first place. For American Jews, this may sound counterintuitive, since Americans are imbued with the value of freedom, whereas this prayer has the highest regard for rules that prompt obedience. Moreover, the majority (Christian) tradition sometimes perceives Jewish law as perverse and legalistic (at best), teaching us to sin or at least to remain ignorant of the spirit that motivated the formation of the law originally. How, then, can God's giving us rules be a manifestation of God's love?

The easiest analogy is the relationship between parents and children. Children who grow up in a home without rules experience apathy, not love. As any parent knows, it takes considerable commitment and energy to frame and enforce reasonable rules. Though rules may become an expression of parental power exerted over the children, they may also be an act of love, demanded by parents to teach children proper behavior. In like manner, this prayer asks God to enable us to experience Torah as an expression of God's love, that we may value learning it ourselves, teaching it to others, and fulfilling its precepts in our own lives.

———◆———

David Ellenson

sake of," from his prayer book. The doctrine in question is a rabbinic notion called *z'khut avot*, meaning "the merit of the ancestors." It held that any given Jew might be rewarded "for the sake of our ancestors," that is, because of the merit stored away by the saintly Abraham, Isaac and Jacob. Wise was a staunch follower of philosopher Immanuel Kant, however, and believed firmly in Kant's doctrine of moral autonomy. The notion that an individual could acquire merit on account of the deeds of another, even one's ancestors, was morally repugnant to him. All persons were, instead, to be judged individually on their own merits. So Wise rewrote the English to say, simply, "Our ancestors trusted in you."

Interestingly, the Reconstructionist *Kol Han'shamah* takes note of the Hebrew word *avotenu*, literally "our fathers," but translated here as "ancestors," and supplements the Hebrew text by adding (in the Hebrew) *ve'imotenu*, "and our mothers," thereby reflecting the Reconstructionist Movement's longstanding sensitivity to and affirmation of gender equality. The translation of *avotenu ve'imotenu* remains, however, "ancestors."

———◆———

JOEL M. HOFFMAN

"Cared for us greatly" Hebrew, *chemlah*. Others: "mercy" or "compassion."

"Even exceedingly" "Even" is required only to make the English readable.

"Whom You therefore taught" Hebrew prefers conjunction over subordination, and so the Hebrew "and," used for many of our more specific conjunctions, is translated here as "therefore."

"Teach them to us" "Them" is absent in the Hebrew, but English requires explicit objects even where Hebrew does not.

"Inspire us to understand" Following Birnbaum. KH provides "place in our hearts" thereby retaining "heart" as a literal equivalent for the Hebrew *lev*. *Lev* does mean "heart," but its metaphoric function is not the same in English as it is in Hebrew (see below, "Your mind and body and strength"). Also, as it stands, the phrase is semantically obtuse, literally, "Let in our hearts to understand" (*ten b'libenu l'havin*).

"In love" It is not clear what "in love" (or perhaps "with love") modifies. It might be how we are to keep etc. the teachings of Torah, or it might be how God might let us do so. The Hebrew is ambiguous, and so the English is too.

"With your Torah" Or, "in your Torah."

"Draw our minds near to You" For "mind" the Hebrew has *lev*, literally, heart. Birnbaum translates, "attach our heart," while GOP suggests "hold fast." But "commandments" seems to be an adverbial phrase, not an object of the verb, and so we must infer the omitted "You" as object. Though it is not unusual to omit objects in Hebrew, the meaning remains unclear.

"Never be shamed" "Never" is too weak to capture the force of the Hebrew *l'olam va'ed*, which is often translated as "forever and ever." The proper meaning here is "never, ever!" but that expression sounds childish, and the original Hebrew does not.

"Rejoice and celebrate" Birnbaum offers the more poetic, "thrill with joy"; GOP: "rejoice and be glad."

———◆———

LAWRENCE A. HOFFMAN

heretics, but apparently, some time in the second century (probably), the Decalogue was replaced with a blessing known as *Birkat Hatorah*, "The blessing over Torah," emphasizing the gift of the entire Torah to Israel.

Many "blessings over Torah" are still extant, scattered throughout the liturgy. A different blessing introduces the evening *Sh'ma* (not *Ahavah rabbah* — "You have loved us most lovingly" — but *Ahavat olam* — "With eternal love"). This allotment goes back to our first prayer book (*Seder Rav Amram*, c. 860). The Sefardi morning blessing follows an alternative precedent set by Saadiah Gaon (d. 942). It starts out like the Ashkenazi evening blessing (*Ahavat olam*) but then reverts to words typical of the Ashkenazi morning prayer.

Many beautiful alternatives can be found in the Genizah fragments. One, for instance, reads, in part, "Blessed are You . . . who provides Torah from the heavens and eternal life on high." Another draws on imagery from Psalm 80, which likens Israel to a vine uprooted from Egypt, and transplanted in the Land of Israel. "God brought forth a vine from Egypt . . . and planted it / Nurturing it with Sinai's waters / With flowing streams from Horeb."

גֶפֶן מִמִּצְרַיִם הֶעֱלָה אֱלֹהֵינוּ נ.‏ . . . נ וַיִּטְעֶהָ מַיִם מִסִּינַי הִשְׁקָה אוֹתָם וְנוֹזְלִים מֵחוֹרֵב.

—◆—

LAWRENCE KUSHNER
NEHEMIA POLEN

yearning is expressed elegantly in the phrase, "Enlighten our eyes with your Torah and cause our hearts to cleave (*dabek*) to your commandments." The sequence begins with understanding, ascends through enlightenment and culminates with cleaving to God's instruction.

In Chasidism, however, the word *dabek* ("cleave") means more than simply remaining close. It comes from the same root letters that give us the noun *d'vekut*, arguably the goal and the fulfillment of Chasidic spirituality. Usually translated as "cleaving," "intimacy," or "staying attached to," *d'vekut* is nothing less than a fusion with God, a loss of self in the enveloping waters of the divine, the *unio mystica*, a kind of amnesia in which we temporarily lose consciousness of where we end and begin, a merging with the Holy One(ness) of all being.

Yechiel Michel of Zlotchov (1731–1786) explained that a person who experiences *d'vekut* loses all self-awareness and considers him or herself to be nothing (*ayin*), like a drop which has fallen into the sea and returned to its source, now one with the waters of the sea, no longer recognizable as a separate entity.

Such a religious loss of self is also described by the contemporary American theologian Richard L. Rubenstein in an "oceanic" metaphor. He suggests that "God is the ocean and we are the waves. In some sense each wave has a moment in which it is distinguishable as a somewhat separate entity. Nevertheless, no wave is entirely distinct from the ocean which is its substantial ground."

In this light we can understand how the phrase *dabek libenu b'mitzvotekha*, "cause our hearts to cleave to, or, unite with, your commandments," means more in Chasidic spirituality than a mere wish to live in accord with God's Torah. Through the observance of the commandments, the worshipper prays to be rewarded with a loss of self, melding into the divine, an experience of the ultimate unity.

Ze'ev Wolf of Zhitomir (d. 1800), in his *Or Hame'ir,* cites a passage in *Chovot Hal'vavot* (*Duties of the Heart,* by Bachya ibn Pakuda, c. 1080, Spain). There we read of a pious Jew who prayed that he be saved from *pizur hanefesh*, literally, "scattering of soul," becoming unfocused, fragmented, not being centered, being "all over the place." Such is the inescapable outcome of trying to own too many things in too many places all at the same time.

But Ze'ev Wolf pushes the notion even further, suggesting that the main idea of having a "scattered soul" goes beyond being "scattered," to the sadness of having a "broken heart." He teaches that the root of our depression is the "dis-unity" of our soul, our inability to be at one, our inability to serve the One God.

Now if you direct your heart toward constantly cleaving to God, then surely your heart will no longer be scattered or fragmented. The power of the cleaving to the One God will necessarily re-unify your broken soul. The world may appear disorganized and broken into pieces, but in truth it conceals the Holy One who sustains and unifies it continually. Everything in creation is but clothing for the divine which animates and nourishes it. It may, in other words, *seem* as if things are unrelated, contradictory, fragmented, "all over the place," but in truth everything is a manifestation of God and therefore the ultimate unity.

Martin Buber calls this "resolution." He teaches the same idea but focuses on the inner fragmentation that afflicts our souls. The person with a "divided, complicated, contradictory soul is not helpless: the core of the soul, the divine force in its depths, is capable of acting upon it, changing it, binding the conflicting forces together, amalgamating the diverging elements — is capable of unifying it."

So it is possible for the scattered soul to cleave to its Creator. And, since God's oneness is the root of all being, then to join oneself with God is to unify oneself. When you feel like you are drowning in a torrent of physical pleasures, dismayed by the multiplicity of your possessions and their demands, you return to the unity of God and heal yourself.

Thus, through Ze'ev Wolf of Zhitomir's deliberate and creative "misreading" of *dabek libenu* ("Cause our hearts to cleave"), we are invited to consider that the source of our alienation from God's commandments and even from God, lies in our personal dis-integration, our fragmentation. In the *Sh'ma*, which this blessing introduces, the reason we are unable to realize God's unity, and therefore the unity of all creation, is on account of our own brokenness. Before we can utter God's unity, then, we must recover our own. What more appropriate introduction to the *Sh'ma*, the declaration of God's unity, could we hope to find?

◆ ◆ ◆

MARC BRETTLER

"*You have chosen us from among all peoples*" This is the fundamental biblical notion of Israel as God's chosen people (see esp. Deut. 7:6–8). It is not fully compatible with the image of God as father (see above, "You have loved us most lovingly") and Israel, therefore, as God's son (also found in the *(p. 76)*

ELLIOT N. DORFF

"*Blessed are You, Adonai, who chooses his people Israel with love*" God is here acknowledged ("blessed") for choosing the People Israel. The Chosen People concept originates *(p. 76)*

LAWRENCE A. HOFFMAN

"*Bring us to peace from the four corners of the earth and lead us upright to our land*" "Bring us to peace" is a literal translation of what we have, but may be a corruption of the original prayer. The Sefardi version retains wording found in *Seder Rav Amram* and *Siddur Saadiah*, and is much clearer: "Adonai our God, let your great grace and mercy never ever abandon us. Quickly bring blessing and peace upon us from the four corners of the earth. Smash the yoke that is upon our neck, and lead us upright to our land." (Some versions *(p. 81)*

וַהֲבִיאֵנוּ לְשָׁלוֹם מֵאַרְבַּע כַּנְ-
פוֹת הָאָרֶץ, וְתוֹלִיכֵנוּ קוֹמְמִיּוּת
לְאַרְצֵנוּ. ‎7 כִּי אֵל פּוֹעֵל יְשׁוּעוֹת
אָתָּה. ‎8 וּבָנוּ בָחַרְתָּ מִכָּל-
עַם וְלָשׁוֹן וְקֵרַבְתָּנוּ לְשִׁמְךָ
הַגָּדוֹל סֶלָה בֶּאֱמֶת, לְהוֹדוֹת

SUSAN L. EINBINDER

"*Blessed are You, Adonai, who chooses his people Israel with love*" The writer and literary scholar C.S. Lewis claimed that the twelfth century "invented" the modern concept of "love." *(p. 77)*

[6] Bring us to peace from the four corners of the earth and lead us upright to our land. [7] It is You who are the God who effects salvation. [8] You have chosen us from among all peoples and nations and brought us closer to your great name with truth, to *(p. 76)*

DANIEL LANDES

"*Bring us to peace from the four corners of the earth*" It is customary here (*v'havi'einu l'shalom . . .*) to collect the four corners of the *tsitsit* in one hand, and hold them awaiting the following occasions *(p. 81)*

DAVID ELLENSON

"*Bring us to peace from the four corners of the earth and lead us upright to our land. . . . You have chosen us from among all peoples and nations*" Liberal liturgists have found these lines troubling, and for two reasons. Rejecting the idea that diasporan Jews live in "exile," and sometimes being anti-Zionist as well, many *(p. 79)*

JUDITH PLASKOW

"*You have chosen us from among all peoples and nations. . . . Blessed are You, Adonai, who chooses his People Israel with love.*" Chosenness is another problematic concept that appears and reappears throughout the prayer book. As Mordecai Kaplan, the great critic of chosenness, argued, the concept is incompatible *(p. 81)*

JOEL M. HOFFMAN

"*Bring us to peace*" The Hebrew, like the English, is ambiguous as to what is to take place. Either "we" who dwell now in the four corners of the earth will be brought to peace, or we will be brought to peace which exists in the four corners of the *(p. 80)* acknowledge You and declare your unity with love. [9] Blessed are You, Adonai, who chooses his people Israel with love.

בְּרוּךְ אַתָּה, יְיָ, [9]לְךָ וּלְיַחֶדְךָ בְּאַהֲבָה. הַבּוֹחֵר בְּעַמּוֹ יִשְׂרָאֵל בְּאַהֲבָה.

MARC BRETTLER

Bible), for it suggests a voluntary association rather than legal familial obligation, but the mixed metaphor highlights the bond between God and Israel. Israel is chosen, perhaps even adopted, into a parent-child relationship that cannot be severed. God becomes a master parent, calling on Israel the child to act responsibly, precisely in ways that the *Sh'ma* will delineate.

—◆—

ELLIOT N. DORFF

in God's choice of Abraham's family (Genesis 15; 17; 18:19) and is reiterated in the Bible with regard to the entire People Israel (e.g., Exodus 19:5; Deuteronomy 7:6–8; 14:2; 26:18; Isaiah 44:1–2, 8–9; Psalms 135:4). It has been the source of much controversy among Jews of the last two centuries. Some have rejected it because it has been used as an excuse for antisemitic attack. Others consider it chauvinistic, implying that we are superior to others, whereas we ought to hold only that we are different. The latter view was forcefully articulated by Mordecai Kaplan, the founder of the Reconstructionist Movement, who substituted the idea of vocation for chosenness, and therefore deleted from his *Sabbath Prayer Book* (1952) all references to the Chosen People, not only here, but even in the blessings surrounding the reading of the Torah.

The issue is frankly hard. We certainly do not want to portray ourselves as haughtily asserting our superiority, and yet we do want to affirm our pride and thankfulness in being a people instructed with, and directed by, God's Torah.

This tension is reminiscent of national allegiance. We feel connected to, and proud of, our country (city, school, etc.); but the feeling may well be objectively unwarranted, and it is certainly morally objectionable to transform that pride for our own group into denigration of, or even a disdain for, others.

Whatever its pitfalls, the concept of the Chosen People is everywhere in our liturgy, but *not* intended as a statement of the inherent superiority of the Jewish People. As the Torah states, "It is not because you are the most numerous of peoples that Adonai set his heart on you and chose you — indeed, you are the smallest of peoples; but it was because Adonai favored you and kept the oath He made to your fathers" (Deut. 7:7–8). The Chosen People concept, as articulated movingly in this prayer, expresses the preciousness of God's gift of the Torah, a gift that the People Israel was lucky to inherit. Moreover, God's love of Israel imposes *obligations* on Israel, not privileges: "You alone have I singled out of all the families of the earth. That is why I will call you to account for all your iniquities" (Amos 3:2).

Israel hopes that obeying the commandments will convince God to bring us back to the Land of Israel and to a state of redemption, but Jewish sources are clear that this divine gift will occur only if Israel does indeed obey (see, for example, Lev. 26, Deut. 28). Thus, even to the extent that possession of the Torah makes the People Israel God's chosen people, and, therefore, the object of God's special love, that status comes with a price: the duty and the privilege of knowing and fulfilling God's commandments.

——◆——

Susan L. Einbinder

While scholars no longer take seriously the possibility that we could suddenly become capable of new emotions previously unknown to human experience, it remains a fact that medieval Europe was very interested in love. In both Islamic Spain and Christian Europe, love inspired men and women to heights of achievement (and depths of degradation!); the etiquette of love fascinated both cultures as much as the physical and emotional symptoms of the age-old malady of "lovesickness." Undoubtedly the humanism of eleventh-century Spain and twelfth-century France, with their intense focus on the individual and what we would call questions of motive and personality, were responsible for some of the interest in love. After all, love is by definition a personal experience, and the one we love is the unique recipient of our idealized and yearning attention.

In a masterful move, the Golden Age poets transferred the language of human love, so exquisitely expressed in their secular compositions, to the description of the relationship between the individual Jew, or the Jewish People, and God. As might be imagined, the *Ahavah* segment of the *Yotser* compositions became a favorite for medieval Andalusian poets. Often tiny gem-like poems, the Andalusian *Ahavah* was written in the meters and rhymes of Arabic love poetry, and offered daring and often erotic metaphors to describe its sacred theme. Scholars have noticed, in fact, the resemblance of some of the motifs of this sacred love poetry to those found in Muslim Sufi verse; some of the Jewish poets were indeed influenced by the work of great Sufi mystics.

Sometimes, the theme is personal, revolving about the poet himself. This form of the *Ahavah* is a quiet and self-contained meditation, in which the poet reflects on the gestures of love that God has made on his behalf and which signal both to him and to the world his status as God's chosen one.

More often, however, the poems composed for insertion before this benediction often rely on a dialogue form between Israel and God. Even where the dialogue form is not used, the Andalusian *Ahavah* is startlingly intimate and human. Israel is a woman whose lover (God) has apparently abandoned or left her; she must demonstrate the depth of her love for Him by suffering in his absence and steadfastly awaiting his return. In the meantime, her rivals, personified as the daughters of Ishmael and Edom (Islam and Christianity), seek to vaunt their apparent triumph over her. What does Israel do? In one poem by Judah Halevi, she ponders the gifts and tokens of her love — the lamp, the Ark, the Law — and consoles herself that her rivals have no claim to match her own. ("She laughed at the daughter of Edom and the daughter of Arabia who covet her beloved. They are nothing but wild asses; how can they compare to the doe who nestled against her gazelle?")

In another Halevi poem, Israel cries out in anguish at the cruelty of her absent or tyrannical lover — can He have forgotten how faithfully she followed him through desert wastes? Sometimes Israel is exhausted in her wanderings after God, and brokenhearted because her lover has abandoned her; sometimes she vows never to mention his name again — but it sears her heart.

> Her lover hurt her heart by leaving her
> for years; she might have died.
> She swore she'd never say his name again
> but in her heart, it burned like fire.
> Why so hostile to her?
> Her mouth is always open to your rain.
> She keeps her faith, does not despair,
> Whether in your name her lot is pain or fame. (Translation, Raymond Scheindlin)

Thus the poets used the *Ahavah* to touch upon a number of theological issues central to the concerns of medieval Jewry — chief among them the claims of Islam and Christianity that the religious truth and special status of the Jews had been superseded. The breathtaking intimacy of the verses also testifies to the powerful way these poets could turn the personal experience of longing, passion and love into a voice for an entire nation.

In contrast, love in Ashkenaz developed in ways that described loyalty and devotion. In the extreme case, the love of the Ashkenaz Jew for God was tested in his or her willingness to be martyred, and we have many martyrological poems which describe Jewish men and women stretching out their necks to be killed in willing sacrifice, or hurrying to the pyre like brides and grooms to the wedding canopy. Interestingly, the description of these acts of martyrdom confirms for historians the emergence of the nuclear family as the primary unit of Jewish life. Within the family unit, love appears clearly as loyalty and tenderness to one's spouse and children, and one must assume that these values colored the Ashkenaz reading of our liturgical passage. We have, for instance, a particularly powerful lament written by Eliezer ben Judah of Worms (c. 1165–c. 1230; named also the *"Roke'ach,"* after the title of his most famous book, a work applying pietistic theory to Halakhah). He wrote it after the slaughter of his wife and two daughters by Crusaders in 1197 (the Third Crusade), and includes the information that his six-year-old, Hannah, not only knew how to weave, sew, embroider and sing, but could recite the first portion of the *Sh'ma* and did so daily — an interesting bit of information about the religious education of young girls at the time.

———◆———

DAVID ELLENSON

of them opposed the call for God to return the people Israel to the Land of Israel. Others condemned the elevation of Israel above all other nations as offensive to their universalistic sensibilities. The first was easier to deal with than the second. Since the blessing is not intrinsically about a return from exile, modern editors could argue that "Bring us . . . to our land" was a late addition to the text, and therefore easily removable without doing damage to the main idea, God's love for Israel. The second was more difficult to handle, since being "chosen from among all peoples and nations" had always been seen as precisely the whole idea: Why else would God give Israel the Torah? Israel was, after all, the "Chosen People."

Abraham Geiger and Isaac Mayer Wise, the builders and leaders of nineteenth-century Reform Judaism in Germany and the United States, just removed "Bring us . . . to our land," and then doctored the statement of being chosen by retaining "You have chosen us," but omitting "from among all peoples and nations." In this way, they purged their texts of Jewish nationalism as well as what they regarded as a noxious particularity bordering on chauvinism. On anti-nationalist grounds, David Einhorn also omitted "Bring us . . . to our land," but unlike Geiger and Wise, he was a firm believer in the uniqueness and particularity of the Jewish People, who, he thought, had been chosen by God for a messianic task of being a "light to the nations." He therefore retained "from among all peoples and nations."

A host of later liberal liturgies have followed the precedents of Geiger and Wise. The *Union Prayer Book* and, more recently, Marcia Falk's *Book of Blessings* omit these lines as they did, and despite their Zionist sympathies and sometimes pronounced particularism, neither *Gates of Prayer* nor *Siddur Lev Chadash*, the major prayer books of twentieth-century North American Reform and British Liberal Jewry, have restored either "Bring us . . . to our land," or "from among all peoples and nations."

Others, like Einhorn, retain a claim to being chosen "from among all peoples and nations." The original *Hamburg Temple Prayer Book* of 1819 did so, but its authors solved the "problem" of Jewish nationalism (posed by the line, "Bring us . . . to our land") in a unique way. They reworded the Hebrew, in accord with the Sefardi rite, to read, "Quickly *bring blessing and peace upon us* from the four corners of the earth, for You are a God of salvation." In this way, they avoided nationalistic claims, but employed Jewish tradition to do so. They were able also to retain the feel of the traditional Hebrew wording so as not to destroy the emotional attachment people had to it.

Not surprisingly, the modern Israeli Progressive Prayer Book, *Ha'avodah Shebalev*, has also preserved the phrase, "from among all peoples and nations." It has also followed the Hamburg precedent of utilizing Sefardi precedent for "Bring us . . . to our land." But it supplements the Sefardi wording with an explicit Zionist wish that restores the pristine Ashkenazi sense of age-old Jewish exile: "Bring blessing and peace upon us *and gather our exiles* from the four corners of the earth, and cause them to walk upright into our land."

Of particular interest to students of American Zionism is the 1963 *Reconstructionist Daily Prayer Book* which renders "Bring us . . . to our land" as, "*O gather the homeless of our people* from the four corners of the earth, and enable them to march erect into our land." American Reconstructionists thus retained the rhythm of the traditional Hebrew wording, and even its idea of bringing home the exiles, but only after transforming it in a very clever way. Like the Ashkenazi original, the Reconstructionist version affirms the centrality of the Land of Israel. But God is no longer beseeched to return *all* Jews there; the Land is envisioned as a haven only for those who are oppressed, not the whole people, and surely not Americans. Here is a liturgical emendation that best captures the benign formulation of Jewish nationalism that has long been the hallmark of the Zionist Movement in the United States.

Even traditional liturgists have had trouble with these lines. In his traditional 1843 *T'fillot Yisra'el*, for instance, Isak Noa Mannheimer (1793–1865) of Vienna changed "our land," to "the land of holiness and blessing." Similarly, the American Conservative Movement's current *Siddur Sim Shalom* translates "our land" as "our holy land." By defining the Land of Israel as uniquely "holy," these liturgists move the text beyond what could be construed as narrow nationalistic concerns. Jewish nationalist hopes for a restoration to the Land are subsumed instead under a spiritual-religious ideal that is consonant with the rhetoric of the larger Christian world. Even for traditionalists, creative translation thus becomes a tool to retain the received Hebrew text while simultaneously transforming and supplementing its meaning.

———◆———

JOEL M. HOFFMAN

earth. Presumably, the former is intended, an expression of the theological doctrine of *kibbutz g'luyot*, "the ingathering of the exiles," but the Hebrew is ambiguous.

"*Effects salvation*" Birnbaum: "performs triumphs."

"*Peoples and nations*" Lit. "peoples and languages."

"*Declare your unity*" From *l'yached*, translated a few lines above as "unite [our mind to love and revere your name]." The verbal pun may be intentional, but the meaning in each case must be different. In the first case (above), God focuses our attention, perhaps, in "uniting our mind" to do our duty. In the second (here) we declare God's unity. Birnbaum agrees, suggesting here, "acclaim thy oneness"; similarly, SSS and Artscroll have "proclaim your oneness" and GOP offers, "proclaim Your unity" — anticipating the upcoming *Sh'ma*.

———◆———

LAWRENCE A. HOFFMAN

are more explicit: "Smash the yoke of the gentile nations [*goyim*] that is upon our neck.")

"Who chooses his People Israel with love" The accent on God's love is noteworthy. Some versions of ancient Christian thought charged that the old covenant of Sinai (the *Old* Testament) was merely the dispensation of law, and was rendered null and void by the new covenant (or *New* Testament) of love, as manifest in Jesus. Second-century Jewish sources thus regularly identify Torah as the sign of God's ultimate love for Israel. This theme of God's love for Israel leads naturally to the *Sh'ma*, which heralds Israel's love, in return, for God.

———◆———

DANIEL LANDES

when they are kissed: 1) in the third paragraph of the *Sh'ma*, during the mention of *tsitsit*; 2) at "true" (*emet*), the word with which the third blessing begins (and the repetition of the *Sh'ma* ends); 3) at the word "true" elsewhere in the third blessing; 4) at "steadfast and desirable forever" (*ne'emanim v'nechemadim la'ad*) in the first paragraph of the third blessing. (See below, "A tassel," "When you see it," "True," "Steadfast and desirable forever.") All these customs are based upon the love of the *mitzvah* so are not, strictly speaking, absolutely necessary (*Arukh Hashulchan*, by Yehiel Michael Epstein, 1829–1908). Some (the Vilna Gaon) require two tassels of the *tsitsit* to remain in the back at all times, so allow taking only the front *tsitsit* and looking at them at appropriate moments (but not kissing them).

"Blessed are You . . . who chooses" Technically a "blessing over Torah" this blessing introduces the Torah reading of the *Sh'ma*. Nothing should interrupt the end of this blessing and the *Sh'ma*, therefore. Worshippers should complete the blessing simultaneously with the prayer leader so as not to have to respond *amen*. (Normally, hearing a blessing evokes the response of *amen*; but Halakhah prohibits saying *amen* to one's own blessings.)

———◆———

JUDITH PLASKOW

with full citizenship in a secular democracy. Without being necessary to Jewish self-respect, it encourages notions of racial and national superiority that lead to divisions among people and foster suspicion and hatred. From a feminist perspective, chosenness is part of a cluster of ideas within Judaism that makes hierarchical separation a central model for understanding difference. The hierarchical distinction between Israel and the nations finds its internal counterpart in the graded separation between men and women, and the distinctions between all those with status and power and any number of groups defined as "Other."

The fact that the blessing thanking God for choosing Israel follows immediately on a plea to be able to understand, teach, and live out Torah points to the challenge in dismantling the notion of election. How can we maintain the distinctiveness of the People of Israel as defined by its connection and allegiance to Torah without claiming the kind of unique relationship to God that sets Israel apart from all other peoples? This question is connected to one of the central challenges facing the human race at the end of the twentieth century. How do we maintain, learn from, and celebrate the richness and diversity of customs, traditions, and beliefs characterizing the world's peoples without ranking that diversity as more and less, better and worse, so that it becomes a source of division, contention, and social injustice?

In the case of Israel, we can rejoice in, offer thanks for, and seek to deepen our relationship to Torah without contrasting it to all the other ways in which the world's peoples connect to God, and without describing ourselves as singled out from among all others. The Reconstructionist liturgy, *Kol Han'shamah*, maintains its founder's suspicion of chosenness, by working around the concept of election very simply. "You have chosen us from among all peoples and nations and brought us closer to your great name" becomes, "For you are the redeeming God and have brought us near to your great name." "Blessed are You, Adonai, who chooses his People Israel with love" becomes, "Blessed are you, abundant One who lovingly cares for your People Israel." In this reworking, Israel's assurance of and gratitude for its own relationship to a loving God is independent of any claims to an unparalleled spiritual destiny.

◆ ◆ ◆

4 | *Sh'ma*
שְׁמַע

A. "Accepting the Yoke of the Kingdom of Heaven" (Deuteronomy 6:4–9)

[Reform congregations say "Hear O Israel . . ." and "Blessed is . . ." standing; others remain seated]

[Before silent recitation, it is customary to say the following three words]

1 (God, steadfast ruler . . .)

2 **H**ear O Israel: Adonai is our God; Adonai is One.

3 Blessed is the One the glory of whose kingdom is renowned forever.

4 **Y**ou shall love Adonai your God with all your mind and body and strength. 5 Keep these words, which I command you today, in mind. 6 Instruct your children about them. 7 Use them when you sit at home and when you walk about, when you lie down and when you stand up. 8 Bind them to your hand as a sign and set them between your eyes as a symbol. 9 Write them on the doorposts of your house and on your gates.

[Reform congregations say "Hear O Israel . . ." and "Blessed is . . ." standing; others remain seated]

[Before silent recitation, it is customary to say the following three words]

¹(אֵל מֶלֶךְ נֶאֱמָן.)

²**שְׁ**מַע יִשְׂרָאֵל. יְיָ אֱלֹהֵינוּ, יְיָ אֶחָד.

³בָּרוּךְ שֵׁם כְּבוֹד מַלְכוּתוֹ לְעוֹלָם וָעֶד.

⁴וְאָהַבְתָּ אֵת יְיָ אֱלֹהֶיךָ בְּכָל-לְבָבְךָ וּבְכָל-נַפְשְׁךָ וּבְכָל-מְאֹדֶךָ. ⁵וְהָיוּ הַדְּבָרִים הָאֵלֶּה, אֲשֶׁר אָנֹכִי מְצַוְּךָ הַיּוֹם, עַל-לְבָבֶךָ. ⁶וְשִׁנַּנְתָּם לְבָנֶיךָ, ⁷וְדִבַּרְתָּ בָּם בְּשִׁבְתְּךָ בְּבֵיתֶךָ וּבְלֶכְתְּךָ בַדֶּרֶךְ, וּבְשָׁכְבְּךָ וּבְקוּמֶךָ. ⁸וּקְשַׁרְתָּם לְאוֹת עַל-יָדֶךָ, וְהָיוּ לְטֹטָפֹת בֵּין עֵינֶיךָ, ⁹וּכְתַבְתָּם עַל-מְזוּזוֹת בֵּיתֶךָ, וּבִשְׁעָרֶיךָ.

B. "Accepting the Yoke of the Commandments" (Deuteronomy 11:13–21)

¹⁰ If you carefully heed my commandments, the ones I command you today, to love Adonai your God and worship Him with all your mind and body, then I shall grant your land's rain in its season, in the autumn and in the spring, that you might gather your grain, wine and oil. ¹¹ I shall grant grass in your fields for your cattle, that you might eat your fill. ¹² Take care lest your mind tempt you to rebel by worshipping other gods and by bowing down to them. ¹³ For then the fire and fury of Adonai will turn against you. ¹⁴ Adonai will stop the flow of the sky. ¹⁵ There will be no rain. ¹⁶ The earth will not grant its produce. ¹⁷ You will quickly perish from the good land that Adonai grants you. ¹⁸ So put these words of mine in charge of your mind and body, bind them to your hand as a sign and set them between your eyes as a symbol; teach them to your children, using them when you sit at home and when you walk about, when you lie down and when you stand up; write them on the doorposts of your house and on your gates — that your days and your children's days in the land that Adonai promised to give to your ancestors may be as numerous as the days that the sky overlooks the earth.

¹⁰ וְהָיָה אִם־שָׁמֹעַ תִּשְׁמְעוּ אֶל־מִצְוֹתַי אֲשֶׁר אָנֹכִי מְצַוֶּה אֶתְכֶם הַיּוֹם לְאַהֲבָה אֶת־יְיָ אֱלֹהֵיכֶם וּלְעָבְדוֹ בְּכָל־לְבַבְכֶם וּבְכָל־נַפְשְׁכֶם. וְנָתַתִּי מְטַר־אַרְצְכֶם בְּעִתּוֹ יוֹרֶה וּמַלְקוֹשׁ וְאָסַפְתָּ דְגָנֶךָ וְתִירֹשְׁךָ וְיִצְהָרֶךָ. ¹¹ וְנָתַתִּי עֵשֶׂב בְּשָׂדְךָ לִבְהֶמְתֶּךָ וְאָכַלְתָּ וְשָׂבָעְתָּ. ¹² הִשָּׁמְרוּ לָכֶם פֶּן־יִפְתֶּה לְבַבְכֶם וְסַרְתֶּם וַעֲבַדְתֶּם אֱלֹהִים אֲחֵרִים וְהִשְׁתַּחֲוִיתֶם לָהֶם. ¹³ וְחָרָה אַף־יְיָ בָּכֶם ¹⁴ וְעָצַר אֶת־הַשָּׁמַיִם ¹⁵ וְלֹא־יִהְיֶה מָטָר ¹⁶ וְהָאֲדָמָה לֹא תִתֵּן אֶת־יְבוּלָהּ ¹⁷ וַאֲבַדְתֶּם מְהֵרָה מֵעַל הָאָרֶץ הַטֹּבָה אֲשֶׁר יְיָ נֹתֵן לָכֶם. ¹⁸ וְשַׂמְתֶּם אֶת־דְּבָרַי אֵלֶּה עַל־לְבַבְכֶם וְעַל־נַפְשְׁכֶם וּקְשַׁרְתֶּם אֹתָם לְאוֹת עַל־יֶדְכֶם וְהָיוּ לְטוֹטָפֹת בֵּין עֵינֵיכֶם. וְלִמַּדְתֶּם אֹתָם אֶת־בְּנֵיכֶם לְדַבֵּר בָּם בְּשִׁבְתְּךָ בְּבֵיתֶךָ וּבְלֶכְתְּךָ בַדֶּרֶךְ וּבְשָׁכְבְּךָ וּבְקוּמֶךָ. וּכְתַבְתָּם עַל־מְזוּזוֹת בֵּיתֶךָ וּבִשְׁעָרֶיךָ.

לְמַעַן יִרְבּוּ יְמֵיכֶם וִימֵי בְנֵיכֶם עַל הָאֲדָמָה אֲשֶׁר נִשְׁבַּע יְיָ לַאֲבֹתֵיכֶם לָתֵת לָהֶם כִּימֵי הַשָּׁמַיִם עַל־הָאָרֶץ.

C. "The Section on Tassels"
(Numbers 15:37–41)

¹⁹ Adonai said to Moses: "Speak to the children of Israel, and tell them to make themselves a tassel on the corners of their clothes in every generation, and to put a blue thread on the tassel of each corner. ²⁰ Let it be a tassel for you. ²¹ When you see it you shall remember all of Adonai's commandments and do them, and not follow your mind or eyes which you follow in false worship. ²² Thus will you remember and do all of my commandments, and so be holy before your God. ²³ I am Adonai, your God, who led you out of the land of Egypt to be your God. ²⁴ I am Adonai your God.

*[Prayer leader adds the first word
of the next prayer, "True"]*

¹⁹ וַיֹּאמֶר יְיָ אֶל־מֹשֶׁה לֵּאמֹר. דַּבֵּר
אֶל־בְּנֵי יִשְׂרָאֵל וְאָמַרְתָּ אֲלֵהֶם
וְעָשׂוּ לָהֶם צִיצִת עַל־כַּנְפֵי בִגְדֵיהֶם
לְדֹרֹתָם וְנָתְנוּ עַל־צִיצִת הַכָּנָף פְּתִיל
תְּכֵלֶת. ²⁰ וְהָיָה לָכֶם לְצִיצִת וּרְאִי־
תֶם אֹתוֹ וּזְכַרְתֶּם אֶת־כָּל־מִצְוֹת יְיָ
וַעֲשִׂיתֶם אֹתָם וְלֹא תָתוּרוּ אַחֲרֵי
לְבַבְכֶם וְאַחֲרֵי עֵינֵיכֶם אֲשֶׁר־אַתֶּם
זֹנִים אַחֲרֵיהֶם. ²² לְמַעַן תִּזְכְּרוּ
וַעֲשִׂיתֶם אֶת־כָּל־מִצְוֹתָי, וִהְיִיתֶם
קְדֹשִׁים לֵאלֹהֵיכֶם. ²³ אֲנִי יְיָ
אֱלֹהֵיכֶם, אֲשֶׁר הוֹצֵאתִי אֶתְכֶם
מֵאֶרֶץ מִצְרַיִם לִהְיוֹת לָכֶם לֵאלֹהִים.
²⁴ אֲנִי יְיָ אֱלֹהֵיכֶם. (אֱמֶת.)

*[Prayer leader adds the first word
of the next prayer, "True"]*

85

MARC BRETTLER

"Hear O Israel" Strange as it may seem to us, the *Sh'ma* (Deut. 6:4) is of no particular significance within the Hebrew Bible. It did, however, rise to prominence in the early post-biblical period, as we see from the Nash papyrus (2nd–1st cent. *(p. 88)*

LAWRENCE A. HOFFMAN

THE CENTRAL FEATURE IN THE SH'MA *AND ITS BLESSINGS IS THE* SH'MA *ITSELF, THE FIRST SECTION OF WHICH (DEUTERONOMY 6:4-9) IS CALLED "ACCEPTING THE YOKE OF THE KINGDOM OF HEAVEN" (*KABBALAT OL MALKHUT SHAMAYIM*). ITS FIRST (p. 91)*

ELLIOT N. DORFF

"Hear O Israel" The three paragraphs that make up the entire *Sh'ma* do not appear consecutively in the Torah, and do not even follow the *(p. 88)*

¹(אֵל מֶלֶךְ נֶאֱמָן.)

²שְׁמַע יִשְׂרָאֵל. יְיָ אֱלֹהֵינוּ, יְיָ אֶחָד.

³בָּרוּךְ שֵׁם כְּבוֹד מַלְכוּתוֹ לְעוֹלָם וָעֶד.

¹ (God, steadfast ruler . . .)

² Hear O Israel: Adonai is our God; Adonai is One.

³ Blessed is the One the glory of whose kingdom is renowned forever.

LAWRENCE KUSHNER
NEHEMIA POLEN

"Adonai is One" The theology of Shneur Zalman of Liadi, the Alter Rebbe of Lubavitch Chasidism (1745–1813, *(p. 93)*

SUSAN L. EINBINDER

"Hear O Israel: Adonai is our God; Adonai is One" The persecutions, expulsions and difficulties experienced by the Jews of Ashkenaz and France gave special meaning to the *Sh'ma*. Familiar with the rabbinic story of R. Akiba, who was said to have uttered these words when he was tortured to death during the Hadrianic persecutions following the Bar Kokhba revolt, Ashkenazi Jews adopted them as a kind of martyrs' creed. The *Sh'ma* thus came to sum up and crown *(p. 90)*

DANIEL LANDES

"God, steadfast ruler" When recited privately, the *Sh'ma* is preceded with *El melekh ne'eman* ("God, steadfast ruler"), because the *Sh'ma* in total has 245 words and the addition *(p. 95)*

JUDITH PLASKOW

"Adonai is One" As the first-learned and most familiar Jewish prayer, the *Sh'ma* comes to the tongue so effortlessly that it is easy to lose sight of what it is affirming. What does it mean to assert *(p. 98)*

JOEL M. HOFFMAN

"God, steadfast ruler" Or perhaps, the affirmation, "God is a steadfast ruler."
"Hear O Israel . . . Adonai is One" Biblically, *Sh'ma* ("hear") is more an introduction than a verb of hearing, like the archaic "Hear ye, hear ye," the collo- *(p. 91)*

MARC BRETTLER

B.C.E.) which contains the decalogue as well as Deuteronomy 6:4–5. The Septuagint, the Greek translation of the Bible from Alexandria, as well as the Nash papyrus introduce the *Sh'ma* with a verse not found in the Hebrew, but intended to highlight the *Sh'ma*'s growing importance: "These are the laws and the rule which Adonai commanded Israel in the desert when they left Egypt."

The introduction ("Hear O Israel") is a typical opening for a speech in Deuteronomy, occurring not only here, but also in vv. 5:1, 9:1, 20:3, and 27:9, and might have been one of the ways of introducing what some have called "a sermon." This particular sermon makes two points: "Adonai is our God" and "You shall love Adonai your God." There then follows a chain of implications: Internalizing these commandments and teaching them to your children, binding them upon your arms and head, and writing them upon your doorposts.

———◆———

ELLIOT N. DORFF

order of the Torah's books (since Numbers, the fourth book of the Torah, precedes Deuteronomy, the fifth). Although all the parts of the *Sh'ma* appear in the Torah, then, the prayer as we have it is not biblical in origin, but rather a prayer created by the Rabbis. Why then did the Rabbis choose these paragraphs, not others (the Ten Commandments, say) for this central prayer? And why did they put these paragraphs in the order they did?

One reason they chose the first two paragraphs is undoubtedly because they contain verses requiring that "you should speak about these things when you lie down and when you stand up." In context, "these things" refers to the entire covenant described in Deuteronomy, which we are to speak of always. I prefer my own translation here ("*Speak of* them" not "*use* them," and "when you lie down and when you *rise* up," not "when you *stand* up") because "when you lie down and when you rise up" is a "merism," a literary device by which the Torah specifies two ends of a spectrum and means everything in between as well. Here, then, we are to think and speak about the words of the Torah during every waking moment. (Another famous example of that literary device is the opening verse of Genesis: "When God began to create the heaven and earth" — meaning everything in between as well.) A narrow reading of these verses, however, leads to the view that every night and every morning we should recite the paragraphs where those verses are embedded, and this is undoubtedly one of the reasons motivating the Rabbis to use the first two paragraphs of the *Sh'ma* as we have it.

That, though, only pushes the question back to the next level, namely, why did the Rabbis choose to interpret these verses in that narrow way rather than in their broader and probably more accurate meaning? And how are we to understand the choice of the third paragraph, where this demand to speak of "them" day and night does not appear?

The Siddur serves as the handbook of theology for the Jewish masses. The Rabbis deliberately chose these paragraphs primarily because *they were convinced that these paragraphs articulated the heart of Jewish faith.* They say explicitly (M. Ber. 2:2) that the first paragraph proclaims the sovereignty of God; the second, the duty to obey the commandments; and the third, the obligation to heed the commandments specific to the day time (because of the verse, "When you see it," which, in the days before electricity, presupposed daylight). I agree with their understanding of the first two paragraphs, although for a somewhat different reason than they provide, but I disagree with their explanation of what the third paragraph was meant to add. After all, if you are already obligated by the second paragraph to obey all the commandments, why do you need the third paragraph to restate your duty to obey only part of them?

Understanding the point of the first two paragraphs demands attention to the antecedents of their pronouns. In each, we are called upon to teach "them" to our children. In the first paragraph, though, the verses preceding that command (which tell us what we should teach) speak of our belief in one God and our duty to love and be loyal to that One God. In the second paragraph, the obligation to teach our children is preceded by the demand that we obey the commandments. We must, then, teach our children, and affirm ourselves, both Jewish beliefs and Jewish practices.

The third paragraph then establishes the educational system by which we are to remember these assertions of faith and these demands of action: we are to use tassels, an unusual dress, as a reminder system — a communal string around our fingers, as it were. The Torah then explicitly spells out the educational process that a tassel will enable: "When you see it, you shall remember all of Adonai's commandments and do them." A concrete and odd object called a tassel will be a physical reminder of your obligations to God; just seeing them will jar your memory of what you are to do. In case you missed the rationale the first time, the paragraph repeats, "Thus you will remember and do all of Adonai's commandments."

That paragraph also specifies the ultimate promise in doing so — that we will be holy to our God. English is a Christian language: those who created it were Christian, and to this day over 90% of those who speak it as their native tongue are Christian. It should not be surprising, then, that English words, especially religious words — like "messiah," "savior," "salvation," and even "holy" — have Christian connotations. Although I am a rabbi and have studied the Jewish tradition extensively, when I say "holy," I still think of "the Holy Ghost." The Hebrew word "*kadosh,*" however, means set apart from all others, as in the Hebrew word for betrothal, *kiddushin,* which declares that bride and groom set each other apart from all other potential mates. The Prophets take this human phenomenon of marriage as the model for the relationship between God and the People Israel. Being holy to God means being in a monogamous relationship together.

The first paragraph of the *Sh'ma* is phrased in the second person *singular,* while the second paragraph refers to some of the same commandments (teaching children, *t'fillin, m'zuzah*) in the second person *plural.* Both individually and collectively, then, we affirm the beliefs and obey the commandments articulated in the *Sh'ma,* so as to merit the promise contained in the third paragraph of being God's People.

◆—

SUSAN L. EINBINDER

the experience of religious martyrdom known technically now as *k'dushat hashem*, "sanctification of the name [of God]."

Ashkenaz Jewry at the end of the eleventh century and into the twelfth was a thriving community of urban centers; recent scholarship stresses the degree that Jewish attitudes and behaviors reflect the general cultural "renaissance" that characterize the period. The intellectual atmosphere gave rise to new critical attitudes towards interpreting texts — hence our great Jewish commentator, Rashi (Solomon ben Isaac of France, 1040–1105) and the school of commentators he developed, known as the Tosafists. It also spawned new types of writing, like the prose narrative, and a new interest in the portrayal of individuals and their inner thoughts. At the same time, however, religious extremism in the Christian culture found expression in a series of crusading expeditions, and these too found their Jewish analogue in an extreme response of martyrdom. The First Crusade, in particular, cut a path of destruction through the major Jewish communities along the Rhine. Both Christian and Jewish chroniclers describe the Christian decision to attack the Jews in the same way: "Behold we travel to a distant land to do battle . . . to kill and to subjugate all those kingdoms that do not believe in the Crucified. How much more so [should we kill and subjugate] the Jews, who killed and crucified him!" (translation, Robert Chazan, *The Destruction of European Jewry*). To a degree even more remarkable for its lack of precedent in Jewish history (medieval Jews did not even know the story of Masada), Jewish men, women and children chose martyrdom, either at their own hands or at the hands of their slaughterers. Over and over, their rallying cry at death is the single verse of the *Sh'ma*. Like their Sefardic counterparts, and medieval Muslims, Ashkenazi Jews understood the Christian concept of the divine Trinity as a case of polytheism; thus their insistence on God's unity is a vehement repudiation of Christian doctrine.

Furthermore, three surviving Hebrew prose records narrate the ravages of the First Crusade (1096) on the Rhine Jewish communities. For all of them, the martyrs' proclamation of God's unity in the *Sh'ma* has a literary force as well, emerging from the multitude of voices that compose a human community — men, women and children; rich and poor; learned and unlearned; communal leaders and marginal characters; those who fight valiantly, those whose defiance is passive, and even those who try to run away. All of this human variety is "unified" itself in the moment it meets its God. The story of the Jews of Worms makes this point vividly. Having sought shelter in the bishop's chambers, the Jews are attacked there by the Christian mob, and they choose willingly to die. Some are killed by the mob and some take their own lives. The chronicle of Solomon ben Simson continues: "Indeed fathers also fell with their children, for they were slaughtered together. They slaughtered brethren, relatives, wives and children. Bridegrooms [slaughtered] their intended and merciful mothers their own children. All of them accepted the heavenly decree unreservedly. As they commended their souls to their Creator, they cried out: "Hear O Israel! Adonai is our God; Adonai is One!" (Chazan translation).

JOEL M. HOFFMAN

quial "listen up," or the scholarly "N.B." Accordingly, a more accurate translation might begin, "Hear this," "Listen up" or "Please note." By the time it was introduced into the liturgy, however, the first line of the *Sh'ma* had became a familiar quotation; so reasonable steps should be taken to ensure that our translation remains familiar. So the usual "hear" is retained, along with the archaic vocative "O Israel" that follows (as in FOP, GOP, SLC, Birnbaum, SSS and Artscroll; KH uses simply "Israel.") As for "Adonai is one," KH has "Adonai alone," an accurate enough rendering of the meaning, but missing the affect of the parallel structure in the Hebrew *Adonai eloheinu, Adonai echad* — which is captured nicely in "Adonai is our God, Adonai is one." Artscroll suggests "the one and only."

"Blessed is the One . . ." Almost every aspect of this line is problematic. At a word-for-word level, the sentence — literally, "Blessed name glory his-kingdom forever" — is almost ungrammatical. The only possible grammatical reading ("Blessed is the One the name of the glory of whose kingdom is everlasting") is so convoluted that it is unlikely to represent the original intention. Lawrence Hoffman suggests that we may have two sentences here, *barukh shem* ("Blessed is the name [of God?]") followed by *k'vod malkhuto l'olam va'ed*, "The glory of his kingdom is everlasting." Birnbaum notes that *Barukh shem k'vod* was "regularly used in the Temple," again suggesting that we have incorrectly punctuated the line by not breaking it up. But because current tradition and practice presupposes a single sentence, we ignore this possibility; for ease of reading, however, the sentence is rewritten.

Other translations include, "Praised be his glorious sovereignty throughout all time" (SS); "Blessed be the name and glory of God's realm, forever" (KH); and "Blessed be the name of his glorious majesty forever and ever" (Birnbaum). We have retained "kingdom," because its connotations are far more majestic than are those of the rivals "realm," "sovereignty" or "majesty."

We also face the particular problem that we do not know fully what "name" (*shem*) connoted in antiquity. It surely meant more than it does today. A change in name was a change in essence, for example (as with Abram/Abraham and Sarai/Sarah), so declaring God's name to be blessed was tantamount to acknowledging God's very being.

———◆———

LAWRENCE A. HOFFMAN

VERSE (DEUT. 6:4), "HEAR O ISRAEL . . ." AND THE RESPONSE, "BLESSED IS . . ." STAND OUT LITURGICALLY AS AN APT SUMMARY OF JUDAISM'S BASIC MONOTHEISTIC PRINCIPLE AND THE HOPE FOR ALL HUMANITY THAT FLOWS FROM IT.

"Reform congregations say 'Hear O Israel . . .' and 'Blessed is . . .' standing" Halakhah prescribes sitting not standing for the *Sh'ma*. The issue goes back to a debate between Bet Hillel and Bet Shammai, in which Bet Hillel ruled (successfully) that the *Sh'ma* should be said in whatever position one happened to be when the time of its recitation arrived. In the ninth century, the Babylonian Gaon, Amram, enforced that position, as part of

his religio-political attack on the Palestinians who still said the *Sh'ma* standing. His successful championing of the Hillelite perspective eventually entered the codes of Jewish law, which justified the Hillelite-Amram position with a variety of *ex post facto* arguments, that became standard Halakhah. When the Crusaders overran Palestine, destroying native Palestinian Jewish custom in the process, the Palestinian practice of standing died too, so that Jews round the world now sat for the *Sh'ma* as Amram had insisted.

Reform Jews, however, saw the *Sh'ma* as central to their claim that Judaism's uniqueness lay in its discovery of ethical monotheism. Wanting to acknowledge the centrality of the *Sh'ma*, and recognizing that people generally stand for the prayers that matter most, they began standing for the *Sh'ma* despite the Halakhah. They justified their position by arguing that the halakhic *act* of sitting for the "watchword of Jewish faith" was inconsistent with the halakhic *principle* of accepting the yoke of heaven: how could one not stand to proclaim God one?

Simultaneously, they began reciting the second line "Blessed be . . ." aloud as well, whereas traditional practice insisted on saying it quietly. They reasoned (with the Halakhah) that the second line was an accessory statement to the first, a verbal acceptance of God's reign, and should likewise be recited with full intentionality, but (against the Halakhah) that doing so could not be accomplished if it was recited quietly.

"God, steadfast ruler (El melekh ne'eman)" The phrase is cited in the midrash and the Talmud, because the Hebrew initials of these three words spell *amen*. "Resh Lakish said, 'If you say *amen* with all your might, the gates to the Garden of Eden will be open to you.' What does *amen* mean? Rabbi Chanina said, 'God steadfast ruler'" (Shab. 119b). The Tosafot (12th-century France) explain, "Whenever you say *amen*, you should think, "God steadfast ruler." By the time of the Tosafot, however, the phrase had become associated with the *Sh'ma* as well, on account of a ninth-century midrashic teaching: "Let the recitation of *Sh'ma* not be light in your eyes, for its 248 words tally with the 248 parts of a human body. God says, 'If you guard the 248 words of the *Sh'ma* by reading them right, I will guard your 248 anatomical parts." Eleventh-century rabbis in Italy and France noted, however, that the midrashist's count was off! The *Sh'ma* has only 245 words. They therefore advocated adding *El melekh ne'eman* to make up the missing three. By the twelfth century, the practice spread to Provence, where a visiting Spanish rabbi, Zerachiah Halevi, encountered it. He brought it back to Spain with him, where he encountered fierce opposition. Most Spanish authorities (including the Zohar) railed against the custom, and by the sixteenth century, it was dying. Joseph Caro omitted it from his *Shulchan Arukh*, and Moses Isserles, the chief Polish authority who made the *Shulchan Arukh* decisive for Ashkenazi Jews too, mentions it only to caution against it. Joel Sirkes of Poland (1561–1640) says, "The custom has ceased; we do not say 'God steadfast ruler.'" Technically speaking, therefore, Neither the Spanish-Portuguese rite nor the Ashkenazi rite officially includes it, but Sefardi custom did retain it, and the practice is so widespread today despite the sources opposing it that we include it here.

"Hear O Israel" The *Sh'ma* comprises three biblical passages: Deuteronomy 6:4–9 — "accepting the yoke of the kingdom of heaven" (*kabbalat ol malkhut shamayim*);

Deuteronomy 11:13–21 — "accepting the yoke of the commandments" (*kabbalat ol hamitzvot*); and Numbers 15:37–41 — "the section on tassels" (*parashat tsitsit*), where *tsitsit* are described as a visible reminder that "I am Adonai your God," precisely what "Hear O Israel: Adonai is our God; Adonai is One" asserts.

Jews were saying the *Sh'ma* twice daily as early as the first century (though possibly without all three paragraphs, at first).

The first line is often written with a large *ayin* (the last letter of *Sh'ma*), and a large *dalet* (the last letter of *echad*). Tradition explains it as an attempt to spell out *ed*, "witness," since the *Sh'ma* is a testimony to the one true God. Others hold that the two enlarged letters prevent heretical error, since the *ayin* might be confused with an *alef* (which sounds similar), and the *dalet* might be read as a *resh* (which looks similar) — giving us, "SHEma (written with *alef*) *yisrael, Adonai eloheinu Adonai acher*, "Maybe, Israel, Adonai our God is another deity."

"Blessed is the One the glory of whose kingdom is renowned forever" Again, a doxology (see above, "Blessed be Adonai who is blessed forever and ever"), this one patterned after the end of the second book of Psalms (Ps. 72:19), "Blessed be his glorious name forever" (*Barukh shem k'vodo l'olam*). It also follows a pattern laid down in Nehemiah 9:5: "The Levites said, 'Arise and bless the Lord your God from everlasting to everlasting; Blessed be your glorious name that is high above all blessing and praise."

The added concept "kingdom" intrudes upon the syntax to make translation difficult, if not impossible. It may be, then, that this new element, a single word in Hebrew (*malkhuto*) is a late addition. Originally, the invitation, "Hear O Israel," evoked a psalm-like doxology without it: "Blessed be his glorious name forever and ever" (*Barukh shem k'vodo l'olam va'ed*).

The accent on God's ultimate reign on earth is usually viewed as a response to Roman rule. Jesus too preached "the coming of the kingdom" which must have been an important doctrine as early as the first century, and became more so, as the wars against Rome were fought.

This particular doxology was said in the Temple, following the high priest's recitation of the ineffable name of God (M. Yoma 3:8), possibly as two sentences: "Blessed be the name" (*Barukh shem*). "The glory of his kingdom is renowned forever" (*K'vod malkhuto l'olam va'ed*).

———◆———

LAWRENCE KUSHNER
NEHEMIA POLEN

known also as *Ba'al Hatanya* — "author of *The Tanya*," the masterwork of Chabad Chasidism) maintains that nothing exists but God. This "acosmism" denies the reality of the cosmos. God is not only the basis of reality, God is the *only* reality; God is all there is. Creation is continuously brought into being through the divine word. If our eyes could truly see reality we would see no material world at all, but instead, behold God's continuous utterance of the Hebrew letters, the real matrix of all being.

In such a radical monism, the *Sh'ma*, the declaration of God's unity, means effectively that nothing exists besides God.

> "In the heavens above and on the earth below, *Ein od* — there is nothing else [besides G-d]."
> This means that even the material earth, which appears to the eyes of all to be actually existing is naught and complete nothingness in relation to the Holy One, blessed be He.

As his editor explains in the English translation: "The unity of God does not mean only that there are no other gods, but that there is nothing apart from God, i.e., there is no existence whatsoever apart from God's existence; the whole Creation is nullified within God as the rays of the sun within the orb of the sun. This is the meaning of *yichuda ila'a* ('higher unity')."

But how do we reconcile the apparent contradiction between this acosmic theory of reality and the inescapable experience of living in an obviously material world? Anyone can have a vision of the unity of all creation. It could be in a forest or by the shore of the sea. It could be during the concluding service of Yom Kippur or at the birth of a child. The questions is how do we bring the awareness of that higher unity into the everyday reality of *this* world? That is the challenge of sacred living: to realize more unity — with patience and devotion, to make *this* world resemble the one on High. And this is where Judaism parts company with the religions of the East. Judaism understands this yearning as a sacred obligation, a requirement for holy living, a commandment.

This is the problem that the Ba'al Hatanya teaches is solved with the second line of the *Sh'ma*, the *Barukh shem* which is not in the biblical text itself, but was added by the Rabbis as a congregational response. The *Barukh shem*, he says, is our attempt to bring back into this world the supernal unity spoken of in the first line. We have a vision of ultimate unity when we utter *Sh'ma Yisra'el Adonai Eloheinu Adonai echad* ("Hear O Israel, Adonai is our God; Adonai is One"). And when we recite *Barukh shem k'vod malkhuto l'olam va'ed* ("Blessed is the One the glory of whose kingdom is renowned forever"), we try to bring that unity into everyday reality.

"We may now understand," he suggests, "the statement in the Zohar (2:134a) that the verse *Sh'ma Yisra'el* is *yichuda ila'a* ('higher Unity'), and *Baruch shem k'vod malkhuto l'olam va'ed* is *yichuda tata'a* ('lower unity')." The Ba'al Hatanya's editor goes on to explain that according to traditional rules of Hebrew grammar, the alphabet is divided into groups of letters, such that the letters in any single group are interchangeable with one another. The letters *alef, hay, vav,* and *yod* fall into one group, permitting *alef* to be interchanged with *vav.* The letters *aleph, chet, hay,* and *ayin* fall into another group, permitting *chet* to be interchanged with *ayin.* In this way *echad* (*alef, chet, dalet*) becomes *va'ed* (*vav, ayin, dalet*).

So the *echad* of the *Sh'ma* is the *yichuda ila'a*, the higher unity, seemingly unattainable in this world, only a dim memory of a sacred moment. But the *va'ed* of the *Baruch shem k'vod* is the *yichuda tata'a*, the lower unity, our bringing the oneness of the Holy One into our daily lives. Now we are ready to recite the *Sh'ma* and its response.

———◆———

DANIEL LANDES

of these 3 make up 248, the number of positive *mitzvot*. In public recitation the prayer leader repeats the last three words, *a-do-nai e-loheikhem emet* to produce the desired total.

"Hear O Israel" The *Sh'ma* is prior to the *Amidah*, not only in the time of its recita-tion, but also in halakhic importance, as the *Sh'ma* comprises two biblically ordained laws while the *Amidah*, and perhaps even prayer itself, is only rabbinically commanded. The habitual recital of the *Sh'ma* (known as *K'riyat Sh'ma*, and sometimes shortened to "the *k'riyah*") renews and confirms the believer's faith, and frames the day by explaining how the world is to be perceived. There are actually two *mitzvot* here, one doctrinal and one ritual.

The *doctrinal mitzvah* is the affirmation of God's unity, as commanded in the first verse (Deut. 6:4). By unity, we mean that God is incorporeal, indivisible and utterly unique (Maimonides [1135–1204], Jacob Emden [1697–1776]) and that the God of Israel will eventually be the God of the entire world (Rashi [1040–1105]).

The *ritual mitzvah* is the actual recitation which is also termed *l'yached et hashem*, "to unify the name [of God]," or *l'kabel ol malkhut shamayim*, "to accept the yoke of the kingdom of heaven." This *mitzvah* applies passively to *B'nai Noah* ("descendants of Noah," that is, covenanted non-Jews) also, for they may not practice idolatry. But unlike Jews, they are not required to affirm God's unity actively. Maimonides calls this the "great principle upon which everything is predicated."

Sh'ma requires *kavvanah*, meaning "direction" (literally), and by extension, "intent." An ongoing halakhic debate questions whether *mitzvot* in general require *kavvanah*, or whether they "count" even if performed without it. But in any case, this *mitzvah* which affirms God's unity presupposes thoughtfulness, so must be accompanied by *kavvanat halev*, "heartfelt intentionality." If we fail to achieve this full intentionality, we do not fulfill the *mitzvah*, and must wait a moment — so as to avoid the semblance of affirming two gods — and then repeat the *Sh'ma* with proper intention.

Minimally, this *kavvanah* must accompany the first sentence of *Sh'ma*, the verse that affirms God's unity. The next line, *Barukh shem*, though post-biblical and therefore recited silently, is also understood as a reflection upon God's unity, so it too requires *kavvanah*. Ritually speaking, people who do not understand Hebrew, and so cannot attain intentionality when they read it, may use any language that they "hear," that is, "understand," but should use the Hebrew names for God. From a doctrinal point of view also, an exact rendering into another language ful-fills the *mitzvah*, but a proper translation may be unavailable or even impossible in practice. Halakhah thus prefers using the original liturgical Hebrew for doctrinal purposes. One need not know the exact translation of the words, since all that is required is a sense of the general content of what is being said, and the liturgical context alone is assumed to provide that basic understanding, since one recognizes at least that this is the liturgical place where we affirm God's unity. The presence of translation and commentaries on the Siddur page enhances *kavvanah* by providing fuller comprehension.

Kavvanah also demands vocal articulation and certain body language. The plain sense of "Hear" implies saying *Sh'ma* loudly enough to be heard, and *kavvanah* generates the requirement to say it ourselves, rather than to depend on "hearing" it from others in the congregation, even the prayer leader. Ordinarily, "hearing a blessing from another obligated person is the same as saying it oneself," but the *Sh'ma* differs, because we require each person's own active acceptance of the yoke of the kingdom of heaven. Custom today actually demands shouting the first verse in a full voice. The loud shout breaking through one's regular whispered chant drives home this special intent of affirming God's unity, and satisfies the characterization of the *Sh'ma* that we find in the *Tur* (code of Jewish law, 14th cent.), where it is called a "proclamation" ordered by our King out of "reverence and trepidation."

Doctrinally speaking, we need only recite the first verse with full *kavvanah*, but ritually considered, we do so as part of a *k'riyah*, a "recitation," that includes three biblical citations and the *Barukh shem* response. Opinions vary on how much of all this is the necessary minimum to count as a *k'riyah*. Early authorities cite either the first verse alone, the first paragraph, or the first two paragraphs. Maimonides includes the third paragraph too, while most everyone else agrees that the third paragraph was included liturgically in order to fulfill the daily commandment to remember the Exodus, but not, strictly speaking, as part of the *mitzvah* of reciting the *Sh'ma*. Some even hold that no specific paragraph is specified, and that any section of Torah would do! The final halakhic decision is that the *k'riyah* requires all three paragraphs.

Rabbi Joseph B. Soloveitchik (1903–1993) differentiates *k'riyat Sh'ma* from other biblically ordained portions that are to be read, the priestly benediction, for instance. These others must be read exactly as they appear in the Torah, so that if even one word or letter is skipped, it is as if we have performed no *mitzvah* at all. With the *Sh'ma*, however, even though we must say it as written, if we do not complete the portion, we still fulfill the obligation of "reciting." To be sure, we do not thereby do all we should: We do not fulfill the complete obligation to recite the three portions. But we do fulfill the *mitzvah* of *k'riyat Sh'ma*.

But Rabbi Soloveitchik differentiates *ex post facto* fulfillment (*b'di'avad*) from the *ab initio* ideal (*l'chatchilah*). Ideally, the *Sh'ma* should be recited with every word pronounced properly. Successive words that share the same consonant at the end of the first and the beginning of the second (like *b'khol l'vav'kha*) should be separated clearly. Words inadvertently slurred, misspoken or omitted should be corrected either on the spot or by returning to the beginning of the verse and continuing again from there. The portions should be read in the order of the Siddur, with its imposed hierarchy of value: first, the *mitzvot* of affirming God's unity, loving God and learning Torah; second, accepting all *mitzvot*; and third, the *mitzvah* of *tsitsit*, specifically, as a reminder of the other *mitzvot*.

Since the *k'riyat Sh'ma* is bracketed by blessings, many authorities extend the biblical obligation to include the blessings as well. Ordinary conversation is banned, for example, in between the paragraphs of the *Sh'ma* (unless it is undertaken out of fear that failure to initiate it will result in punishment from the person slighted, or if the conversation is a response to someone who deserves honor); so too it is disallowed between the *Sh'ma* and its blessings, or between the blessings themselves.

The integrity of the *Sh'ma* and Its Blessings raises other issues too. Why, for example, is there no introductory blessing of command, as we find with other ritual obligations: Something like, " . . . who has sanctified us with his commandments and has commanded us to recite the *Sh'ma*"? Moreover, we saw above that the *mitzvah* of affirming God's unity (in the first sentence) requires *kavvanat halev*, deep intention of the heart. There is, however, a simpler form of intentionality to consider: *kavvanah latseit*, the intention simply to fulfill the *mitzvah* in question. The *Chazon Ish* rules that if someone recites *k'riyat Sh'ma* in the proper liturgical order, even without the intention of fulfilling the *mitzvah*, the obligation has nonetheless been fulfilled, since the very doing of the *mitzvah* (that is, reciting the blessings with the biblical paragraphs embedded within them) assumes that one had the prior purpose of fulfilling it, at least implicitly. Regarding the absent blessing, then, we might say that the explicit formulation of command that a blessing would convey is implicitly present in the very saying of the *Sh'ma* within its liturgical structure.

Various customs are attached to the recitation of the first line.

1. It is said in a loud voice, initiated by the prayer leader, with all following together as befits the coronation of the King.
2. Care is taken not to run words together, especially *Yisra'el* and *A-do-nai*, and *A-do-nai* and *echad*.
3. *Echad* is recited with a slight elongation of the *chet*, and greater elongation of the *dalet*, emphasizing that the last letter is not a *resh*, since instead of *echad* ("one") we would have *acher* ("other") as if to say that God is "the other deity." The *dalet*, however, should not be pronounced with excessive force, lest it become gibberish, like *echadeh*.
4. *Sh'ma Yisra'el* is recited with the right hand covering the eyes, to achieve *kavvanah*.
5. We say it in awe and trepidation, with a sense of newly proclaiming God king, and with the resolve that we would give up life rather than violate this belief.

Other than the doctrinal and the ritual *mitzvot* mentioned above, we find in the *Sh'ma* also the following commandments: 1) Loving God ("You shall love A-do-nai your God" [Deut. 6:5]). This means directing one's heart to the reality of God as our ultimate source of joy. Desire for any material object or affirming any spiritual goal that does not make love for God central violates this commandment. 2) *Talmud torah*, "learning and teaching Torah" ("Instruct them to your children" [Deut. 6:7]). Our obligation is first to our own children, but students become honorary children. We should learn Torah all our life and teach Torah to all Jews. The community is obliged to establish schools that every Jew may learn the texts and practices of our people.

Some say the *Sh'ma* while using the following words within it to remind them of the Ten Commandments (not in order of the Decalogue itself):

From paragraph 1: "A-do-nai your God" = 1st commandment ("I am A-do-nai your God"); "A-do-nai is One" = 2nd commandment ("You shall have no other Gods before Me"); "You shall love" = 3rd commandment ("Do not take A-do-nai's name in vain"); "Your house" = 10th commandment ("Do not covet your neighbor's house)."

From paragraph 2: "Gather your grain" = 8th commandment ("Do not steal"); "You will quickly perish" = 6th commandment ("Do not murder"); "That your days and your children's days . . . may be numerous" = 5th commandment ("Honor your father and mother that your days may be numerous").

From paragraph 3: "And not follow your mind and eyes" = 7th commandment ("Do not commit adultery"); "Thus will you remember" = 4th commandment ("Remember the Sabbath Day"); "I am A-do-nai your God" = 9th commandment ("Do not bear false witness" — the Midrash explains, "God knows when we lie").

"Blessed is the One . . ." Being post-biblical, *Barukh shem* is recited in an undertone, after a short pause, with the intent of saying that God's reign is eternal.

———◆———

JUDITH PLASKOW

that God is One? On the simplest level, the *Sh'ma* can be understood as a passionate rejection of polytheism. In the context of the commandment, "You shall have no other gods besides Me," it is a polemic against foreign worship. It is reminiscent of the familiar midrash (which, like the *Sh'ma*, is also often learned early) that depicts Abraham destroying his father's idols because he knows instinctively that there is only one deity.

Viewed in this way, the *Sh'ma* supports a popular (although inaccurate) reading of Jewish history, according to which Israel, from its very beginnings, brought to the world the idea of one God who was creator and ruler of the universe.

This understanding of the *Sh'ma*, however, does not address the issue of God's oneness. It defines "one" in opposition to "many," but it never really specifies what it means to say that God/Adonai/the One who is and will be is one. Is God's oneness mere numerical singularity? Does it signify simply that rather than many forces ruling the universe, there is only one? A simple numerical definition of oneness is compatible with idolatry, if it is just the worship of one finite God imaged as infinite — as if the chief deity of the Canaanite pantheon were suddenly elevated to the only one, the king of all the earth.

We can, of course, say that we associate numerical uniqueness with our particular God, Adonai, affirming here both 1) that there is only one God, and 2) that Adonai is his (sic) name. On this view, however, attempts to name God in new ways or to broaden the range of imagery used for God are experienced as assaults on monotheism. If God is so singular as to necessitate identification with a particular image, other images must be assumed to refer to other deities.

There is another way to understand oneness, however, and that is as inclusiveness. In Marcia Falk's words, "The authentic expression of an authentic monotheism is not a singularity of image but an embracing unity of a multiplicity of images." Rather than being the chief deity in the pantheon, God includes the qualities and characteristics of the whole pantheon, with nothing remaining outside. God is all in all. This is the God who "forms light and creates darkness, who makes peace and creates everything," because there can be no power other than or in opposition to God who could possibly be responsible for evil. This is the God who is male and female, both and neither, because there is no genderedness outside of God that is not made in God's image. On this understanding of oneness, extending the range of images we use for God challenges us to find God in ever-new aspects of creation. Monotheism is about the capacity to glimpse the One in and through the changing forms of the many, to see the whole in and through its infinite images. "Hear O Israel": despite the fractured, scattered, and conflicted nature of our experience, there is a unity that embraces and contains our diversity and that connects all things to each other.

◆ ◆ ◆

MARC BRETTLER

"*You shall love Adonai your God*" The central, and most misunderstood, section of the *Sh'ma* is its commandment to love God fully and completely. As in the previous "You have loved us most lovingly" (see above) a particular kind of love is intended. In its current liturgical framework, Israel is the child returning appropriate love to the loving, caring father. As such, the passage is likely subsumed under the metaphor of God as father (e.g. Exod. 4:22; Deut. 32:6). But that metaphor is relatively rare in the Bible, and in any event, it is quite *(p. 101)*

LAWRENCE A. HOFFMAN

THE REST OF DEUTERONOMY 6:4-9 NOW FOLLOWS.

———◆———

DANIEL LANDES

"*You shall love*" Some congregations sing the entire *Sh'ma* or read it in unison. Either custom is proper, as long as it is not discordant or distracting.

"*Today, in mind*" We pause after "today" (*hayom*) so as not to imply that only "today" we keep the commandments "in mind."

"*When you lie down and when you stand up*" This verse refers to the time of reciting *Sh'ma*, not the position in which it is recited. The traditional practice is thus to sit, not stand. The *Tur* contrasts God's demand that we proclaim Him king with a similar order by earthly kings, who ask that their kingship be affirmed "while standing," as a sign of a person's servility.

The halakhic point of sitting is not sitting per se, but the absence of a requirement to stand. Thus, if we are *(p. 103)*

⁴וְאָהַבְתָּ אֵת יְיָ אֱלֹהֶיךָ בְּכָל־לְבָבְךָ וּבְכָל־נַפְשְׁךָ וּבְכָל־מְאֹדֶךָ. ⁵וְהָיוּ הַדְּבָרִים הָאֵלֶּה, אֲשֶׁר אָנֹכִי מְצַוְּךָ הַיּוֹם, עַל־לְבָבֶךָ. ⁶וְשִׁנַּנְתָּם לְבָנֶיךָ, ⁷וְדִבַּרְתָּ בָּם בְּשִׁבְתְּךָ בְּבֵיתֶךָ וּבְלֶכְתְּךָ בַדֶּרֶךְ, וּבְשָׁכְבְּךָ וּבְקוּמֶךָ. ⁸וּקְשַׁרְתָּם

DAVID ELLENSON

"*You shall love*" The major twentieth-century prayer books of American Reform Judaism — *The Union Prayer Book* and *Gates of Prayer*— follow the example set by David Einhorn's *Olath Tamid* from over a century ago, by including as their *Sh'ma* only the first of the three traditional paragraphs (Deut. 6:4–9), along with the conclusion of the third (Num. 15:41). In so doing, they affirmed only those parts of the *(p. 102)*

⁴ You shall love Adonai your God with all your mind and body and strength. ⁵ Keep these words, which I command you today, in mind. ⁶ Instruct your children about them. ⁷ Use them when you sit at home and when you walk about, when you lie down and when you stand up. ⁸ Bind them to *(p. 101)*

JOEL M. HOFFMAN

"*You shall love*" "Love" (*v'ahavta*) is functionally an imperative, even though grammatically a future verb. We maintain "shall" to attempt to capture the ancient style (ancient even for the Rabbis).

"*Mind and body and strength*" The Hebrew *levav*, *nefesh*, and *m'od* suggest that the Bible conceived of human-ness differently than we do. We divide ourselves into "mind," "body" and (perhaps) "soul," representing, respectively, our cognitive capacity, our physical matter and our holy essence. We also distinguish between thought *(p. 102)* your hand as a sign and set them between your eyes as a symbol. [9] Write them on the doorposts of your house and on your gates.

לְאוֹת עַל־יָדֶךָ, וְהָיוּ לְטֹטָפֹת בֵּין עֵינֶיךָ,
[9] וּכְתַבְתָּם עַל־מְזֻזוֹת בֵּיתֶךָ, וּבִשְׁעָרֶיךָ.

MARC BRETTLER

odd to command a child to love a parent. It thus seems appropriate to understand this love in a different way.

The covenant of Deuteronomy arose originally within the context of the vassal-suzerain (dependent-overlord) treaties of the ancient Semitic world. (Indeed, the Hebrew word *b'rit* means not just "covenant" but "treaty" in some contexts.) Thus, Israel is God's vassal, and the commandments of Deuteronomy are obligations owed toward God, the overlord. In return, God as suzerain has treaty obligations toward the vassal, such as protection from third-party invasions.

These treaties customarily use the term "love." For example, the vassal treaties of the early-seventh-century B.C.E. Assyrian (northern Mesopotamian) king, Esarhaddon, which have significant similarities to Deuteronomy, call on the vassal to "love the crown prince designated Ashurbanipal, son of your lord, Esarhaddon, king of Assyria as you do your own lives." In fact, the main point of the text is that Ashurbanipal alone shall be recognized as king, an idea quite close to the initial verse of the *Sh'ma*.

"Love" here is therefore a technical term for acceptance of treaty obligations. In our case of Deuteronomy, the expected love is quite extreme. We are to "love" God with all of our "mind, body and strength"; express this love by keeping the commandments in mind always ("when you sit, walk about, lie down and stand up"); and instruct them to the next generation. We are expected also to surround body and house with reminders of them: "Bind them to your hand . . . and set them between your eyes . . . Write them on the doorposts of your house and on your gates."

The ancient near east had amulets, but these written signs, symbols or door-writings are not among them, since these have no protective power. They are to remind Israel, as vassal, that God is the overlord (see above, "You shall love Adonai your God"). The measures are intentionally extreme, in part because Deuteronomy was written to remind Israel not to imagine there were other deities as well as Adonai (see esp. 1 Kgs. 18:21). In addition, the *Sh'ma* makes the point that God is more powerful than other human political overlords, for God controls earthly kings.

The use of a political metaphor here is therefore subversive, undermining loyalty to human rulers, relative to God. It is God's commandments which must be fully obeyed.

---◆---

DAVID ELLENSON

Sh'ma that they thought had been part of the original liturgy, and that, coincidentally, they believed with all their heart anyway: the Jewish community's wholehearted devotion to God and the central event in Jewish history — the Exodus from Egypt.

———◆———

JOEL M. HOFFMAN

(cognition) and feeling (emotion). The Bible, however, groups thought and feeling together under *levav*; soul and body together under *nefesh*; and perhaps physical strength or endurance under *m'od*. When *levav* (or *lev*, from the same root) refers to an organ, it is the heart but the heart is metaphorically akin to the English "mind." For example, when biblical characters "think," they say they have something "in *lev*" (see, e.g., Deut: 15:9) — roughly translatable as "said to himself," or, less idiomatically, "said in his mind." For something to be "on your *levav*" (below) is what we would call to "have it in mind." *Levav*, then, refers at once to emotion and to intellect, a conceptual combination that English lacks. *Nefesh*, most often translated here as "soul" (SSS, Birnbaum, SLC, FOP) or "breath" (KH) is used biblically the way we might use "person": Deut. 24:7 speaks of a "person who steals another person," using *ish* "man" in the first instance but *nefesh* in the second. Similarly, it is the *nefesh* that transgresses (Lev. 4:2) and eats (Lev. 7:27). Yet every creature, it seems, has (or is) a *nefesh*. God's covenant with Noah is established with every *nefesh* ("every living being"?) and the laws of *kashrut* forbid eating any "living *nefesh* in the water" (Lev 11:10). *Nefesh*, then, is paradigmatically a person, yet refers to that which people have in common with all animals. Neither "breath of life," nor "soul" captures this meaning. (We use "soul" with a vaguely similar notion of "person" in the English expression "not a soul.")

Furthermore, *nefesh* and *levav* together form an idiom in biblical Hebrew (here, Deut. 11:13, 11:18, and 13:4; Josh. 22:5 and Josh. 23:14 etc.), probably used to represent the entirety of human existence, much the way we use "mind and body," or sometimes, "body and soul" depending on the context, but always in order to mean "the whole person." In Joshua, the combined term "*nefesh* and *levav*" modifies both "to serve" and later "to know," suggesting that the connection between "love" here and "heart" is at most a play on words, and probably a coincidence of our modern understanding of these words. Accordingly, we use the common English phrase "mind and body" for the corresponding Hebrew "*levav* and *nefesh*."

M'odekha seems to have been tacked on here, since it is missing from Deut. 11:13, for instance, which follows. Similarly secondary, relative to "mind and body" is our English "strength." SSS, Birnbaum, SLC and FOP have "might"; GOP offers "being," KH "what you have" and Artscroll "your resources."

"In mind" Levav, translated here, as above, as "mind." The repetition of *levav* raises the interesting conjecture that this paragraph is a three-fold elaboration of the ways God

is to be loved: 1) keeping God's instruction in mind (representing *levav*); 2) teaching children or acting on them ourselves (perhaps what one does with the *nefesh*); and 3), associating them with hand, eye and doorpost (the *m'od*).

"Instruct your children about them" Not "teach"; "teach" is reserved below for a different verb. The Hebrew verb here (*v'shinantem*) derives from the root for "tooth," a connotation missed in the English translation. The frequently used adverb "diligently" would add little, and so is omitted here.

"Use them" The usual translation is "speak of them," from *v'dibarta bam*. The verb *v'dibarta* (from the root *d.b.r*) usually refers to the communicative aspect of language, in contrast to *amar*, the vocal aspect of language. For instance, the common phrase, *Vaydaber adonai el Moshe leimor*, usually translated, "God spoke to Moses, saying," is really, "God communicated to Moses, using speech to do so." But *d.b.r* does not take a *bet* before its object, whereas here, we have just that *bet* (*bam*, not *otam*). We assume that the *bet* is instrumental, giving us, "Communicate, using them [these words]," or equivalently, "Use them."

"When you sit at home . . . when you stand up" The four Hebrew words rendered by "sit," "walk," "lie down" and "stand" represent four postures, and ought to do so in English. "When you . . ." is used to create the possibility of mimicking the Hebrew parallel structure: thus, "when you sit, when you walk, when you lie down, when you stand up." Others prefer "rise (up)," but the emphasis here seems to be on bodily posture, not the act of rising.

"To your hand . . . between your eyes" Both "to your hand" and "between your eyes" are almost certainly idioms, and so might be better translated idiomatically in English ("keep them at hand and in sight") were it not for the (current, but probably not biblical) association between these phrases and *t'fillin*.

"As a symbol" Others, "frontlets." But for most readers "frontlets" is enigmatic. Is is not clear that the original intention was anything more than metaphoric.

———◆———

DANIEL LANDES

out walking when the time arrives to say *Sh'ma*, we need not sit down. We just halt momentarily, and say it standing. Even a worker up a tree just pauses from work. A driver in an automobile can say *Sh'ma* without stopping, as long as proper intent is present. We may not lie down, however, since lying face-down is servile, and lying face-up is arrogant.

"Bind them to your hand as a sign and set them between your eyes" Wearing *t'fillin* constitutes testimony to the *Sh'ma*'s doctrine. Traditionally, not to wear them is held to constitute self-indictment as giving false testimony. When reference is made to the

arm, we touch the arm *t'fillin* (*t'fillin shel yad*); similarly, with the *t'fillin* on the forehead (*t'fillin shel rosh*). Then we kiss our fingertips.

The *t'fillin* are boxes that contain paragraphs from the Torah written by a scribe on parchment. They are considered two separate *mitzvot*, but a person fulfills the dual *mitzvah* by using only one, if a) only one is available, or b) in cases of physical disability, such as a paralyzed arm. Since they are "a sign" they are not worn on Shabbat and holidays which themselves are signs of the covenant between God and Israel. The wearing of *t'fillin* requires physical cleanliness and pure thoughts.

"Doorposts" "Doorposts" implies the *m'zuzah*, a cylinder attached to the upper right doorpost of the gates of the city, the outer doorways of our homes, and all residential rooms there. The first and second paragraphs of the *Sh'ma* are placed within it.

◆ ◆ ◆

MARC BRETTLER

"*If you carefully heed my commandments*" With the commandments (or treaty stipulations) given in the first paragraph of the *Sh'ma*, we move on in the second paragraph to the implications of observing or not observing them. The reward *(p. 106)*

LAWRENCE A. HOFFMAN

WE ARRIVE AT THE SECOND BIBLICAL SECTION OF THE SH'MA: *DEUTERONOMY 11:31-21, KNOWN AS "ACCEPTANCE OF THE YOKE OF THE COMMANDMENTS" (*KABBALAT OL HAMITZVOT*).*

———◆———

ELLIOT N. DORFF

"*If you carefully heed my commandments*" Abiding by God's commandments seems to guarantee reward; disobeying them incurs God's punishment. As the Rabbis themselves painfully noted, this poses the problem that in life "the righteous suffer and the evil prosper" (*tzaddik v'ra lo, rasha v'tov lo*). They consequently devised a variety of ways *(p. 107)*

¹⁰וְהָיָה אִם-שָׁמֹעַ תִּשְׁמְעוּ אֶל-
מִצְוֹתַי אֲשֶׁר אָנֹכִי מְצַוֶּה אֶתְכֶם
הַיּוֹם לְאַהֲבָה אֶת-יְיָ אֱלֹהֵיכֶם
וּלְעָבְדוֹ בְּכָל-לְבַבְכֶם וּבְכָל-
נַפְשְׁכֶם. וְנָתַתִּי מְטַר-אַרְצְכֶם
בְּעִתּוֹ יוֹרֶה וּמַלְקוֹשׁ וְאָסַפְתָּ
דְגָנֶךָ וְתִירֹשְׁךָ וְיִצְהָרֶךָ. ¹¹וְנָתַתִּי

¹⁰If you carefully heed my commandments, the ones I command you today, to love Adonai your God and worship Him with all your mind and body, then I shall grant your land's rain in its season, in the autumn and in the spring, that you might gather your grain, wine and oil. ¹¹I shall *(p. 106)*

DANIEL LANDES

"*Today, to love*" We pause after "today" (*hayom*) so as not to imply that we "love" God only "today."

———◆———

JUDITH PLASKOW

"*If you carefully heed my commandments . . .*" The second paragraph of the *Sh'ma* asserts a connection precious to the Deuteronomist but disputed elsewhere in the Bible and contested by everyday experience: "As you sow, so shall you reap." Reward and punishment flow directly from human deserving; those who obey God prosper, and those who defy God perish. This theology of suffering — "for our sins we are punished" — has *(p. 109)*

DAVID ELLENSON

"*If you carefully heed my commandments*" The commentary in the present-day Reconstructionist *Kol Han'shamah* aptly describes the problem in this paragraph: Its detailed description of the "bountiful or *(p. 108)*

JOEL M. HOFFMAN

"*I command you*" Plural ("ye" or "y'all"), perhaps in contrast to the singular above. Here it is particularly unfortunate that Modern Standard English cannot convey this distinction, because the paragraph alternates oddly (and perhaps even in error) between singular and plural. *(p. 109)* grant grass in your fields for your cattle, that you might eat your fill. 12 Take care lest your mind tempt you to rebel by worshipping other gods and by bowing down to them. 13 For then the fire and fury of Adonai will turn against you. 14 Adonai will stop the flow of the sky. 15 There will be no rain. 16 The earth will not grant its produce. 17 You will quickly perish from the good land that Adonai grants you. 18 So put these words of mine in charge of your mind and body, bind them to your hand as a sign and set them between your eyes as a symbol; teach them to your children, using them when you sit at home and when you walk about, when you lie down and when you stand up; write them on the doorposts of your house and on your gates — that your days and your children's days in the land that Adonai promised to give to your ancestors may be as numerous as the days that the sky overlooks the earth.

עֵשֶׂב בְּשָׂדְךָ לִבְהֶמְתֶּךָ וְאָכַלְתָּ וְשָׂבָעְתָּ. ¹²הִשָּׁמְרוּ לָכֶם פֶּן־יִפְתֶּה לְבַבְכֶם וְסַרְ־תֶּם וַעֲבַדְתֶּם אֱלֹהִים אֲחֵרִים וְהִשְׁ־תַּחֲוִיתֶם לָהֶם. ¹³וְחָרָה אַף־יְיָ בָּכֶם ¹⁴וְעָצַר אֶת־הַשָּׁמַיִם ¹⁵וְלֹא־יִהְיֶה מָטָר ¹⁶וְהָאֲדָמָה לֹא תִתֵּן אֶת־יְבוּלָהּ ¹⁷וַאֲבַדְ־תֶּם מְהֵרָה מֵעַל הָאָרֶץ הַטֹּבָה אֲשֶׁר יְיָ נֹתֵן לָכֶם. ¹⁸וְשַׂמְתֶּם אֶת־דְּבָרַי אֵלֶּה עַל־לְבַבְכֶם וְעַל־נַפְשְׁכֶם וּקְשַׁרְתֶּם אֹתָם לְאוֹת עַל־יֶדְכֶם וְהָיוּ לְטוֹטָפֹת בֵּין עֵינֵיכֶם. וְלִמַּדְתֶּם אֹתָם אֶת־בְּנֵיכֶם לְדַבֵּר בָּם בְּשִׁבְתְּךָ בְּבֵיתֶךָ וּבְלֶכְתְּךָ בַדֶּרֶךְ וּבְשָׁכְבְּךָ וּבְקוּמֶךָ. וּכְתַבְתָּם עַל־מְזוּזוֹת בֵּיתֶךָ וּבִשְׁעָרֶיךָ.

לְמַעַן יִרְבּוּ יְמֵיכֶם וִימֵי בְנֵיכֶם עַל הָאֲדָמָה אֲשֶׁר נִשְׁבַּע יְיָ לַאֲבֹתֵיכֶם לָתֵת לָהֶם כִּימֵי הַשָּׁמַיִם עַל־הָאָרֶץ.

MARC BRETTLER

for proper behavior is agricultural productivity and securing the Land of Israel, while infraction of the treaty through the worship of other gods (which would be like dallying with a rival political alliance) will occasion agricultural disaster and exile. Human sovereigns too might threaten exile, but only God has the power to wipe out agriculture as well.

The Hebrew here is plural, referring to the whole community, because Deuteronomy is typically concerned with the covenant with Israel the nation, not its individuals. The punishments enumerated (exile and agricultural disaster) are therefore national in scope. Elsewhere, of course (e.g., Ezek. 18), where the metaphoric model is not a treaty, the Bible emphasizes personal responsibility, and individual punishment or reward.

ELLIOT N. DORFF

to justify God ("theodicies") in the face of the apparent failure of Deuteronomy's neat moral calculus, as expressed here in the *Sh'ma*, believing, for instance, in a world to come, where people's moral accounts would be righted. Sometimes, though, they simply said that we cannot fathom God's justice.

Why did they include this troublesome belief in the *Sh'ma*, when they could have left it out? And how could the Deuteronomist assert it in the first place? Surely the righteous and wicked were not justly compensated in biblical times either.

Rabbi Robert Gordis pointed out that the problem was less acute for biblical Jews who lived before the rise of individualism, a doctrine that developed after the coming of Greek culture. Most biblical authors — certainly in the First Temple period — applied the doctrine of God's justice to communities, not individuals (it was "communal providence" not "individual providence"). That is why the rewards and punishments mentioned here are rain and crops, which affect whole groups, not matters that apply to individuals alone. The story of Abraham arguing with God for the righteous individuals in Sodom (Gen. 18:22–33) indicates that even First-Temple literature was not completely at home with collective rewards and punishments, but the doctrine of communal providence at least enables us to understand how God could be just even if individually speaking, some righteous people suffer and some wicked ones prosper. God considers us all as interwoven within our communities and therefore responsible for, and the beneficiaries of, what the rest of the community does.

This is a much stronger sense of community than contemporary Jews, nourished on the Enlightenment ideology of individualism, are used to. We may therefore find the doctrine of communal providence insufficient to justify God's morality.

Moreover, as the Shoah demonstrates, but as Jews have known in other times as well — the Crusades, for instance — entire communities are sometimes unjustly rewarded or punished. Yes, in all these cases, the perpetrators of evil abused free will, but Deuteronomy's promises do not make exception for the behavior of others. And even if we restrict the discussion to the kind of natural rewards and punishments that are specified in Deuteronomy, are we really willing to say that every people victimized by drought or famine must be wicked or disobedient?

How, then, can we continue to affirm the belief in God's justice contained in the second paragraph of the *Sh'ma*?

Contemporary Jewish environmentalists answer the objection by pointing out that when we sin against God's world, pollution results, with the result that clean water and safe food become scarce. This is undoubtedly true, but Deuteronomy connects reward and punishment to *all* the commandments, not just those connected to the environment.

My own approach combines two doctrines of the Rabbis. I too admit that in the end, we cannot fathom God's justice: whether we are talking about individuals or communities, it is simply not true that the righteous always prosper and the wicked suffer; and I do not know why that is. I also believe that "the reward of performing a commandment is [the propensity and opportunity to perform another] commandment, and the result of doing a wicked thing is [the propensity and opportunity to do another] wicked thing" (M. Avot 4:2). That is, we should do the right thing because it is the right thing and not out of hope for reward, and we should avoid evil acts because they are evil and not out of fear of punishment.

This approach is a far cry from the direct, reward-and-punishment thinking of the second paragraph of the *Sh'ma*, and yet I recite the *Sh'ma* each day because it proclaims God's justice, and justice must be a critical element in the God I affirm. The calculus of reward and punishment articulated in this paragraph may be too simple and ultimately inaccurate, and, for that matter, it may be immoral in the first place to do the right thing and avoid the wrong out of concern for consequences. Nevertheless, I find this paragraph, with all its problems, central to my beliefs, for it insists starkly (even if too starkly) that God is ultimately just.

Somehow, justice is an inherent part of the world and of God; and since God is the model for human beings, the possibility of justice must be inherent in us as well. The Rabbis too had problems with the doctrine of justice announced in this paragraph, but they included it anyway because they too had a deep faith in the ultimate justice of God as the metaphysical backdrop and support for human acts of justice.

———◆———

DAVID ELLENSON

devastating consequences of Israel's collective relationship to the *mitzvot* . . . offers a supernatural theology that many contemporary Jews find difficult." Simply put, it presents a doctrine of reward and punishment that most liberal Jews have found problematic, if not offensive. It has therefore been removed from most liberal prayer books in the modern era.

Usually, no alternative is provided, but the Reconstructionist liturgy of 1945 substitutes Deuteronomy 28:1–6: "If you will truly give heed to the voice of the Lord your God, by being careful to observe all of His commandments which I am giving you this day, then all these blessings will come upon you: Blessed will you be in the city, and blessed will you be in the country; blessed will be your basket and your kneading trough; blessed will you be in your coming, and blessed will you be in your going." *Kol Han'shamah* follows suit, but only as an alternative, saying that Deuteronomy 28:1–6 encourages "observance in the same language [as Deut. 11], but concentrates on the positive ways in which observance of the *mitzvot* focuses our attention on God's presence."

The Israeli *Ha'avodah Shebalev* provides a similar option: Deuteronomy 30:15–20: "See, I set before you this day life and good, death and evil. For I command you this day to love the Lord your God. . . . I put before you life and death, blessing and curse. Choose life — if you and your offspring would live — by loving the Lord your God, heeding his commandments, and holding fast to Him. For thereby you shall have life and shall long endure upon the soil that the Lord your God swore to Abraham, Isaac and Jacob to give to them." This passage is more consonant than the traditional one with modern ethical sensibilities, and it concludes with a promise of long and prosperous life in Israel. Like *Kol Han'shamah*, however, *Ha'avodah Shebalev* offers it only as an alternative, not a substitute.

JOEL M. HOFFMAN

"Mind and body" As above.

"Land's rain in its season, in the autumn and in the spring" The Hebrew presupposes the existence of the rain. God's promise is to bring it at the right time, a fact that our translation tries to capture. We have no words for the Hebrew *yoreh* and *malkosh*. Birnbaum offers "autumn rains" and "spring rains," while JPS has "early rain" and "late rain." The *yoreh* falls immediately after Sukkot, the *malkosh* in the Spring.

"That you might gather" Singular "you" again. One wonders why.

"I shall grant" Hebrew, *natati*.

"Eat your fill" As in JPS. Birnbaum offers the more literal "eat and be satisfied."

"Take care" Again plural.

"Lest your mind tempt you" In keeping with "mind" for *levav* (see above, "Mind, body, and strength"), we translate *yifteh* as "tempt," with the correlative connotations of folly, deception and persuasion.

"The fire and fury . . . will turn against you" From *ch.r.h*, "to burn," but used with anger, as an expression for getting angry. Others, "anger flare up" or "anger blaze."

"When you sit" Again singular.

"That your days" Plural.

"As the days that the sky overlooks the earth" Probably a deliberate simile (not just an idiom), so best translated word for word. Both Birnbaum and JPS have "for as long as," which misses the connection between "your days," and "the days that the sky overlooks the earth." A less literal translation might read: ". . . that your stay in the land . . . will be as permanent as the sun's dominion over the earth."

———◆———

JUDITH PLASKOW

been very powerful in Jewish history, as again and again in the face of exile and destruction, Jews accused themselves of disobedience and looked to their own behavior as the source of their affliction. Yet, for all its importance, the notion of suffering as just punishment never entirely eclipsed other interpretations of the nature and purpose of evil. The Book of Job constitutes a passionate attack on any simple correlation between misery and wrongdoing, and, after the destruction of the Second Temple, the Rabbis imagined God as going into exile with God's People. In the aftermath of the Holocaust, during which it was the most pious segments of European Jewry who were most systematically slaughtered, it is difficult to see the Deuteronomistic perspective as anything but a misguided attempt to vindicate God at the expense of suffering human beings.

But it is not necessary to read this paragraph of the *Sh'ma* as a literal statement about divine reward and punishment. In a world whose survival depends partly on the human capacity to value creation and care for it wisely, it is possible to interpret the passage more naturalistically. If we are able to develop an ecological consciousness, if we treat the earth with respect, if we are aware that we are embedded in a great web of life of which God is the ultimate source and sustainer, then the earth will bear fruit for us and the rain will come in its season. But if we believe we can trample on or transcend the constraints of nature, if we forget the sacredness of all things and make idols of our own wealth and power, "the earth will not grant its produce," and both we and our world may perish. *Siddur Birkat Shalom* expresses these ideas in a lovely meditation on the *Sh'ma:* "Israel, your covenant with God is made of choices: holiness or profanity, life or its destruction; you can never keep from choosing. If you set yourself to love God with everything you have . . . God's gifts will be yours: a vital earth, its seas and continents moving slowly in their own way; the rain and sun and snow and clouds forming and changing. . . . But if you forget God and choose instead to fashion gods of your own . . ., you may lose everything you have. . . . This blue-green earth, so beautiful, so solitary, is as fragile as you are and as precious. Beware lest in giving way to excess you risk too much. . . ."

MARC BRETTLER

"Adonai said to Moses" This section shares some of the themes of the prior ones, such as the need to manifest love of God through visible tokens (here, the tassels) and meticulous adherence to God's word. However, as a non-Deuteronomy text that *(p. 112)*

ELLIOT N. DORFF

"Speak to the children of Israel" Not to the elders alone, but to the entire People Israel. Jewish tradition is *not* to be an esoteric religion, whose beliefs and practices are known by an elite group of people alone, but rather a religion of the masses. Similarly, the first two paragraphs of the *Sh'ma* tell us that we must teach our children this heritage so that *(p. 112)*

¹⁹וַיֹּאמֶר יְיָ אֶל-מֹשֶׁה לֵּאמֹר. דַּבֵּר אֶל-בְּנֵי יִשְׂרָאֵל וְאָמַרְתָּ אֲלֵהֶם וְעָשׂוּ לָהֶם צִיצִת עַל-כַּנְפֵי בִגְדֵיהֶם לְדֹרֹתָם וְנָתְנוּ עַל-צִיצִת הַכָּנָף פְּתִיל תְּכֵלֶת. ²⁰וְהָיָה לָכֶם לְצִיצִת ²¹וּרְאִיתֶם אֹתוֹ וּזְכַרְתֶּם אֶת-כָּל-מִצְוֹת יְיָ

¹⁹ Adonai said to Moses: "Speak to the children of Israel, and tell them to make themselves a tassel on the corners of their clothes in every generation, and to put a blue thread on the tassel of each corner. ²⁰ Let it be a tassel for you. ²¹ When you see it you shall remember all of Adonai's *(p. 112)*

DAVID ELLENSON

"Make themselves a tassel" As Reform Jews have generally not worn a *tallit*, most of its liturgies have excluded this passage from their *Sh'ma*. Isaac Mayer Wise retained the Deut. 11 passage but left out this one. Scholarship seemed to support *(p. 114)*

LAWRENCE A. HOFFMAN

THE FINAL BIBLICAL SECTION IS NUMBERS 15:37-41, "THE SECTION ON TASSELS" (PARASHAT TSITSIT).

"I am Adonai your God" It was already the custom in talmudic times to join the last two words of the *Sh'ma (Adonai eloheikhem)* to the first word of the following blessing (*emet*, "True"), imitating Jeremiah 10:10, "For Adonai your God is a true God." In the thirteenth century, Spanish leaders were trying to make the total number of *(p. 115)*

DANIEL LANDES

"A tassel" At the mention of "tassel" *(tsitsit)*, the *tsitsit* are kissed. These *tsitsit* are made by being passed through the *tallit*, then *(p. 115)*

JUDITH PLASKOW

"Make themselves a tassel" With the third paragraph of the *Sh'ma*, we seem to descend from the sublime to the ridiculous. Whether or not one agrees with the theology of the second paragraph, at least it deals with cosmic issues. But why *(p. 115)*

JOEL M. HOFFMAN

"Make themselves a tassel" Others, the usual "fringes," used as a technical term. But if a technical term is to be used, it may as well be "*tsitsit*" (as in Artscroll). Also, *tsitsit* may be used here to mean a lock of hair. Finally, one wonders why the word isn't plural.

(p. 114)

commandments and do them, and not follow your mind or eyes which you follow in false worship. 22 Thus will you remember and do all of my commandments, and so be holy before your God. 23 I am Adonai your God, who led you out of the land of Egypt to be your God. 24 I am Adonai your God."

[Prayer leader adds the first word of the next prayer, "True"]

וַעֲשִׂיתֶם אֹתָם וְלֹא תָתוּרוּ אַחֲרֵי לְבַבְכֶם וְאַחֲרֵי עֵינֵיכֶם אֲשֶׁר־אַתֶּם זֹנִים אַחֲרֵיהֶם. ²²לְמַעַן תִּזְכְּרוּ וַעֲשִׂיתֶם אֶת־כָּל־מִצְוֹתָי, וִהְיִיתֶם קְדֹשִׁים לֵאלֹ־הֵיכֶם. ²³אֲנִי יְיָ אֱלֹהֵיכֶם, אֲשֶׁר הוֹצֵאתִי אֶתְכֶם מֵאֶרֶץ מִצְרַיִם לִהְיוֹת לָכֶם לֵאלֹהִים. ²⁴אֲנִי יְיָ אֱלֹהֵיכֶם. (אֱמֶת.)

[Prayer leader adds the first word of the next prayer, "True"]

MARC BRETTLER

arose within priestly circles, its concerns are different. Through its last two verses, it adds the crucial theological idea of Israel's holiness, and an accent on the role of God as liberator of Israel from Egypt. The latter idea is central to the Torah as a whole, but is missing in the two Deuteronomy paragraphs which this citation from Numbers "corrects," not only for its own sake, but in order to lead into the final blessing (on the theme of "redemption") which follows.

"A tassel" The origin and meaning of these tassels (mentioned also in Deut. 22:12) is unclear.

Various ancient near-eastern reliefs suggest that garments, especially those worn by the nobility, could be elaborately fringed. Yet this text calls upon all Israel to wear such tassels, and to dye them with blue thread, most likely from the murex snail, an expensive dye usually reserved for the upper classes. The tassels, therefore, may represent a democratization process in which all Israel is seen "a nation of priests" (Exod. 19:6).

In any case, like the *t'fillin* or *m'zuzah* of the previous passages, these tassels represent a sacralization of the mundane, where everyday objects surround the Jews, as reminders of God's power and sovereignty, and the need for Israel to uphold its part of the covenant.

ELLIOT N. DORFF

they too can practice it and pass it on to their children. We are all together "a kingdom of priests and a holy nation," worthy to be partners with God.

"I am Adonai your God, who led you out of the land of Egypt to be your God" The trilogy of creation, revelation, and redemption that marks the three-fold blessing

structure occurs within the very paragraphs of the *Sh'ma* itself, albeit reordered stylistically to fit the blessings surrounding them. The first two blessings move from creation to revelation, and so the first paragraph of the *Sh'ma* picks up the revelation theme, telling us to "teach the commandments to our children," bequeathing the revelation to them. The second paragraph returns to creation, reflecting on God's use of nature to reward obedience and punish rebellion. The third paragraph now concludes with redemption, by saying, "I am Adonai your God who led you out of Egypt," thus forming a redemption couplet with the final blessing which is about redemption also.

If "a"=creation, "b"=revelation, and "c"=redemption, the overall structure is thus "abbacc." (The blessings before *Sh'ma* speak of "a," then "b"; the *Sh'ma* starts with "b," then returns to "a" and then progresses to "c"; and the blessing after *Sh'ma* reiterates "c"). The first unit ("abba") illustrates a common rhetorical structure (called "chiastic") whereby a pattern is executed and then reversed (e.g., 135531, or, here, "abba"). The second is a couplet on the third theme ("cc").

This trilogy of creation-revelation-redemption was first noted by Rabbi Isaac Arama (c. 1420–1494) in his *Akedat Yitzchak* (Bialystok ed., 1849, pp. 285–289), but was made famous in Franz Rosenzweig's *Star of Redemption* (New York: Holt, Rinehart, Winston, 1970, pp. 308–315). It occurs elsewhere too — the three motifs of the pilgrimage festivals, for instance. Its importance can be gleaned from a comparison with another way of looking at the world, common in Greco-Roman times, and articulated even in the biblical Book of Kohelet (Ecclesiastes). On that view, history is circular, with everything happening today exactly as it occurred yesterday and will occur tomorrow. "All is vanity and a chasing after wind," for nothing that you do today will have any lasting effect on what will be true for tomorrow (Ecc. 2:17, and in general, all of chap. 1). Under these circumstances, one can become cynical and morose (like the Stoics and Cynics), or, like Kohelet, one can decide merely to enjoy life as much as possible, taking care only not to overdo things so that you do not get into trouble with human beings or with God. Why strive to make things different when that is impossible (Ecc. 7:15–18; 8:15; 9:7–10)?

In sharp contrast, the dominant biblical view, and the view the Rabbis adopted, is that history has meaning precisely because it is not circular, but linear: we progress from creation through revelation to ultimate redemption. Since the Garden of Eden, we human beings are in the intermediate stage, between revelation and redemption. We may not live our lives as if we already live in a state of redemption, as Christians do, but we should forever strive to create a world worthy of being redeemed, for the promise of future redemption is real, confirmed by none other than God.

Consequently, this sequence of creation-revelation-redemption does no less than proclaim that history is meaningful, that our current efforts to make a better world can bear fruit, and that life itself has meaning.

David Ellenson

Reform efforts in this direction, since it was generally believed that the Numbers passage was the last to be added to the *Sh'ma*, and Reform liturgists tended anyway to privilege pristine parts of the liturgy while deleting late additions that they felt had crept in through time. Both *Hamburg Temple Prayer Books* (1819 and 1841) retained the passage, however. All Reconstructionist prayer books keep it also, since Reconstructionist Jews have always worn a *tallit*.

———◆———

Joel M. Hoffman

"Each corner" Lit., "the tassel on the corner." Perhaps it was clear which corner was meant.

"Let it be a tassel for you" "Let it [the tassel] be a tassel" is most odd; what else would it be? JPS offers, "that [the tassel] shall be your [tassel]." Either way, it is clear that the convention of using tassels was sufficiently widespread as to need no explanation. The point here is how to make Jewish tassels. Plaut notes that pictures predating the Bible depict garments with tassels. But *tsitsit* also means "lock [of hair]," so that we might have "the lock of hair shall be a tassel." Deuteronomy 22:12 repeats the requirement, asking that we make *g'dilim* ("twisted cords"), but immediately before we are warned against *sha'atnez* (mixing wool and linen together), further suggesting that the crux of the issue may be the nature of the tassels, not their existence.

"Not follow your mind or eyes" Meaning uncertain. *Taturu* is usually "to spy," but it appears here (and only here) with the preposition *acharei*. We can guess at its meaning from other contexts, but in general, verbs change meaning when they change prepositions (cf. the English "pick," "pick up," "pick on," and "pick up on.")

"Which you follow in false worship" Hebrew, *zonim*, used elsewhere in the sense of worshipping false gods, but also used in the sense of "lust," suggesting a second possible translation: ". . . which you lust after."

"Remember and do" JPS: "remember to do."

"To be your God" Or "become your God."

"I am Adonai your God" This phrase is repeated over and over again. Perhaps it was rhetoric used as part of a rallying speech, the way Martin Luther King, Jr. used "I have a dream."

———◆———

LAWRENCE A. HOFFMAN

words in the *Sh'ma* (245) tally with what they thought to be the total number of bodily parts (248). Rejecting the Ashkenazi solution, adding the three words "God faithful ruler" (see above), they hit on the notion that the repetition of these three words by the prayer leader on behalf of the entire congregation would suffice, and the practice has held ever since.

——◆——

DANIEL LANDES

doubled over and tied in a prescribed and intricate pattern with special knots. One double thread per corner is to be made from *t'khelet,* a special blue dye that was lost for millennia, but believed by some contemporary groups to be rediscovered now.

"When you see it" At these words, we pass the *tsitsit* before our eyes, to fulfill the commandment, "Remember all of A-do-nai's commandments" (Num. 15:39). The numerical value of the Hebrew letters of "*tsitsit*" add up to 600, and, when added to the 8 doubled threads and 5 knots, make up 613, the number of *mitzvot.*

"And not follow your mind or eyes" The command to detach ourselves from heretical or immoral thoughts: to be internalized by the regular recitation of the *Sh'ma.*

"A-do-nai your God (A-do-nai E-loheikhem). True (emet)" The last two words of the *Sh'ma (A-do-nai E-loheikhem)* and the first word of the following blessing (*emet*) are recited by the prayer leader so as to bring the total number of words to 248. (See above, "God, faithful King.") Also, we affirm this truth: "A-do-nai is your true God."

——◆——

JUDITH PLASKOW

should the creator of the universe care whether we put a "tassel on the corners of [our] clothes in every generation," and what possible difference can it make to God whether the thread in that tassel is green or red or blue?

In moving from the global to the ordinary and concrete, the paragraph on *tsitsit* addresses the power and importance of symbols. The *Sh'ma's* exhortations to love God and follow God's will, even its threats and promises, remain on the level of the abstract and the general. In our everyday experience, there are a thousand things that get between us and our capacity to focus on the sacred; we are continually distracted from awareness of God as we "follow [our] mind or eyes." Symbols provide us with tangible reminders of our obligations and of their roots in our history. Sometimes, as with the symbols on the Seder plate, these reminders seem integrally related to the history they recall; other times, as with *tsitsit,* they seem more arbitrary. In either case, however, symbols make up part of the common vocabulary of a particular community through which it constitutes itself and gives concreteness to its beliefs. Again, the *Birkat Shalom* "Meditation on the *Sh'ma*" captures the essence of this paragraph: "Gather up some things that remind you of Me, things that speak of the earth and the sky, solid and shimmering, light sand and blue air. . . . Whatever these things may be, agree upon them. Choose them together and be one people."

◆ ◆ ◆

5 | *G'ullah*
גְּאוּלָה
Blessing on Redemption

[1] True and established and accurate and enduring and right and steadfast and beloved and precious and desirable and pleasant and awesome and mighty and correct and accepted and good and beautiful for us are these words for ever and ever. [2] True it is that the everlasting God is our ruler; the rock of Jacob is our saving shield. [3] From generation to generation He endures, and his name endures, and his decrees are accurate and his reign and faithfulness endure forever; and his words live and endure, steadfast and desirable, forever and to the ends of time, for our ancestors and for us, for our children and for our generations, and for all of the generations of the progeny of Israel, your servants.

[4] For the first and for the last, these words are good and enduring for ever and ever; truth and faith, a law that will not pass. [5] True it is that You are Adonai our God, and our ancestors' God; our ruler, our ancestors' ruler; our redeemer, our ancestors' redeemer; our creator, our saving rock; our deliverer and our rescuer. [6] Your name is eternal. [7] There is no god but You.

[1] אֱמֶת וְיַצִּיב וְנָכוֹן וְקַיָּם וְיָשָׁר וְנֶאֱמָן וְאָהוּב וְחָבִיב וְנֶחְמָד וְנָעִים וְנוֹרָא וְאַדִּיר וּמְתֻקָּן וּמְקֻבָּל וְטוֹב וְיָפֶה הַדָּבָר הַזֶּה עָלֵינוּ לְעוֹלָם וָעֶד. [2] אֱמֶת אֱלֹהֵי עוֹלָם מַלְכֵּנוּ צוּר יַעֲקֹב מָגֵן יִשְׁעֵנוּ. [3] לְדוֹר וָדוֹר הוּא קַיָּם וּשְׁמוֹ קַיָּם וְכִסְאוֹ נָכוֹן וּמַלְכוּתוֹ וֶאֱמוּנָתוֹ לָעַד קַיֶּמֶת. וּדְבָרָיו חָיִים וְקַיָּמִים נֶאֱמָנִים וְנֶחֱמָדִים לָעַד וּלְעוֹלְמֵי עוֹלָמִים. עַל-אֲבוֹתֵינוּ וְעָלֵינוּ, עַל-בָּנֵינוּ וְעַל-דּוֹרוֹתֵינוּ, וְעַל כָּל-דּוֹרוֹת זֶרַע יִשְׂרָאֵל עֲבָדֶיךָ.

[4] עַל הָרִאשׁוֹנִים וְעַל הָאַחֲרוֹנִים דָּבָר טוֹב וְקַיָּם לְעוֹלָם וָעֶד, אֱמֶת וֶאֱמוּנָה, חֹק וְלֹא יַעֲבֹר. [5] אֱמֶת, שָׁאַתָּה הוּא יְיָ אֱלֹהֵינוּ וֵאלֹהֵי אֲבוֹתֵינוּ, מַלְכֵּנוּ מֶלֶךְ אֲבוֹתֵינוּ, גֹּאֲלֵנוּ גֹּאֵל אֲבוֹתֵינוּ, יוֹצְרֵנוּ צוּר יְשׁוּעָתֵנוּ, פּוֹדֵנוּ וּמַצִּילֵנוּ. [6] מֵעוֹלָם שְׁמֶךָ, [7] אֵין אֱלֹהִים זוּלָתֶךָ.

8 You have always been our ancestors' help, protecting and saving their children after them in each and every generation. 9 High above the world lies your habitation, and your justice and righteousness reach the ends of the earth. 10 Happy is the one who obeys your commandments, taking your Torah and your words to heart. 11 True it is that You are lord over your people, and a mighty ruler to battle their battle. 12 True it is that You are the first and You are the last, and other than You we have no king who redeems and saves.

13 You redeemed us from Egypt, Adonai our God, and You set us free from the House of Bondage. 14 You killed all their first-born, and redeemed your first-born, and You parted the Red Sea and drowned the insolent and brought the precious across the water, and the water covered up their foes. 15 Not one of them was left. 16 The beloved lauded and praised God for this, and the precious offered hymns, songs and praises, blessings and thanks to our ruler, the living and eternal God, high and exalted, great and revered, humbling the proud and raising the humble, freeing the captive and redeeming the meek, helping the poor and answering his people when they cry out to Him for help. 17 All praise to God on high, most blessed be He.

עֶזְרַת אֲבוֹתֵינוּ אַתָּה הוּא מֵעוֹלָם, מָגֵן וּמוֹשִׁיעַ לִבְנֵיהֶם אַחֲרֵיהֶם בְּכָל דּוֹר וָדוֹר. בְּרוּם עוֹלָם מוֹשָׁבֶךָ, וּמִשְׁפָּטֶיךָ וְצִדְקָתְךָ עַד אַפְסֵי אָרֶץ. אַשְׁרֵי אִישׁ שֶׁיִּשְׁמַע לְמִצְוֹתֶיךָ, וְתוֹרָתְךָ וּדְבָרְךָ יָשִׂים עַל לִבּוֹ. אֱמֶת, אַתָּה הוּא אָדוֹן לְעַמֶּךָ, וּמֶלֶךְ גִּבּוֹר לָרִיב רִיבָם. אֱמֶת, אַתָּה הוּא רִאשׁוֹן וְאַתָּה הוּא אַחֲרוֹן, וּמִבַּלְעָדֶיךָ אֵין לָנוּ מֶלֶךְ גּוֹאֵל וּמוֹשִׁיעַ.

מִמִּצְרַיִם גְּאַלְתָּנוּ, יְיָ אֱלֹהֵינוּ, וּמִבֵּית עֲבָדִים פְּדִיתָנוּ. כָּל־ בְּכוֹרֵיהֶם הָרַגְתָּ, וּבְכוֹרְךָ גָּאָלְתָּ, וְיַם סוּף בָּקַעְתָּ, וְזֵדִים טִבַּעְתָּ, וִידִידִים הֶעֱבַרְתָּ. וַיְכַסּוּ מַיִם צָרֵיהֶם, אֶחָד מֵהֶם לֹא נוֹתָר. עַל זֹאת שִׁבְּחוּ אֲהוּבִים וְרוֹמְמוּ אֵל, וְנָתְנוּ יְדִידִים זְמִירוֹת, שִׁירוֹת וְתִשְׁבָּחוֹת, בְּרָכוֹת וְהוֹדָאוֹת לְמֶלֶךְ, אֵל חַי וְקַיָּם. רָם וְנִשָּׂא, גָּדוֹל וְנוֹרָא, מַשְׁפִּיל גֵּאִים וּמַגְבִּיהַּ שְׁפָלִים, מוֹצִיא אֲסִירִים וּפוֹדֶה עֲנָוִים, וְעוֹזֵר דַּלִּים, וְעוֹנֶה לְעַמּוֹ בְּעֵת שַׁוְּעָם אֵלָיו. תְּהִלּוֹת לְאֵל עֶלְיוֹן, בָּרוּךְ הוּא וּמְבֹרָךְ.

118

¹⁸ Moses and the children of Israel most joyfully answered You in song, all of them singing:

Who is like You among the gods, Adonai!

Who is like You, adorned in holiness,

Revered in praise, worker of wonders!

¹⁹ At the seashore the redeemed sang a new song to your name. ²⁰ Together they all gave thanks, exalting You with these words:

Adonai will reign for ever and ever.

²¹ Rock of Israel, arise to help Israel, and deliver Judah and Israel, as you promised. ²² Our redeemer, Lord of Hosts is his name, Israel's holy one. ²³ Blessed are You, Adonai, who redeemed Israel.

¹⁸מֹשֶׁה וּבְנֵי יִשְׂרָאֵל לְךָ עָנוּ שִׁירָה בְּשִׂמְחָה רַבָּה, וְאָמְרוּ כֻלָּם.

מִי־כָמְכָה בָּאֵלִם יְיָ.

מִי כָּמְכָה נֶאְדָּר בַּקֹּדֶשׁ,

נוֹרָא תְהִלֹּת, עֹשֵׂה פֶלֶא.

¹⁹שִׁירָה חֲדָשָׁה שִׁבְּחוּ גְאוּלִים לְשִׁמְךָ עַל שְׂפַת הַיָּם. ²⁰יַחַד כֻּלָּם הוֹדוּ וְהִמְלִיכוּ וְאָמְרוּ.

יְיָ יִמְלֹךְ לְעֹלָם וָעֶד.

²¹צוּר יִשְׂרָאֵל, קוּמָה בְּעֶזְרַת יִשְׂרָאֵל, וּפְדֵה כִנְאֻמֶךָ יְהוּדָה וְיִשְׂרָאֵל. ²²גֹּאֲלֵנוּ יְיָ צְבָאוֹת שְׁמוֹ, קְדוֹשׁ יִשְׂרָאֵל. ²³בָּרוּךְ אַתָּה יְיָ, גָּאַל יִשְׂרָאֵל.

MARC BRETTLER

"*True and established*" God's nature as "true" or "reliable" is the major theme here. The first part of the blessing has been carefully constructed to draw liberally on words like *emet* ("true"), *emunah* ("faithfulness") and *ne'emanim* ("steadfast"), and is *(p. 122)*

DANIEL LANDES

"*True*" At each mention of "true" (*emet*) in this blessing, we kiss the *tsitsit*.

"*Steadfast and desirable, forever*" We kiss the *tsitsit* here.

—◆—

JOEL M. HOFFMAN

"*True and established*" As elsewhere, the flavor conveyed by this prayer comes not so much from the individual meanings of the words but from the intense repetition. Therefore, little mention is made of possible alternative translations for the individual words.

"*From generation to generation*" Or "in each and every generation." *(p. 122)*

אֱמֶת וְיַצִּיב וְנָכוֹן וְקַיָּם וְיָשָׁר¹
וְנֶאֱמָן וְאָהוּב וְחָבִיב וְנֶחְמָד
וְנָעִים וְנוֹרָא וְאַדִּיר וּמְתֻקָּן
וּמְקֻבָּל וְטוֹב וְיָפֶה הַדָּבָר הַזֶּה
עָלֵינוּ לְעוֹלָם וָעֶד. ²אֱמֶת
אֱלֹהֵי עוֹלָם מַלְכֵּנוּ צוּר יַעֲקֹב
מָגֵן יִשְׁעֵנוּ. ³לְדוֹר וָדוֹר הוּא

¹ True and established and accurate and enduring and right and steadfast and beloved and precious and desirable and pleasant and awesome and mighty and correct and accepted and good and beautiful for us are these words for ever and ever. *(p. 122)*

JUDITH PLASKOW

"*True and established and accurate and enduring. . . .*" This blessing after the *Sh'ma* raises the same problems of male imagery, hierarchy, and supernaturalism as the blessings before it (see above, "King over the kings of kings"; "Our protector"; "Worker of wonder") Again, Marcia Falk rewrites in a much more immanentist fashion: "Let *(p. 123)*

LAWRENCE A. HOFFMAN

A FINAL BLESSING CONCLUDES THE MORNING SH'MA AND ITS BLESSINGS: THE "BLESSING OF REDEMPTION" (G'ULLAH) WHICH ACKNOWLEDGES GOD'S PARTICIPATION IN THE PROCESS OF HISTORY.

"*True and established*" The first part of this lengthy blessing (up to "There is no god but You") has nothing to do with the theme of redemption. Its original purpose was probably to affirm the creed as given thus far — as if, having recited the *Sh'ma*, we now say, "All of this is true; we really believe it." Some time in the first or second century, the prayer expanded to include our faith in redemption.

With the theme of redemption added, the final order of the blessings recapitulates the history of the universe: from creation, to Sinai, and eventually to history's end.

—◆—

² True it is that the everlasting God is our ruler, the rock of Jacob is our saving shield. ³ From generation to generation He endures, and his name endures, and his decrees are accurate and his reign and faithfulness endure forever, and his words live and endure, steadfast and desirable, forever and to the ends of time, for our ancestors and for us, for our children and for our generations, and for all of the generations of the progeny of Israel, your servants.

קַיָּם וּשְׁמוֹ קַיָּם וְכִסְאוֹ נָכוֹן וּמַלְכוּתוֹ וֶאֱמוּנָתוֹ לָעַד קַיֶּמֶת. וּדְבָרָיו חָיִים וְקַיָּמִים נֶאֱמָנִים וְנֶחֱמָדִים לָעַד וּלְעוֹלְמֵי עוֹלָמִים. עַל־אֲבוֹתֵינוּ וְעָלֵינוּ, עַל־בָּנֵינוּ וְעַל־דּוֹרוֹתֵינוּ, וְעַל כָּל־דּוֹרוֹת זֶרַע יִשְׂרָאֵל עֲבָדֶיךָ.

MARC BRETTLER

filled with examples of God's covenantal reliability, especially in the role of liberator. It therefore connects the final verse of the *Sh'ma* ("I am Adonai your God, who led you out of the land of Egypt") to the end of this blessing which is the Song of the Sea (Exod. 15:11 — "Who is like You among the gods, Adonai!"). But the emphasis here is the future. If the first blessing focused on creation, and therefore highlighted the past, this one anticipates redemption in the future. But that redemption harks back to the Exodus, a prior sign of God's truth and reliability.

Thematically, this section may be modeled after Deutero-Isaiah (see above, "Who forms light and creates darkness, makes peace and creates everything"), who preached to the Babylonian exiles about God's reliability. He frequently reminds his hearers of how God has fulfilled his initial promises (*rishonot* — e.g. 42:9 and 48:3), and thus may be reliably counted on to fulfill his latter ones too. Moreover, God will redeem the exiles in what is nothing less than a second exodus, even more miraculous than the earlier one (e.g. 52:11–12).

JOEL M. HOFFMAN

"His decrees" Lit., "chair," but probably used metonymically to denote God's throne whence royal decrees are issued.

"His reign and faithfulness" Birnbaum: "truth." We prefer "faithfulness" following "reign" (the word it accompanies), as an extension of the metonymic *kis'o* ("throne"). The whole paragraph portrays an extended metaphor of God as an absolute sovereign who issues eternal decrees and keeps faith with his subject people, Israel.

"Forever and to the ends of time" Forever is *l'ad*, not the more common *l'olam*. "Ends of time" is *l'olamei olamim*, stronger than simply *l'olam*, and much stronger coming as it does after *l'ad*.

"For our generations" Perhaps the intent is "future generations."

"Progeny" Lit., "seed."

—◆—

JUDITH PLASKOW

us bless the source of life, / source of faith and daring, / wellspring of new song / and the courage to mend."

SUSAN L. EINBINDER

"*There is no god but You*" This phrase gives its name to the *piyyut* insertion known as the *Zulat* (sometimes also called the *Emet*). Some of the surviving compositions of this form are choral.

———◆———

LAWRENCE A. HOFFMAN

"*Our creator, our saving rock*" (*yotsreinu, tsur yeshu'ateinu*) A play on the similar sounding *yotser* ("creator") and *tsur* ("rock"). Sefardi liturgy actually reads *tsureinu tsur yeshu'ateinu* ("Our rock, our saving rock").

———◆———

⁴עַל הָרִאשׁוֹנִים וְעַל הָאַחֲרוֹנִים
דָּבָר טוֹב וְקַיָּם לְעוֹלָם וָעֶד,
אֱמֶת וֶאֱמוּנָה, חֹק וְלֹא יַעֲבֹר.
⁵אֱמֶת, שָׁאַתָּה הוּא יְיָ אֱלֹהֵינוּ
וֵאלֹהֵי אֲבוֹתֵינוּ, מַלְכֵּנוּ מֶלֶךְ
אֲבוֹתֵינוּ, גֹּאֲלֵנוּ גֹּאֵל אֲבוֹתֵינוּ,
יוֹצְרֵנוּ צוּר יְשׁוּעָתֵנוּ, פּוֹדֵנוּ

⁴For the first and for the last, these words are good and enduring for ever and ever, truth and faith, a law that will not pass. ⁵True it is that You are Adonai our God, and our ancestors' God; our ruler, our ancestors' ruler; our redeemer, our ancestors' redeemer; our creator, our saving rock; our *(p. 125)*

JOEL M. HOFFMAN

"*These words*" *Davar*, singular in the Hebrew, probably denoting "communication" in general, from the root *d.b.r* (see above, "Use them"). But "this communication" is the wrong register here.

"*A law that will not pass*" Or perhaps, "a law He [God] will not break."

"*Our ancestors' God*" Others, "God of our ancestors" or "God of our fathers." The word order used here ("our God and our ancestors' God") more closely captures the parallelism of the Hebrew.

"*Our creator, our saving rock*" The Hebrew *yotsreinu* and *tsur* sound similar, particularly in a language where vowels matter less than consonants. A vaguely similar effect in English results from, "our designer, our saving sign."

"*Eternal*" The Hebrew *me'olam* indicates "forever (in the past) up to now," but English does not distinguish between "forever up to now," and "forever forth." *(p. 125)* deliverer and our rescuer. [6] Your name is eternal. [7] There is no god but You.

[8] You have always been our ancestors' help, protecting and saving their children after them in each and every generation. [9] High above the world lies your habitation, and your justice and righteousness reach the ends of the earth. [10] Happy is the one who obeys your commandments, taking your Torah and your words to heart. [11] True it is that You are lord over your people, and a mighty ruler to battle their battle. [12] True it is that You are the first and You are the last, and other than You we have no king who redeems and saves.

וּמַצִּילֵנוּ. [6] מֵעוֹלָם שְׁמֶךָ, [7] אֵין אֱלֹהִים זוּלָתֶךָ.

[8] עֶזְרַת אֲבוֹתֵינוּ אַתָּה הוּא מֵעוֹלָם, מָגֵן וּמוֹשִׁיעַ לִבְנֵיהֶם אַחֲרֵיהֶם בְּכָל דּוֹר וָדוֹר. [9] בְּרוּם עוֹלָם מוֹשָׁבֶךָ, וּמִשְׁפָּטֶיךָ, וְצִדְקָתְךָ עַד אַפְסֵי אָרֶץ. [10] אַשְׁרֵי אִישׁ שֶׁיִּשְׁמַע לְמִצְוֹתֶיךָ, וְתוֹרָתְךָ וּדְבָרְךָ יָשִׂים עַל לִבּוֹ. [11] אֱמֶת, אַתָּה הוּא אָדוֹן לְעַמֶּךָ, וּמֶלֶךְ גִּבּוֹר לָרִיב רִיבָם. [12] אֱמֶת, אַתָּה הוּא רִאשׁוֹן וְאַתָּה הוּא אַחֲרוֹן, וּמִבַּלְעָדֶיךָ אֵין לָנוּ מֶלֶךְ גּוֹאֵל וּמוֹשִׁיעַ.

JOEL M. HOFFMAN

"Lies" Hebrew, "is."

"Your Torah" Or, "your teachings."

"To heart" The Hebrew idiom, too, involves the heart.

"A mighty ruler to battle their battle" Birnbaum's "champion their cause" is both more poetic and less violent, but also less accurate. God appears here not only as "ruler," but as "mighty," in the military sense of being the one and only king who can be counted on to deliver us. (The graphic military imagery increases with the destruction of the Egyptians, at the paragraph's end.)

"The first and . . . the last" Perhaps an idiom; if so, "the one and only" might serve better.

◆ ◆ ◆

ELLIOT N. DORFF

"*You redeemed us from Egypt*" Why does the Siddur specify just the Exodus from Egypt, not other instances of God's deliverance?

I suggest the Exodus matters most because it is the birth event of our people. Individuals and nations take birth events seriously and mark them publicly, not because nothing significant has happened since then, but because who we are at birth often sets the stage for who we are in later life. For individuals, new genetic discoveries only reinforce this *(p. 127)*

DAVID ELLENSON

"*You redeemed us from Egypt . . . Not one of them was left*" This graphic description of divine chastisement has offended the moral beliefs and rationalistic sensibilities of many liberal prayerbook authors. Such a vengeful God has seemed inappropriate to Jews who enjoy the liberty and tolerance offered by western Emancipation. The Talmud, however, explicitly *(p. 127)*

DANIEL LANDES

"*All praise to God on high*" (*t'hillot l'el elyon*) The *Sh'ma* and Its Blessings is directly connected to the *Amidah*. Halakhah calls it *s'michat g'ulah lit'filah*, "connecting redemption (the final blessing of *Sh'ma*) to the *T'fillah* (the *Amidah*)." We may not say anything at all between the two; nor may we even pause there. We therefore rise at this point in the blessing to get ready for the *Amidah*.

In some congregations, worshippers recite the last line of the *G'ullah* along with the prayer leader so as to obviate even *(p. 128)*

JUDITH PLASKOW

"*You redeemed us from Egypt*" The new element here is the reference to redemption from Egypt, which Emil Fackenheim calls one of the "root experiences" of Judaism. A root experience is an epoch-making historical event every generation recalls and reenacts as a present reality. As the words of the blessing make clear (and as the Passover Haggadah explicitly reminds *(p. 129)*

13 מִמִּצְרַיִם גְּאַלְתָּנוּ, יְיָ אֱלֹהֵינוּ, וּמִבֵּית עֲבָדִים פְּדִיתָנוּ. 14 כָּל־בְּכוֹרֵיהֶם הָרַגְתָּ, וּבְכוֹרְךָ גָּאָלְתָּ, וְיַם סוּף בָּקַעְתָּ, וְזֵדִים טִבַּעְתָּ, וִידִידִים הֶעֱבַרְתָּ. וַיְכַסּוּ מַיִם צָרֵיהֶם, 15 אֶחָד מֵהֶם לֹא נוֹתָר. 16 עַל זֹאת שִׁבְּחוּ אֲהוּבִים

13 You redeemed us from Egypt, Adonai our God, and You set us free from the House of Bondage. 14 You killed all their first-born, and redeemed your first-born, and You parted the Red Sea and drowned the insolent and brought the precious across the water, and the water covered up their foes. 15 Not one of them was left. 16 The beloved *(p. 127)*

JOEL M. HOFFMAN

"*House of Bondage*" Probably a proper noun, equivalent to Egypt, and so translated here as the more popular "House of Bondage," rather than the more literal "house of slaves."

"*Red Sea*" "Sea of Reeds" is surely too literal.

"*Insolent . . . precious*" Perhaps these were technical terms, similar to "enemy" and "friendly" in our "enemy fire" and "friendly fire," but more likely merely an instance of the then-popular poetic style of using adjectives to refer to known groups of people. *(p. 128)*

lauded and praised God for this, and the precious offered hymns, songs and praises, blessings and thanks to our ruler, the living and eternal God, high and exalted, great and revered, humbling the proud and raising the humble, freeing the captive and redeeming the meek, helping the poor and answering his people when they cry out to Him for help. [17] All praise to God on high, most blessed be He.

וְרוֹמְמוּ אֵל, וְנָתְנוּ יְדִידִים זְמִירוֹת, שִׁירוֹת וְתִשְׁבָּחוֹת, בְּרָכוֹת וְהוֹדָאוֹת לְמֶלֶךְ, אֵל חַי וְקַיָּם. רָם וְנִשָּׂא, גָּדוֹל וְנוֹרָא, מַשְׁפִּיל גֵּאִים וּמַגְבִּיהַּ שְׁפָלִים, מוֹצִיא אֲסִירִים וּפוֹדֶה עֲנָוִים, וְעוֹזֵר דַּלִּים, וְעוֹנֶה לְעַמּוֹ בְּעֵת שַׁוְּעָם אֵלָיו. [17] תְּהִלּוֹת לְאֵל עֶלְיוֹן, בָּרוּךְ הוּא וּמְבֹרָךְ.

ELLIOT N. DORFF

truth. For whole peoples, we have the evidence of mythology. The Romans, for instance, explained their military might by recalling how their founders, Romulus and Remus, were descended from powerful animals. Even we Americans explain our commitment to fight oppression by stories of the Revolution and the writing of the Constitution in the hot summer days of Philadelphia in 1789. In the same way, the Exodus story clearly articulates who we Jews are by recollecting how we came into being: a people born into slavery, redeemed by a miraculous act of God on our behalf, taken to Sinai to become "a kingdom of priests and a holy nation."

Birth stories also act as paradigms for what is important. God redeemed us from Egypt not because of our size, power, or worth (Deut. 7) but because God chose to love us and to do special things for us, so that — indeed, on condition that — we carry out the God-given mission articulated at Sinai. More than freedom from slavery, the Jewish birth-story of redemption is freedom to become responsible partners with God in the ongoing divine acts of creation, revelation, and redemption.

DAVID ELLENSON

demands the inclusion of just these elements at this point in the service, so that modern liturgies have had to struggle with the tension between Jewish tradition and contemporary ethics.

As with other "difficult" passages, many Reform and Reconstructionist liturgies omitted these lines altogether, following David Einhorn's *Olath Tamid* which set the standard in doing so. By omitting the entire passage (including the beginning, "You redeemed us from Egypt, Adonai our God, and You set us free from the House of Bondage"), they reject the depiction of a vengeful deity and also any hint of chauvinism or particularism which might imply that God redeems only Israel. God emerges instead as the redeemer of all humanity.

Other prayer books, as disparate as *The Hamburg Temple Prayer Book* of 1841, the present Reconstructionist *Kol Han'shamah,* the British Liberal *Lev Chadash,* and the Israeli Progressive *Ha'avodah Shebalev* retain "You redeemed us from Egypt," but omit the details of slaying the first-born and drowning the Egyptians. They stop short of presenting God as a punishing deity, but they freely highlight Jewish particularity, seeing the Exodus as *the* redemptive moment in Jewish history.

Prayer books of the Conservative Movement, here as elsewhere, retain the traditional Ashkenazi text, but provide metaphoric or non-literal translations to mute the image of a vengeful deity. "You killed all their first-born" is rendered in the 1962 Conservative Prayer Book and in *Siddur Sim Shalom* as, "The first-born of the Egyptians were slain." "You . . . drowned the insolent," becomes "the wicked drowned." The Egyptian first-born were killed and the pursuers drowned, apparently, on account of their own wickedness.

———◆———

JOEL M. HOFFMAN

"Our ruler" Simply "the ruler" in Hebrew, but Hebrew often omits possessive pronouns when the possessor is required in English.

"All praise" "All" is absent from the Hebrew, but required to make the English readable.

"Most blessed be He" The English cannot capture the two words for "bless" used here: *barukh* and *m'rovakh.* We would like to use "blessed" (two syllables) for the first and "blessed" (one syllable) for the latter, but we have no way to write this. And so we resort to "most blessed."

———◆———

DANIEL LANDES

having to say *amen* when the blessing ends. (Normally, any blessing evokes the necessary response of *amen;* but Halakhah prohibits saying *amen* to one's own blessings.) Others have the custom for the prayer leader to drop his voice so that this blessing is not heard. Still others begin their own *Amidah* before the prayer leader finishes the *G'ullah,* since they need not interrupt the *Amidah* to say *amen.*

———◆———

JUDITH PLASKOW

us), it was not only our ancestors who experienced the Exodus, but "[God] redeemed us from Egypt . . . and set us free from the house of bondage."

It is in the context of the Exodus that the hierarchical God emerges most clearly as God the liberator. The imagery of this blessing is filled with reversals as God overturns the expected order of things. The proud are humbled while the meek are redeemed, and those who were enslaved go forth in freedom. There is none of the restraint that we find in the Passover Seder, where wine is removed from the second cup as the ten plagues are recited. All is celebration and thanksgiving. The mighty God has performed miracles; a lowly group of slaves is raised up and their powerful enemies punished. This imagery is very compelling. Yet it depicts a world of "us" and "them," with God on "our" side, that makes it very difficult to confront and disentangle the complexities of oppression or the reversibility of meekness and arrogance. Perhaps the challenge confronting us is to find a way to give thanks for the "root experience" of liberation and at the same time imagine a world in which the liberation of some is not dependent on the destruction of others, and in which God is the "source of faith and daring" (Marcia Falk) rather than the great and exalted God on high.

◆ ◆ ◆

MARC BRETTLER

"*W*ho is like You among the gods [elim], Adonai!*" From the Song of the Sea (Exod. 15), one of the earliest pieces of biblical literature. When it was written, *elim* certainly meant real gods, but by the time it was incorporated into the liturgy, Judaism had long accepted "radical monotheism" and would not even admit the *theoretical* possibility of other deities. *Elim* was thus reinterpreted as "divine beings" like angels, or just as "mighty ones."

From here until the end of the blessing, we find grammatical tenses used in a particularly *(p. 131)*

LAWRENCE A. HOFFMAN

"*W*ho is like You*" The Song of the Sea celebrates God's paradigmatic entry into history. Reciting it here celebrates the belief that God will enter history again, to inaugurate divine rule in the world to come.

"*Who redeemed Israel*" The final benediction, "Redemption," presents the Jewish response to a theme in Greek philosophy ever since Aristotle, who posited the existence of a god, but only as a logical necessity. Aristotle believed that every event has a cause immediately antecedent to it. Such a view results in an infinite *(p. 133)*

מֹשֶׁה¹⁸ וּבְנֵי יִשְׂרָאֵל לְךָ עָנוּ שִׁירָה בְּשִׂמְחָה רַבָּה, וְאָמְרוּ כֻּלָּם.

מִי־כָמֹכָה בָּאֵלִם יְיָ.

מִי כָּמֹכָה נֶאְדָּר בַּקֹּדֶשׁ,

SUSAN L. EINBINDER

"*B*lessed are You, Adonai, who redeemed Israel*" The *G'ullah* is the last *piyyut* insertion in the *Yotser* set. Many poets exploited its theme to give voice to a collective yearn- *(p. 132)*

¹⁸ Moses and the children of Israel most joyfully answered You in song, all of them singing:

Who is like You among the gods, Adonai!

Who is like You, adorned in holiness,

(p. 131)

LAWRENCE KUSHNER
NEHEMIA POLEN

"*W*ho is like You*" Elimelekh of Grodzisk (d. 1892), in his *Divrei Elimelekh,* offers an extraordinary insight into the meaning of redemption. It is based on a deliberate misreading of the *Mi kamokha,* and a daring Zoharic interpretation of Adam and Eve's sin in the Garden of Eden. Elimelekh begins with a traditional reading: *Mi kamokha ba'elim Adonai,* "Who is like You among the gods, Adonai!" This, he says, is an exclamatory question: "God, You are incomparable, inconceivable and incomprehensible. You are beyond any *(p. 133)*

DAVID ELLENSON

"*M*oses and the children of Israel*" In response to the modern demand for gender equality, a whole host of liturgies (the British *Lev Chadash,* the Reconstructionist *Kol Han'shamah,* and the Reform Movement's gender-sensitive *Gates of Prayer*) have added the name of Miriam to that of *(p. 132)*

JOEL M. HOFFMAN

"*S*inging*" Lit., "saying," but the verb "saying" does not refer to any particular modality, being used rather in place of quotation marks, which had not been invented yet.

(p. 132)

Revered in praise, worker of wonders!

[19] At the seashore the redeemed sang a new song to your name. [20] Together they all gave thanks, exalting You with these words:

Adonai will reign for ever and ever.

[21] Rock of Israel, arise to help Israel, and deliver Judah and Israel, as You promised. [22] Our redeemer, Lord of Hosts is his name, Israel's holy one. [23] Blessed are You, Adonai, who redeemed Israel.

נוֹרָא תְהִלֹּת, עֹשֵׂה פֶלֶא.

[19]שִׁירָה חֲדָשָׁה שִׁבְּחוּ גְאוּלִים לְשִׁמְךָ עַל שְׂפַת הַיָּם. [20]יַחַד כֻּלָּם הוֹדוּ וְהִמְלִיכוּ וְאָמְרוּ.

יְיָ יִמְלֹךְ לְעֹלָם וָעֶד.

[21]צוּר יִשְׂרָאֵל, קוּמָה בְּעֶזְרַת יִשְׂרָאֵל, וּפְדֵה כִנְאֻמֶךָ יְהוּדָה וְיִשְׂרָאֵל. [22]גֹּאֲלֵנוּ יְיָ צְבָאוֹת שְׁמוֹ, קְדוֹשׁ יִשְׂרָאֵל. [23]בָּרוּךְ אַתָּה יְיָ, גָּאַל יִשְׂרָאֵל.

MARC BRETTLER

significant way. God's actions in the past are recalled with quotations from the Song of the Sea given in the past tense ("sang a new song"), and the *chatimah* (the closing line of the blessing) too is in the past ("who redeemed Israel"). But it contains a set of commands dealing with the present ("arise," "deliver") and uses present participles (like "our redeemer"). The climactic hope for a new exodus (Exod. 15:18), however, is given in the future ("Adonai will reign for ever and ever"). This alternation of tenses cleverly reinforces the theme of Deutero-Isaiah (see above, "True and established") that the promised new redemption will mimic the past one. Indeed, it will occur not in the distant future, but in the near present, as all time periods — past, present and future — converge.

"Adonai will reign for ever and ever" Also from the Song of the Sea (see above, "Who is like You among the gods, Adonai!"), serving as its climactic conclusion (Exod. 15:18), a role which it plays in its liturgical recontextualization as well. The metaphor of God as king recapitulates the same image in the blessings before the *Sh'ma*, and recapitulates the idea of covenant or vassal-suzerain treaty which is central to the *Sh'ma* (see above, "You shall love Adonai your God").

"Our redeemer, Lord of Hosts is his name, Israel's holy one" It may not be accidental that this is a quotation of Isaiah 47:4 (Deutero-Isaiah), whose theology concerning the reliability of God in bringing about a second exodus so infused the preceding unit (see above, "True and established"). But the end of the blessing is also linked to the first two blessings (the ones before the *Sh'ma*) which describe the heavenly praise of God. The combination of heavenly praise before the *Sh'ma* and earthly praise after it are a powerful reminder of the *Sh'ma*'s central message of Israel's responsibility to be loyal to the one true God.

"Rock . . . redeemer, Lord of Hosts" All images that unequivocally highlight God's tremendous power, and in this context serve as an introduction to the petitions of the *Amidah*. God is, moreover, *Israel's* Holy One, so it is right and proper for this God to accept petitions from individual Jews, with every possibility that they will be granted.

———◆———

SUSAN L. EINBINDER

ing for redemption, mingling their sense of longing for a lost state of harmony with a hope that soon, they would be restored to their rightful place as God's people and in God's world.

———◆———

DAVID ELLENSON

Moses here, acknowledging her role in leading the Israelites in song and dance at the sea.

"And deliver Judah and Israel, as you promised" Reform liturgies have often objected to the nationalistic overtones of this passage. Both *Hamburg Temple Prayer Books, Olath Tamid,* and *Minhag America* all omitted the troublesome promise of Jewish national deliverance. Even some twentieth-century prayer books (like *Lev Chadash*) have not restored it, although others (like *Gates of Prayer*) have readmitted it, to reflect their new-found positive attitude towards Zionism.

———◆———

JOEL M. HOFFMAN

"Who is like You . . . Adonai!" Certainly an exclamation, not a question.

"Adorned . . . wonders" We have three sets of two words in Hebrew, and so, in English, three parallel phrases. Other translations of this famous line include: "glorious in holiness, awe-inspiring in renown, doing wonders" (Birnbaum), "majestic in holiness, awesome in splendor, working wonders" (SSS), "mighty in holiness, too awesome for praise, doing wonders" (Artscroll) and "majestic among the holy-ones, Feared-One of praises, Doer of Wonders" (Fox). We prefer "wonders" to "miracles," because "miracles" departs too greatly from the most likely biblical point of view, a view which combined the dual present-day notions of God's miracles and other natural wonders into one concept.

"As You promised" Lit., "as [in] your speeches."

———◆———

LAWRENCE A. HOFFMAN

regress, since everything must be caused by something else. To extricate himself from the endless search for prior causes, Aristotle posited the existence of a First Cause: a single "something" that is the cause of everything that comes afterward, but is itself not caused by anything else. That First Cause is Aristotle's God. A similar notion of a purely impersonal deity who cared nothing for human destiny was preached also by the school of thought known as the Epicureans, who held also a pre-Aristotelian view that the universe consists of atoms swirling endlessly through space and colliding with each other. This doctrine of physical reality, which, incidentally, was remarkably consistent with modern physics, was easily adopted by the Rabbis. They, however, felt obliged to polemicize against the parallel Epicurean denial of a personal God and the denial, therefore, of a system of morality in which divine will plays a role. In contrast to the Epicureans, the Rabbis insist on a moral God who enters history to right wrongs and bring about a better age.

Since the Epicureans denied an end to history in the form of a world to come, the Rabbis ruled that even though the righteous of all nations receive a share in the world to come, the Epicureans do not. To this day, the Hebrew *Apikoros* means a particularly loathsome form of heresy, because of its denial of a God who cares enough to be active in the world of human affairs.

———◆———

LAWRENCE KUSHNER
NEHEMIA POLEN

name or euphemism." In the words of the Kabbalists, God is *Ein Sof,* "the One without end," or *Ayin,* "Nothing." Nevertheless, as a concession to the needs of humanity and for our own good, God clothes Godself with qualities and names and actions, with *yesh,* "something." In this way we can know in a concrete manner how to serve and comprehend God.

People too need to maintain this balance between *Ayin,* "Nothing," and *yesh,* "something." In human terms *Ayin* or Nothingness, is egolessness, selflessness, radical humility. One needs to strip away all corporeality and substance, and be, in one's own eyes, simply nothing. But this also creates a religious problem since radical humility or egolessness is also debilitating. How can one who is utterly nothing serve the Holy One of All Being? How could an ant serve an eagle? Somehow therefore, without losing our sense of Nothingness, we must, at the same time, inflate ourselves with the notion that our actions, our service, might actually be like sweet fragrances of the sacrificial altar in the Temple, ascending to God. Otherwise there would be no need for human action. Through humility and selflessness we must, therefore, be *Ayin,* "Nothing," while through our deeds and service, striving also to be *yesh,* "something."

This also finds a kabbalistic parallel to the two trees in the Garden of Eden. The tree of life corresponds in mystical imagery to *Ein Sof,* "the One without end," *Ayin,* "Nothing" (the top of the sefirotic diagram). The tree of knowledge of good and evil corresponds to this world of multiplicity, division, corporeality, and tangible reality — *yesh,* "something" (the bottom of the sefirotic diagram), the world of action. The goal is to balance the two trees. And that, says the Zohar — in a daring teaching — was the sin of Adam and Eve: They only "ate from the tree of knowledge but *not* from the tree of life!" The goal is to eat from *both* trees, to restore the balance between *Ayin* and *yesh,* "Nothing" and "something," and, in so doing, to repair the sin of Adam and Eve.

And just this is the real meaning of *Mi kamokha,* "Who is like You among the gods, Adonai!" For the Kabbalists, the word *mi* is not an interrogative "who," but another name for God. And *ba'elim* "among the gods" can also be read as *bet ilan* ב' אִילָן "two trees." So now the *Mi kamokha* reads not as a question but as a statement: "'Who' [i.e., God] is two trees," the tree of life which is *Ayin,* "Nothingness," and the tree of knowledge of good and evil, which is *yesh,* "something," *ne'dar bakodesh, nora tehilot, oseh fele,* "adorned in holiness, revered in praise, worker of miracles."

And when we balance our power to act, our self-assertion, our *yesh,* our something, with the humility of being selfless, *Ayin,* Nothing, then we too can perform wonders. And this is redemption.

◆ ◆ ◆

About the Commentators

MARC BRETTLER

Marc Brettler, PhD, is Dora Golding Professor of Biblical Studies in the Department of Near Eastern and Judaic Studies at Brandeis University. His major areas of research are biblical historical texts, religious metaphors, and gender issues in the Bible. Brettler is author of *God Is King: Understanding an Israelite Metaphor* (Sheffield Academic Press), *The Creation of History in Ancient Israel* (Routledge), *The Book of Judges* (Routledge), *How to Read the Bible* (Jewish Publication Society), and *How to Read the Jewish Bible* (Oxford University Press), as well as a variety of articles on the Bible. He is also associate editor of the new edition of the *Oxford Annotated Bible* and coeditor of the *Jewish Study Bible* (Oxford University Press).

ELLIOT N. DORFF

Elliot N. Dorff, PhD, is rector and Sol and Anne Dorff Distinguished Professor of Philosophy at American Jewish University (formerly the University of Judaism) in Los Angeles. His book *Knowing God: Jewish Journeys to the Unknowable* (Rowman and Littlefield) includes an extensive analysis of the nature of prayer. Ordained a rabbi at The Jewish Theological Seminary of America, Dorff is vice-chair of the Conservative Movement's Committee on Jewish Law and Standards, and he contributed to the Conservative Movement's Torah commentary, *Etz Hayim.* He has chaired the Jewish Law Association, the Society of Jewish Ethics, and the Academy of Jewish Philosophy, and he is immediate past president of Jewish Family Service of Los Angeles. He has served on several federal and California government commissions on issues in bioethics. Winner of the National Jewish Book Award for *To Do the Right and the Good: A Jewish Approach to Modern Social Ethics,* he has written numerous books and more than 150 articles on Jewish thought, law, and ethics. His latest books are *The Way Into* Tikkun Olam *(Repairing the World),* a finalist for the National Jewish Book Award; *The Jewish Approach to Repairing the World* (Tikkun Olam): *A Brief Introduction for Christians* (both Jewish Lights); and *The Unfolding Tradition: Jewish Law After Sinai* (Aviv Press of the Rabbinical Assembly).

SUSAN L. EINBINDER

Susan L. Einbinder, PhD, is professor of Hebrew literature at the Cincinnati campus of the Hebrew Union College–Jewish Institute of Religion. She is the author of *Beautiful Death: Jewish Poetry and Martyrdom in Medieval France* (Princeton University Press) and *No Place of Rest: Medieval Jewish Literature and the Memory of France* (University of Pennsylvania Press). She is currently at work on a study of medieval Jewish physicians from Provence and their writings.

DAVID ELLENSON

David Ellenson, PhD, is president of Hebrew Union College–Jewish Institute of Religion. He holds the Gus Waterman Herrman Presidential Chair and is the I. H. and Anna Grancell Professor of Jewish Religious Thought. Ordained a rabbi by Hebrew Union College–Jewish Institute of Religion, he has served as a visiting professor at Hebrew University in Jerusalem, at The Jewish Theological Seminary in New York, and at the University of California at Los Angeles. Ellenson has also taught at the Pardes Institute of Jewish Studies and at the Shalom Hartman Institute, both in Jerusalem. Ellenson has published and lectured extensively on diverse topics in modern Jewish thought, history, and ethics. His most recent book, *After Emancipation* (HUC Press), won the National Jewish Book Award in the category of Modern Jewish Thought and Experience.

JOEL M. HOFFMAN

Joel M. Hoffman, PhD, lectures around the globe on popular and scholarly topics spanning history, Hebrew, prayer, and Jewish continuity. He has served on the faculties of Brandeis University, the Academy for Jewish Religion, and Hebrew Union College–Jewish Institute of Religion in New York. Hoffman writes about Hebrew for the international *Jerusalem Post*, and is the author of *In the Beginning: A Short History of Hebrew Language* and *God Said: How Translations Conceal the Bible's Original Meaning*. He contributed to *My People's Passover Haggadah: Traditional Texts, Modern Commentaries* (Jewish Lights). He lives in Westchester, New York.

LAWRENCE A. HOFFMAN

Lawrence A. Hoffman, PhD, was ordained by and received his doctorate from Hebrew Union College–Jewish Institute of Religion. He has served in its New York campus for more than three decades, most recently as the Barbara and Stephen Friedman Professor of Liturgy, Worship and Ritual. Widely recognized for his scholarship and classroom teaching, Hoffman has combined research with a passion for the spiritual renewal of contemporary Judaism. He has written and edited over thirty books, including *Who by Fire, Who by Water*—Un'taneh Tokef and *All These Vows*—Kol Nidre, the first two volumes in the Prayers of Awe series; *My People's Passover Haggadah: Traditional Texts,*

Modern Commentaries, in two volumes (all Jewish Lights); *The Art of Public Prayer, Not for Clergy Only* (SkyLight Paths), now used nationally by Jews and Christians as a handbook for liturgical planners in church and synagogue; and a revision of *What Is a Jew?*, the best-selling classic that remains the most widely read introduction to Judaism ever written in any language. He is also the author of *Israel — A Spiritual Travel Guide: A Companion for the Modern Jewish Pilgrim* and *The Way Into Jewish Prayer* (both Jewish Lights). Hoffman is a founder of Synagogue 2000 (now renamed Synagogue 3000), a transdenominational project designed to transform synagogues into the moral and spiritual centers of the twenty-first century. His book *Rethinking Synagogues: A New Vocabulary for Congregational Life* (Jewish Lights), an outgrowth of that project, was a finalist for the National Jewish Book Award.

LAWRENCE KUSHNER

Lawrence Kushner is the Emanu-El scholar at Congregation Emanu-El in San Francisco, an adjunct faculty member at Hebrew Union College–Jewish Institute of Religion, and a visiting professor of Jewish spirituality at the Graduate Theological Union in Berkeley, California. He served as spiritual leader of Congregation Beth El in Sudbury, Massachusetts, for twenty-eight years and is widely regarded as one of the most creative religious writers in America. Ordained a rabbi by Hebrew Union College–Jewish Institute of Religion, Kushner led his congregants in publishing their own prayer book, *V'tahaer Libenu* (Purify Our Hearts), the first gender-neutral liturgy ever written. Through his lectures and many books, including *Filling Words with Light: Hasidic and Mystical Reflections on Jewish Prayer* (with Nehemia Polen); *The Way Into Jewish Mystical Tradition*; *Invisible Lines of Connection: Sacred Stories of the Ordinary*; *The Book of Letters: A Mystical Hebrew Alphabet*; *Honey from the Rock: An Introduction to Jewish Mysticism*; *God Was in This Place and I, i Did Not Know: Finding Self, Spirituality, and Ultimate Meaning*; *Eyes Remade for Wonder: A Lawrence Kushner Reader*; *Jewish Spirituality: A Brief Introduction for Christians*; and most recently, *I'm God; You're Not: Observations on Organized Religion and Other Disguises of the Ego*, all published by Jewish Lights, he has helped shape the Jewish community's present focus on personal and institutional spiritual renewal. He has also published a novel, *Kabbalah: A Love Story.*

DANIEL LANDES

Daniel Landes is director and Rosh HaYeshivah of the Pardes Institute of Jewish Studies in Jerusalem and was an adjunct professor of Jewish law at Loyola University Law School in Los Angeles. Ordained a rabbi by Rabbi Isaac Elchanan Theological Seminary, Landes was a founding faculty member of the Simon Wiesenthal Center and the Yeshiva of Los Angeles, and served as a judge in the Los Angeles Orthodox Beith Din. He has lectured and written various popular and scholarly articles on the subjects of Jewish thought, social ethics, and spirituality.

JUDITH PLASKOW

Judith Plaskow, PhD, is professor of religious studies at Manhattan College and co-founder and former coeditor of the *Journal of Feminist Studies in Religion*. She is the author of *Standing Again at Sinai: Judaism from a Feminist Perspective* (Harper and Row); *The Coming of Lilith: Essays on Feminism, Judaism, and Sexual Ethics* (Beacon); and a contributor to *Lifecycles, V. 2: Jewish Women on Biblical Themes in Contemporary Life* (Jewish Lights). Plaskow writes and lectures widely on feminist issues in religion.

NEHEMIA POLEN

Nehemia Polen is professor of Jewish thought and director of the Hasidic Text Institute at Boston's Hebrew College. He is the author of *The Holy Fire: The Teachings of Rabbi Kalonymus Shapira, the Rebbe of the Warsaw Ghetto* (Jason Aronson) as well as many academic and popular articles on Chasidism and Jewish spirituality, and coauthor of *Filling Words with Light: Hasidic and Mystical Reflections on Jewish Prayer* (Jewish Lights). He received his PhD from Boston University, where he studied with and served as teaching fellow for Nobel laureate Elie Wiesel. In 1994 he was Daniel Jeremy Silver Fellow at Harvard University, and he has also been a visiting scholar at the Hebrew University in Jerusalem. He was ordained a rabbi at the Ner Israel Rabbinical College in Baltimore, Maryland, and served as a congregational rabbi for twenty-three years. From 1998–1999 he was a National Endowment for the Humanities Fellow, working on the writings of Malkah Shapiro (1894–1971), the daughter of a noted Chasidic master, whose Hebrew memoirs focus on the spiritual lives of women in the context of prewar Chasidism in Poland. This work is documented in his book *The Rebbe's Daughter* (Jewish Publication Society), winner of the National Jewish Book Award.

List of Abbreviations

Artscroll	*Siddur Kol Ya'akov,* 1984.
Birnbaum	*Daily Prayer Book: Hasiddur Hashalem,* 1949.
FOP	*Forms of Prayer,* 1997.
Fox	Everett Fox, *The Five Books of Moses* (New York: Schocken Books, 1995).
GOP	*Gates of Prayer,* 1975
SSS	*Siddur Sim Shalom,* 1985.
KH	*Kol Han'shamah,* 1994.
JPS	*Jewish Publication Society Bible* (Philadelphia: Jewish Publication Society, 1962).
NRSV	*New Revised Standard Bible,* 1989.
SLC	*Siddur Lev Chadash,* 1995.
SOH	*Service of the Heart,* 1967.
UPB	*Union Prayer Book,* 1894–1895.

Glossary

The following glossary defines Hebrew words used regularly throughout this volume and the way the words are pronounced. Sometimes two pronunciations are common, in which case, the first is the way the word is sounded in proper Hebrew, and the second is the way it is sometimes heard in common speech under the influence of Yiddish, the folk language of Jews in northern and eastern Europe (it is a combination, mostly, of Hebrew and German). Our goal is to provide the way that many Jews actually use these words, not just the technically correct version.

- The pronunciations are divided into syllables by dashes.
- The accented syllable is written in capital letters.
- "Kh" represents a gutteral sound, similar to the German "ch" (as in "sprach").
- The most common vowel is "a" as in "father," which appears here as "ah."
- The short "e" (as in "get") is written either "e" (when it is in the middle of a syllable) or "eh" (when it ends a syllable).
- Similarly, the short "i" (as in "tin") is written either "i" (when it is in the middle of a syllable) or "ih" (when it ends a syllable).
- The long "o" (as in "Moses") is written "oe" (as in "toe") or "oh" (as in "oh!").

Alenu (pronounced ah-LAY-noo): The first word, and, therefore, the title of a major prayer compiled in the second or third century as part of the New Year (*Rosh Hashanah*) service, but, from about the fourteenth century on, used also as part of the concluding section of every daily service as well. *Alenu* means "It is incumbent upon us . . ." and introduces the prayer's theme: our duty to praise God.

Amidah (pronounced either ah-mee-DAH, or, commonly, ah-MEE-dah): One of three commonly used titles for the second of two central units in the worship service, the first being The *Sh'ma* and Its Blessings. It is composed of a series of blessings, many of which are petitionary, except on Sabbaths and holidays, when the petitions are removed out of deference to the holiness of the day. Also called *T'fillah* and *Sh'moneh Esreh*. *Amidah* means "standing," and refers to the fact that the prayer is said standing up.

Arvit (pronounced ahr-VEET, or, commonly, AHR-veet): From the Hebrew word *erev* (pronounced EH-rev) meaning "evening": One of two titles used for the evening worship service (also called *Ma'ariv*).

Ashkenazi (pronounced ahsh-k'-nah-ZEE, or, commonly, ahsh-k'-NAH-zee): From the Hebrew word *Ashkenaz*, meaning the geographic area of northern and eastern Europe; *Ashkenazi* is the adjective, describing the liturgical rituals and customs practiced there, as opposed to *Sefardi*, meaning the liturgical rituals and customs that are derived from *Sefarad*, Spain (see *Sefardi*).

Ashre (pronounced ahsh-RAY, or, commonly, AHSH-ray): The first word, and, therefore, the title of a prayer said three times each day, composed primarily of Psalm 145. *Ashre* means "Happy" and introduces the phrase, "Happy are they who dwell in your [God's] house."

Bar'khu (pronounced bah-r'-KHOO, or, commonly, BOH-r'-khoo): The first word, and, therefore, the title of the formal call to prayer with which the section called The *Sh'ma* and Its Blessings begins. *Bar'khu* means "Praise," and introduces the invitation to the assembled congregation to praise God.

Benediction (also called Blessing): One of two terms used for the Rabbis' favorite prose formula for composing prayers. The worship service is composed of many different literary genres, but most of it is benedictions. Long benedictions end with a summary line that begins, *Barukh atah Adonai . . .* "Blessed are You, Adonai. . . ." Short blessings have only the summary line alone.

Birkat Hatorah (pronounced beer-KAHT hah-toe-RAH): Literally, "Blessing of Torah," the title for the second blessing in the liturgical section called The *Sh'ma* and Its Blessings; its theme is the revelation of the Torah to Israel on Mt. Sinai.

Birkhot Hashachar (pronounced beer-KHOTE hah-SHAH-khar): Literally, "Morning Blessings," the title of the first large section in the morning prayer regimen of Judaism; originally said privately upon arising in the morning, but now customarily recited immediately upon arriving at the synagogue. Composed primarily of benedictions thanking God for the everyday gifts of health and wholeness, as well as study sections taken from the Bible and rabbinic literature.

B'rakhah (pronounced b'-rah-KHAH): The Hebrew word for "benediction" or "blessing." See "Benediction." Plural ("benedictions") is *B'rakhot* (pronounced b'-rah-KHOTE).

Chasidism (pronounced KHAH-sih-dizm): The doctrine generally traced to an eighteenth-century Polish Jewish mystic and spiritual leader known as the Ba'al Shem Tov (called also the BeSHT, an acronym composed of the initials of his name B, SH, and T.) Followers are called *Chasidim* (pronounced khah-see-DEEM or khah-SIH-dim; singular: *Chasid* (pronounced khah-SEED, or, commonly, KHAH-sid) from the Hebrew word *chesed* (pronounced KHEH-sed), meaning "loving-kindness" or "piety."

Chatimah (pronounced khah-tee-MAH): The final summary line of a benediction (see *Benediction*).

Doxology: Technical term for a congregational response to an invitation to praise God; generally a single line of prayer affirming praise of God forever and ever. Examples in The *Sh'ma* and Its Blessings are the responses to the Call to Prayer and to the *Sh'ma* itself. From the Greek word *doxos* meaning "glory."

Eretz Yisrael (pronounced EH-retz yis-rah-AYL): Hebrew for "The Land of Israel."

Gaon (pronounced gah-OHN; plural: *Geonim*, pronounced g'-oh-NEEM): Title for the leading rabbis in Babylon (present-day Iraq) from about 750 to 1038. From a biblical word meaning "glory," equivalent, in a title, to saying "Your Excellence."

Genizah (pronounced g'-NEE-zah): A cache of documents (in particular, the one discovered at the turn of the twentieth century in an old synagogue in Cairo), the source of our knowledge about how Jews prayed in the Land of Israel and vicinity prior to the twelfth century. From a word meaning "to store or hide away"; "to archive."

G'ullah (pronounced g'-oo-LAH): Literally, "redemption" or "deliverance," and the title of the third blessing in The *Sh'ma* and Its Blessings; its theme affirms God's redemptive act of delivering the Israelites from Egypt, and promises ultimate deliverance from suffering and want, at the end of time.

Haftarah (pronounced hahf-tah-RAH, or, commonly, hahf-TOE-rah): The section of Scripture taken from the prophets and read publicly as part of Shabbat and holiday worship services. From a word meaning "to conclude," since it is the "concluding reading," that is, it follows a reading from the Torah (the five books of Moses).

Haggadah (pronounced hah-gah-DAH, or, commonly, hah-GAH-dah): The liturgical service for the Passover eve *Seder* meal. From a Hebrew word meaning "to tell," since the *Haggadah* is a telling of the Passover narrative.

Halakhah (pronounced hah-lah-KHAH, or, commonly, hah-LAH-khah): The Hebrew word for "Jewish law." Used as an anglicized adjective, *halakhic* (pronounced hah-LAH-khic), meaning "legal." From the Hebrew word meaning "to walk, to go," so denoting the way on which a person should walk through life.

143

Hallel (pronounced hah-LAYL, or, commonly, HAH-layl): A Hebrew word meaning "praise," and, by extension, the name given to sets of psalms that are recited liturgically in praise of God: Psalms 145–150, the Daily *Hallel* is recited each morning; Psalm 136, The Great *Hallel* is recited on Shabbat and holidays, and is part of the Passover *Seder;* Psalms 113–118, the best-known *Hallel,* known more fully as the Egyptian *Hallel,* is recited on holidays, and gets its name from Psalm 114:1, which celebrates the moment "When Israel left Egypt."

Kabbalah (pronounced kah-bah-LAH, or, commonly, kah-BAH-lah): A general term for Jewish mysticism, but used properly for a specific mystical doctrine that began in western Europe in the eleventh or twelfth centuries, was recorded in the *Zohar* (see *Zohar*) in the thirteenth century, and then was further elaborated, especially in the Land of Israel (in Safed), in the sixteenth century. From a Hebrew word meaning "to receive" or "to welcome," and, secondarily, "tradition," implying the receiving of tradition from one's past.

Kabbalat Shabbat (pronounced kah-bah-LAHT shah-BAHT): Literally, "Welcoming the Sabbath," and, therefore, a term for the introductory synagogue prayers that lead up to the arrival of the Sabbath at sundown Friday night.

Kaddish (pronounced kah-DEESH, or, commonly, KAH-dish): One of several prayers from a Hebrew word meaning "holy," and, therefore, the name given to a prayer affirming God's holiness. This prayer was composed in the first century, but later found its way into the service in several forms, including one known as the Mourners' *Kaddish,* and used as a mourning prayer.

Kavvanah (pronounced kah-vah-NAH): From a word meaning "to direct," and, therefore, used technically to denote the state of directing one's words and thoughts sincerely to God, as opposed to the rote recitation of prayer.

K'dushah (pronounced k'-doo-SHAH, or, commonly, k'-DOO-shah): From the Hebrew word meaning "holy," and, therefore, one of the several prayers from the first or second century, occurring in several places and versions, all of which have in common the citing of Isaiah 6:3 *Kadosh, kadosh kadosh . . .,* "Holy, holy, holy is the Lord of hosts. The whole earth is full of his glory."

K'dushat Hashem (pronounced k'-doo-SHAHT hah-SHEM): Literally, "Sanctification of the name [of God]"), and the full name for the prayer that is generally called *K'dushah* (see *K'dushah*). Used also in variant form *kiddush hashem* (pronounced kee-DOOSH hah-SHEM) as a term to describe dying for the sanctification of God's name; that is, martyrdom.

Keva (pronounced KEH-vah): A Hebrew word meaning "fixity, stability," and, therefore, the aspect of a service that is fixed and immutable: the words on the page, perhaps, or the time at which the prayer must be said. In the early years, when prayers were delivered orally and improvised on the spot, *keva* meant the fixed order in which the liturgical themes had to be expressed.

K'riyat Sh'ma (pronounced k'-ree-YAHT sh'-MAH): Literally, "Reciting the *Sh'ma*," and, therefore, a technical term for the liturgical act of reading the prayer known as the *Sh'ma* (see *Sh'ma*).

Liturgy: Public worship, from the Greek word *leiturgia*, meaning "public works." Liturgy in ancient Greece was considered a public work, the act of sacrificing or praising the gods, from which benefit would flow to the body politic.

Ma'ariv (pronounced mah-ah-REEV, or, commonly, MAH-ah-reev): From the Hebrew word *erev* (pronounced EH-rev) meaning "evening"; one of two titles used for the evening worship service (also called *Arvit*).

Midrash (pronounced meed-RAHSH, or, commonly, MID-rahsh): From a Hebrew word meaning "to ferret out the meaning of a text," and, therefore, a rabbinic interpretation of a biblical word or verse. By extension, a body of rabbinic literature that offers classical interpretations of the Bible.

Minchah (pronounced meen-KHAH, or, more commonly, MIN-khah): Originally the name of a type of sacrifice, then the word for a sacrifice offered during the afternoon, and now the name for the afternoon synagogue service, usually scheduled just before nightfall. *Minchah* means "afternoon."

Minhag (pronounced meen-HAHG, or, commonly, MIN-hahg): The Hebrew word for custom, and, therefore, used liturgically to describe the customary way that different groups of Jews pray. By extension, *Minhag* means a "rite," as in *Minhag Ashkenaz*, meaning "the rite of prayer, or the customary way of prayer for Jews in *Ashkenaz*" — that is, northern and eastern Europe.

Minyan (pronounced meen-YAHN, or, commonly, MIN-y'n): A quorum, the minimum number of people required for certain prayers. *Minyan* comes from the Hebrew word meaning "to count."

Mishnah (pronounced meesh-NAH, or, commonly, MISH-nah): The first written summary of Jewish law, compiled in the Land of Israel in approximately 200 C.E., and, therefore, our first overall written evidence for the state of Jewish prayer in the early centuries.

Mitzvah (pronounced meetz-VAH, or, commonly, MITZ-vah; plural, *mitzvot*, pronounced meetz-VOTE): A Hebrew word used commonly to mean "good deed," but in the more technical sense, denoting any commandment from God, and, therefore, by extension, what God wants us to do. Reciting the *Sh'ma*, morning and evening, for instance, is a *mitzvah*.

Musaf (pronounced moo-SAHF, or, commonly, MOO-sahf): The Hebrew word meaning "extra" or "added," and, therefore, the title of the additional sacrifice that was offered in the Temple on Shabbat and holy days; now the name given to an added service of worship appended to the morning service on those days.

M'zuzah (pronounced m'-zoo-ZAH, or, commonly, m'-ZOO-zah): The Hebrew word in the Bible, meaning "doorpost," and, by extension, the term now used for a small casement that contains the first two sections of the *Sh'ma* (Deut. 6:4–9, 11:13–21), and is affixed to the doorposts of Jewish homes.

Payy'tan (pronounced pah-y'-TAHN; plural: *Payy'tanim*, pronounced pah-y'-tah-NEEM): a poet; the name given particularly to classical and medieval poets whose work is inserted into the standard prayers on special occasions.

Perek (pronounced PEH-rek; plural: *p'rakim*, pronounced p'-rah-KEEM): Literally, a "section" or "chapter" of a written work, and used liturgically to mean the sections of the *Sh'ma*. Each of its three biblical sections is a different *perek*.

Piyyut (pronounced pee-YOOT; plural: *piyyutim*, pronounced pee-yoo-TEEM): Literally, "a poem," but used technically to mean liturgical poems composed in classical and medieval times, and inserted into the standard prayers on special occasions.

P'sukei D'zimrah (pronounced p'-soo-KAY d'-zeem-RAH, or, commonly, p'-SOO-kay d'-ZIM-rah): Literally, "verses of song," and, therefore, the title of a lengthy set of opening morning prayers that contain psalms and songs, and serve as spiritual preparation prior to the official call to prayer.

Rosh Chodesh (pronounced rohsh KHOH-desh): Literally, "the head of the month," and, therefore, the Hebrew name for the one- or two-day new-moon period with which lunar months begin; marked as a holiday in Jewish tradition, a period of new beginnings.

Rubric (pronounced ROO-brick): A technical term for any discrete section of liturgy, whether a prayer or a set of prayers. The *Sh'ma* and Its Blessings is one of several large rubrics in the service; within that large rubric, the *Sh'ma* or any one of its accompanying blessings may be called a rubric as well.

Seder (pronounced SEH-der, or, commonly, SAY-der): The Hebrew word meaning "order," and, therefore, 1) the name given to the ritualized meal eaten on Passover eve, and 2) an early alternative term for the order of prayers in a prayer book. The word *Siddur* (see *Siddur*) is now preferred for the latter.

Sefardi (pronounced s'-fahr-DEE, or, commonly, s'-FAHR-dee): From the Hebrew word *Sefarad* (pronounced s'-fah-RAHD) meaning the geographic area of modern-day Spain and Portugal: *Sefardi* is the adjective, describing the liturgical rituals and customs that are derived from Sefarad, prior to the expulsion of Jews from there at the end of the fifteenth century, as opposed to *Ashkenazi* (see *Ashkenazi*), meaning the liturgical rituals and customs common to northern and eastern Europe. Nowadays, *Sefardi* refers also to the customs of Jews from North Africa and the Arab lands, whose ancestors came from Spain.

S'firot (pronounced s'-fee-ROTE; singular: *s'firah*, pronounced s'-fee-RAH): According to the Kabbalah (Jewish mysticism; see *Kabbalah*), the universe came into being by a process of divine emanation, whereby the divine light, as it were, expanded into empty space, eventually becoming physical matter. At various intervals, this light was frozen in time, as if captured by containers, each of which is called a *s'firah*. Literally, *s'firah* means "number," because early theory conceptualized the stages of creation as primordial numbers.

Shabbat (pronounced shah-BAHT): The Hebrew word for "Sabbath," from a word meaning "to rest."

Shacharit (pronounced shah-khah-REET, or, commonly, SHAH-khah-reet): The name given to the morning worship service; from the Hebrew word *shachar* (SHAH-khar) meaning "morning."

Sh'ma (pronounced sh'-MAH): The central prayer in the first of the two main units in the worship service, the second being the *Amidah* (see *Amidah*). The *Sh'ma* comprises three citations from the Bible, and the larger unit in which it is embedded (called the *Sh'ma* and Its Blessings) is composed of a formal call to prayer (see *Bar'khu*) and a series of blessings on the theological themes that, together with the *Sh'ma*, constitute a liturgical creed of faith. *Sh'ma*, meaning "Hear," is the first word of the first line of the first biblical citation, "Hear O Israel: Adonai is our God; Adonai is One," which is the paradigmatic statement of Jewish faith, the Jew's absolute commitment to the presence of a single and unique God in time and space.

Sh'liach Tsibbur (pronounced sh'-LEE-ahkh tsee-BOOR): Literally, the "agent of the congregation," and, therefore, the name given to the person who leads the prayer service.

Sh'moneh Esreh (pronounced sh'-MOE-neh ES-ray): A Hebrew word meaning "eighteen," and, therefore, a name given to the second of the two main units in the worship service, which once had 18 benedictions in it (it now has 19); known also as the *Amidah* (see *Amidah*).

Shulchan Arukh (pronounced shool-KHAN ah-ROOKH, or, commonly, SHOOL-khan AH-rookh): The name given to the best-known code of Jewish law, compiled by Joseph Caro in the Land of Israel, and published in 1565. *Shulchan Arukh* means "The Set Table," and refers to the ease with which the various laws are set forth — like a table prepared with food for ready consumption.

Siddur (pronounced see-DOOR, or, commonly, SIH-d'r): From the Hebrew word *seder* (see *Seder*) meaning "order," and, therefore, by extension, the name given to the "order of prayers," or prayer book.

Tachanun (pronounced TAH-khah-noon): A Hebrew word meaning "supplications," and, therefore, by extension, the title of the large unit of prayer that follows the *Amidah*, and which is largely supplicatory in character.

Tallit (pronounced tah-LEET; plural: *tallitot*, pronounced tah-lee-TOTE): The prayer shawl equipped with tassels (see *Tsitsit*) on each corner, and generally worn during the morning (*Shacharit*) and additional (*Musaf*) synagogue service.

Talmud (pronounced tahl-MOOD, or, commonly, TAHL-m'd): The name given to each of two great compendia of Jewish law and lore compiled over several centuries and, ever since, the literary core of the rabbinic heritage. The *Talmud Yerushalmi* (pronounced y'-roo-SHAHL-mee), the "Jerusalem Talmud," is earlier, a product of the Land of Israel, generally dated about 400 C.E. The better-known *Talmud Bavli* (pronounced BAHV-lee), or "Babylonian Talmud," took shape in Babylonia (present-day Iraq), and is traditionally dated about 550 C.E. When people say "The" Talmud, without specifying which one they mean, they are referring to the Babylonian version. *Talmud* means "Teaching."

Tetragrammaton: The technical term for the four-letter name of God that appears in the Bible, it is treated as sacred. Jews stopped pronouncing it centuries ago, so that the actual pronunciation has been lost; instead of reading it according to its letters, it is replaced in speech by the alternative name of God, Adonai.

T'fillah (pronounced t'-fee-LAH, or, commonly, t'-FEE-lah): A Hebrew word meaning "prayer," but used technically to mean a specific prayer, namely, the second of the two main units in the worship service; known also as the *Amidah* or the *Sh'moneh Esreh* (see *Amidah*).

T'fillin (pronounced t'-fee-LEEN, or, commonly, t'-FIH-lin): Two cube-shaped black boxes containing biblical quotations (Ex. 13:1–10; 13:11–16; Deut. 6:4–9; Deut. 11:13–21), and affixed by means of attached leather straps to the forehead and left arm (right arm for left-handed people) during morning prayer.

Tsitsit (pronounced tsee-TSEET): A Hebrew word meaning "tassel," or "fringe," and used to refer to the tassels affixed to the four corners of the *tallit* (the prayer shawl; see *tallit*) as Numbers 15:38 instructs.

Tur (pronounced TOOR): The shorthand title applied to a fourteenth-century code of Jewish law, compiled by Jacob ben Asher in Spain, and the source for much of our knowledge about medieval liturgical practice. *Tur* means "row" or "column." The full name of the code is *Arba'ah Turim* (pronounced ahr-bah-AH too-REEM) "The four Rows," each row, or *Tur* being a separate section of law on a given broad topic.

Yotser (pronounced yoe-TSAYR, or, commonly, YOE-tsayr): The Hebrew word meaning "creator," and, by extension, the title of the first blessing in the *Sh'ma* and Its Blessings, which is on the theme of God's creation of the universe.

Zohar (pronounced ZOE-hahr): A shorthand title for *Sefer Hazohar* (pronounced SAY-fer hah-ZOE-hahr), literally, "The Book of Splendor," which is the primary compendium of mystical thought in Judaism; written mostly by Moses de León in Spain, near the end of the thirteenth century, and, ever since, the chief source for the study of *Kabbalah* (see *Kabbalah*).

A Note on the Border
The border decoration used in this book is from the
Sarajevo Haggadah, one of the best-known Hebrew
illuminated manuscripts; Spain, Barcelona (?), 14th century.

Bar/Bat Mitzvah

The JGirl's Guide: The Young Jewish Woman's Handbook for Coming of Age
By Penina Adelman, Ali Feldman and Shulamit Reinharz This inspirational, interactive guidebook helps pre-teen Jewish girls address the many issues surrounding coming of age. 6 x 9, 240 pp, Quality PB, 978-1-58023-215-9 **$14.99** *For ages 11 & up*

The JGirl's Teacher's and Parent's Guide 8½ x 11, 56 pp, PB, 978-1-58023-225-8 **$8.99**

The Bar/Bat Mitzvah Memory Book, 2nd Edition: An Album for Treasuring the Spiritual Celebration *By Rabbi Jeffrey K. Salkin and Nina Salkin*
8 x 10, 48 pp, 2-color text, Deluxe HC, ribbon marker, 978-1-58023-263-0 **$19.99**

For Kids—Putting God on Your Guest List, 2nd Edition: How to Claim the Spiritual Meaning of Your Bar or Bat Mitzvah *By Rabbi Jeffrey K. Salkin*
6 x 9, 144 pp, Quality PB, 978-1-58023-308-8 **$15.99** *For ages 11–13*

Putting God on the Guest List, 3rd Edition: How to Reclaim the Spiritual Meaning of Your Child's Bar or Bat Mitzvah *By Rabbi Jeffrey K. Salkin*
6 x 9, 224 pp, Quality PB, 978-1-58023-222-7 **$16.99**; HC, 978-1-58023-260-9 **$24.99**

Putting God on the Guest List Teacher's Guide
8½ x 11, 48 pp, PB, 978-1-58023-226-5 **$8.99**

Tough Questions Jews Ask: A Young Adult's Guide to Building a Jewish Life
By Rabbi Edward Feinstein 6 x 9, 160 pp, Quality PB, 978-1-58023-139-8 **$14.99** *For ages 11 & up*

Tough Questions Jews Ask Teacher's Guide
8½ x 11, 72 pp, PB, 978-1-58023-187-9 **$8.95**

Bible Study/Midrash

Sage Tales: Wisdom and Wonder from the Rabbis of the Talmud
By Rabbi Burton L. Visotzky Illustrates how the stories of the Rabbis who lived in the first generations following the destruction of the Jerusalem Temple illuminate modern life's most pressing issues. 6 x 9, 256 pp, HC, 978-1-58023-456-6 **$24.99**

The Modern Men's Torah Commentary: New Insights from Jewish Men on the 54 Weekly Torah Portions *Edited by Rabbi Jeffrey K. Salkin*
A major contribution to modern biblical commentary. Addresses the most important concerns of modern men by opening them up to the messages of Torah.
6 x 9, 368 pp, HC, 978-1-58023-395-8 **$24.99**

The Genesis of Leadership: What the Bible Teaches Us about Vision, Values and Leading Change *By Rabbi Nathan Laufer; Foreword by Senator Joseph I. Lieberman*
6 x 9, 288 pp, Quality PB, 978-1-58023-352-1 **$18.99**

Hineini in Our Lives: Learning How to Respond to Others through 14 Biblical Texts and Personal Stories *By Rabbi Norman J. Cohen, PhD* 6 x 9, 240 pp, Quality PB, 978-1-58023-274-6 **$16.99**

A Man's Responsibility: A Jewish Guide to Being a Son, a Partner in Marriage, a Father and a Community Leader *By Rabbi Joseph B. Meszler*
6 x 9, 192 pp, Quality PB, 978-1-58023-435-1 **$16.99**

Moses and the Journey to Leadership: Timeless Lessons of Effective Management from the Bible and Today's Leaders *By Rabbi Norman J. Cohen, PhD*
6 x 9, 240 pp, Quality PB, 978-1-58023-351-4 **$18.99**; HC, 978-1-58023-227-2 **$21.99**

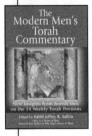

Righteous Gentiles in the Hebrew Bible: Ancient Role Models for Sacred Relationships *By Rabbi Jeffrey K. Salkin; Foreword by Rabbi Harold M. Schulweis; Preface by Phyllis Tickle* 6 x 9, 192 pp, Quality PB, 978-1-58023-364-4 **$18.99**

The Wisdom of Judaism: An Introduction to the Values of the Talmud
By Rabbi Dov Peretz Elkins 6 x 9, 192 pp, Quality PB, 978-1-58023-327-9 **$16.99**

The Wisdom of Judaism Teacher's Guide 8½ x 11, 18 pp, PB, 978-1-58023-350-7 **$8.99**

Or phone, fax, mail or e-mail to: **JEWISH LIGHTS Publishing**
An imprint of Turner Publishing Company
4507 Charlotte Ave. • Suite 100 • Nashville, Tennessee 37209
Tel: (615) 255-2665 • www.jewishlights.com
Prices subject to change.

Congregation Resources

Empowered Judaism: What Independent Minyanim Can Teach Us about Building Vibrant Jewish Communities
By Rabbi Elie Kaunfer; Foreword by Prof. Jonathan D. Sarna
Examines the independent minyan movement and the lessons these grassroots communities can provide. 6 x 9, 224 pp, Quality PB, 978-1-58023-412-2 **$18.99**

Spiritual Boredom: Rediscovering the Wonder of Judaism *By Dr. Erica Brown*
Breaks through the surface of spiritual boredom to find the reservoir of meaning within. 6 x 9, 208 pp, HC, 978-1-58023-405-4 **$21.99**

Building a Successful Volunteer Culture
Finding Meaning in Service in the Jewish Community
By Rabbi Charles Simon; Foreword by Shelley Lindauer; Preface by Dr. Ron Wolfson
Shows you how to develop and maintain the volunteers who are essential to the vitality of your organization and community. 6 x 9, 192 pp, Quality PB, 978-1-58023-408-5 **$16.99**

The Case for Jewish Peoplehood: Can We Be One?
By Dr. Erica Brown and Dr. Misha Galperin; Foreword by Rabbi Joseph Telushkin
6 x 9, 224 pp, HC, 978-1-58023-401-6 **$21.99**

Inspired Jewish Leadership: Practical Approaches to Building Strong Communities
By Dr. Erica Brown 6 x 9, 256 pp, HC, 978-1-58023-361-3 **$24.99**

Jewish Pastoral Care, 2nd Edition: A Practical Handbook from Traditional & Contemporary Sources *Edited by Rabbi Dayle A. Friedman, MSW, MAJCS, BCC*
6 x 9, 528 pp, Quality PB, 978-1-58023-427-6 **$30.00**

Rethinking Synagogues: A New Vocabulary for Congregational Life
By Rabbi Lawrence A. Hoffman, PhD 6 x 9, 240 pp, Quality PB, 978-1-58023-248-7 **$19.99**

The Spirituality of Welcoming: How to Transform Your Congregation into a Sacred Community *By Dr. Ron Wolfson* 6 x 9, 224 pp, Quality PB, 978-1-58023-244-9 **$19.99**

Children's Books

Around the World in One Shabbat
Jewish People Celebrate the Sabbath Together
By Durga Yael Bernhard
Takes your child on a colorful adventure to share the many ways Jewish people celebrate Shabbat around the world.
11 x 8½, 32 pp, HC, 978-1-58023-433-7 **$18.99** *For ages 3–6*

What You Will See Inside a Synagogue
By Rabbi Lawrence A. Hoffman, PhD, and Dr. Ron Wolfson; Full-color photos by Bill Aron
A colorful, fun-to-read introduction that explains the ways and whys of Jewish worship and religious life.
8¼ x 10¾, 32 pp, Full-color photos, Quality PB, 978-1-59473-256-0 **$8.99** *For ages 6 & up*
(A book from SkyLight Paths, Jewish Lights' sister imprint)

Because Nothing Looks Like God
By Lawrence Kushner and Karen Kushner Introduces children to the possibilities of spiritual life. 11 x 8½, 32 pp, Full-color illus., HC, 978-1-58023-092-6 **$17.99** *For ages 4 & up*

The Book of Miracles: A Young Person's Guide to Jewish Spiritual Awareness
Written and illus. by Lawrence Kushner
6 x 9, 96 pp, 2-color illus., HC, 978-1-879045-78-1 **$16.95** *For ages 9–13*

In God's Hands *By Lawrence Kushner and Gary Schmidt* 9 x 12, 32 pp, Full-color illus., HC, 978-1-58023-224-1 **$16.99** *For ages 5 & up*

In Our Image: God's First Creatures *By Nancy Sohn Swartz*
9 x 12, 32 pp, Full-color illus., HC, 978-1-879045-99-6 **$16.95** *For ages 4 & up*

The Kids' Fun Book of Jewish Time
By Emily Sper 9 x 7½, 24 pp, Full-color illus., HC, 978-1-58023-311-8 **$16.99** *For ages 3–6*

What Makes Someone a Jew? *By Lauren Seidman*
Reflects the changing face of American Judaism.
10 x 8½, 32 pp, Full-color photos, Quality PB, 978-1-58023-321-7 **$8.99** *For ages 3–6*

Judaism / Christianity / Interfaith

Christians & Jews—Faith to Faith: Tragic History, Promising Present, Fragile Future   *By Rabbi James Rudin*
A probing examination of Christian-Jewish relations that looks at the major issues facing both faith communities.   6 x 9, 288 pp, HC, 978-1-58023-432-0 **$24.99**

How to Do Good & Avoid Evil: A Global Ethic from the Sources of Judaism   *By Hans Küng and Rabbi Walter Homolka*   Explores how the principles of Judaism provide the ethical norms for all religions to work together toward a more peaceful humankind.   6 x 9, 224 pp, HC, 978-1-59473-255-3 **$19.99***

Getting to the Heart of Interfaith: The Eye-Opening, Hope-Filled Friendship of a Pastor, a Rabbi and a Sheikh
By Rabbi Ted Falcon, Pastor Don Mackenzie and Imam Jamal Rahman
Presents ways we can work together to transcend the differences that have divided us historically.   6 x 9, 192 pp, Quality PB, 978-1-59473-263-8 **$16.99***

Claiming Earth as Common Ground: The Ecological Crisis through the Lens of Faith   *By Rabbi Andrea Cohen-Kiener*   6 x 9, 192 pp, Quality PB, 978-1-59473-261-4 **$16.99***

Modern Jews Engage the New Testament: Enhancing Jewish Well-Being in a Christian Environment   *By Rabbi Michael J. Cook, PhD*   6 x 9, 416 pp, HC, 978-1-58023-313-2 **$29.99**

The Changing Christian World: A Brief Introduction for Jews
By Rabbi Leonard A. Schoolman   5½ x 8½, 176 pp, Quality PB, 978-1-58023-344-6 **$16.99**

Christians & Jews in Dialogue: Learning in the Presence of the Other
By Mary C. Boys and Sara S. Lee
6 x 9, 240 pp, Quality PB, 978-1-59473-254-6 **$18.99**; HC, 978-1-59473-144-0 **21.99***

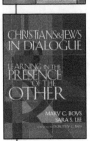

Disaster Spiritual Care: Practical Clergy Responses to Community, Regional and National Tragedy   *Edited by Rabbi Stephen B. Roberts, BCJC, and Rev. Willard W. C. Ashley Sr., DMin, DH*
6 x 9, 384 pp, HC, 978-1-59473-240-9 **$40.00***

Healing the Jewish-Christian Rift: Growing Beyond Our Wounded History
By Ron Miller and Laura Bernstein   6 x 9, 288 pp, Quality PB, 978-1-59473-139-6 **$18.99***

How to Be a Perfect Stranger, 5th Edition: The Essential Religious Etiquette Handbook   *Edited by Stuart M. Matlins and Arthur J. Magida*
6 x 9, 432 pp, Quality PB, 978-1-59473-294-2 **$19.99***

InterActive Faith: The Essential Interreligious Community-Building Handbook
Edited by Rev. Bud Heckman with Rori Picker Neiss
6 x 9, 304 pp, Quality PB, 978-1-59473-273-7 **$16.99**; HC, 978-1-59473-237-9 **$29.99***

Introducing My Faith and My Community
The Jewish Outreach Institute Guide for the Christian in a Jewish Interfaith Relationship
By Rabbi Kerry M. Olitzky   6 x 9, 176 pp, Quality PB, 978-1-58023-192-3 **$16.99**

The Jewish Approach to Repairing the World (*Tikkun Olam*)
A Brief Introduction for Christians   *By Rabbi Elliot N. Dorff, PhD, with Rev. Cory Willson*
5½ x 8½, 256 pp, Quality PB, 978-1-58023-349-1 **$16.99**

The Jewish Connection to Israel, the Promised Land: A Brief Introduction for Christians   *By Rabbi Eugene Korn, PhD*   5½ x 8½, 192 pp, Quality PB, 978-1-58023-318-7 **$14.99**

Jewish Holidays: A Brief Introduction for Christians   *By Rabbi Kerry M. Olitzky and Rabbi Daniel Judson*   5½ x 8½, 176 pp, Quality PB, 978-1-58023-302-6 **$16.99**

Jewish Ritual: A Brief Introduction for Christians   *By Rabbi Kerry M. Olitzky and Rabbi Daniel Judson*   5½ x 8½, 144 pp, Quality PB, 978-1-58023-210-4 **$14.99**

A Jewish Understanding of the New Testament   *By Rabbi Samuel Sandmel;*
Preface by Rabbi David Sandmel   5½ x 8½, 368 pp, Quality PB, 978-1-59473-048-1 **$19.99***

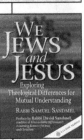

Righteous Gentiles in the Hebrew Bible: Ancient Role Models for Sacred Relationships   *By Rabbi Jeffrey K. Salkin; Foreword by Rabbi Harold M. Schulweis; Preface by Phyllis Tickle*
6 x 9, 192 pp, Quality PB, 978-1-58023-364-4 **$18.99**

Talking about God: Exploring the Meaning of Religious Life with Kierkegaard, Buber, Tillich and Heschel   *By Rabbi Daniel F. Polish, PhD*   6 x 9, 160 pp, Quality PB, 978-1-59473-272-0 **$16.99***

We Jews and Jesus: Exploring Theological Differences for Mutual Understanding
By Rabbi Samuel Sandmel; Preface by Rabbi David Sandmel
6 x 9, 192 pp, Quality PB, 978-1-59473-208-9 **$16.99**

*A book from SkyLight Paths, Jewish Lights' sister imprint

Social Justice

Confronting Scandal
How Jews Can Respond When Jews Do Bad Things
By Dr. Erica Brown

A framework to transform our sense of shame over reports of Jews committing crime into actions that inspire and sustain a moral culture.
6 x 9, 192 pp, HC, 978-1-58023-440-5 **$24.99**

There Shall Be No Needy
Pursuing Social Justice through Jewish Law and Tradition
By Rabbi Jill Jacobs; Foreword by Rabbi Elliot N. Dorff, PhD; Preface by Simon Greer

Confronts the most pressing issues of twenty-first-century America from a deeply Jewish perspective. 6 x 9, 288 pp, Quality PB, 978-1-58023-425-2 **$16.99**

There Shall Be No Needy Teacher's Guide 8½ x 11, 56 pp, PB, 978-1-58023-429-0 **$8.99**

Conscience
The Duty to Obey and the Duty to Disobey
By Rabbi Harold M. Schulweis

Examines the idea of conscience and the role conscience plays in our relationships to government, law, ethics, religion, human nature, God—and to each other.
6 x 9, 160 pp, Quality PB, 978-1-58023-419-1 **$16.99**; HC, 978-1-58023-375-0 **$19.99**

Judaism and Justice
The Jewish Passion to Repair the World
By Rabbi Sidney Schwarz; Foreword by Ruth Messinger

Explores the relationship between Judaism, social justice and the Jewish identity of American Jews. 6 x 9, 352 pp, Quality PB, 978-1-58023-353-8 **$19.99**

Spirituality/Women's Interest

New Jewish Feminism
Probing the Past, Forging the Future
Edited by Rabbi Elyse Goldstein; Foreword by Anita Diamant

Looks at the growth and accomplishments of Jewish feminism and what they mean for Jewish women today and tomorrow.
6 x 9, 480 pp, Quality PB, 978-1-58023-448-1 **$19.99**; HC, 978-1-58023-359-0 **$24.99**

The Divine Feminine in Biblical Wisdom Literature
Selections Annotated & Explained
Translation & Annotation by Rabbi Rami Shapiro
5½ x 8½, 240 pp, Quality PB, 978-1-59473-109-9 **$16.99**
(A book from SkyLight Paths, Jewish Lights' sister imprint)

The Quotable Jewish Woman
Wisdom, Inspiration & Humor from the Mind & Heart
Edited by Elaine Bernstein Partnow
6 x 9, 496 pp, Quality PB, 978-1-58023-236-4 **$19.99**

The Women's Haftarah Commentary
New Insights from Women Rabbis on the 54 Weekly Haftarah Portions, the 5 Megillot & Special Shabbatot
Edited by Rabbi Elyse Goldstein

Illuminates the historical significance of female portrayals in the Haftarah and the Five Megillot. 6 x 9, 560 pp, Quality PB, 978-1-58023-371-2 **$19.99**

The Women's Torah Commentary
New Insights from Women Rabbis on the 54 Weekly Torah Portions
Edited by Rabbi Elyse Goldstein

Over fifty women rabbis offer inspiring insights on the Torah, in a week-by-week format.
6 x 9, 496 pp, Quality PB, 978-1-58023-370-5 **$19.99**; HC, 978-1-58023-076-6 **$34.95**

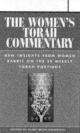

See Passover for *The Women's Passover Companion: Women's Reflections on the Festival of Freedom* and *The Women's Seder Sourcebook: Rituals & Readings for Use at the Passover Seder.*

Life Cycle

Marriage/Parenting/Family/Aging

The New Jewish Baby Album: Creating and Celebrating the Beginning of a Spiritual Life—A Jewish Lights Companion
By the Editors at Jewish Lights; Foreword by Anita Diamant; Preface by Rabbi Sandy Eisenberg Sasso
A spiritual keepsake that will be treasured for generations. More than just a memory book, *shows you how—and why it's important—*to create a Jewish home and a Jewish life. 8 x 10, 64 pp, Deluxe Padded HC, Full-color illus., 978-1-58023-138-1 **$19.95**

The Jewish Pregnancy Book: A Resource for the Soul, Body & Mind during Pregnancy, Birth & the First Three Months *By Sandy Falk, MD, and Rabbi Daniel Judson, with Steven A. Rapp* Medical information, prayers and rituals for each stage of pregnancy. 7 x 10, 208 pp, b/w photos, Quality PB, 978-1-58023-178-7 **$16.95**

Celebrating Your New Jewish Daughter: Creating Jewish Ways to Welcome Baby Girls into the Covenant—New and Traditional Ceremonies *By Debra Nussbaum Cohen; Foreword by Rabbi Sandy Eisenberg Sasso* 6 x 9, 272 pp, Quality PB, 978-1-58023-090-2 **$18.95**

The New Jewish Baby Book, 2nd Edition: Names, Ceremonies & Customs—A Guide for Today's Families *By Anita Diamant* 6 x 9, 320 pp, Quality PB, 978-1-58023-251-7 **$19.99**

Parenting as a Spiritual Journey: Deepening Ordinary and Extraordinary Events into Sacred Occasions *By Rabbi Nancy Fuchs-Kreimer, PhD*
6 x 9, 224 pp, Quality PB, 978-1-58023-016-2 **$17.99**

Parenting Jewish Teens: A Guide for the Perplexed
By Joanne Doades Explores the questions and issues that shape the world in which today's Jewish teenagers live and offers constructive advice to parents.
6 x 9, 176 pp, Quality PB, 978-1-58023-305-7 **$16.99**

Judaism for Two: A Spiritual Guide for Strengthening and Celebrating Your Loving Relationship *By Rabbi Nancy Fuchs-Kreimer, PhD, and Rabbi Nancy H. Wiener, DMin; Foreword by Rabbi Elliot N. Dorff, PhD*
Addresses the ways Jewish teachings can enhance and strengthen committed relationships. 6 x 9, 224 pp, Quality PB, 978-1-58023-254-8 **$16.99**

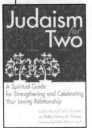

The Creative Jewish Wedding Book, 2nd Edition: A Hands-On Guide to New & Old Traditions, Ceremonies & Celebrations *By Gabrielle Kaplan-Mayer*
9 x 9, 288 pp, b/w photos, Quality PB, 978-1-58023-398-9 **$19.99**

Divorce Is a Mitzvah: A Practical Guide to Finding Wholeness and Holiness When Your Marriage Dies *By Rabbi Perry Netter; Afterword by Rabbi Laura Geller*
6 x 9, 224 pp, Quality PB, 978-1-58023-172-5 **$16.95**

Embracing the Covenant: Converts to Judaism Talk About Why & How
By Rabbi Allan Berkowitz and Patti Moskovitz 6 x 9, 192 pp, Quality PB, 978-1-879045-50-7 **$16.95**

The Guide to Jewish Interfaith Family Life: An InterfaithFamily.com Handbook
Edited by Ronnie Friedland and Edmund Case
6 x 9, 384 pp, Quality PB, 978-1-58023-153-4 **$18.95**

A Heart of Wisdom: Making the Jewish Journey from Midlife through the Elder Years
Edited by Susan Berrin; Foreword by Rabbi Harold Kushner
6 x 9, 384 pp, Quality PB, 978-1-58023-051-3 **$18.95**

Introducing My Faith and My Community: The Jewish Outreach Institute Guide for the Christian in a Jewish Interfaith Relationship
By Rabbi Kerry M. Olitzky 6 x 9, 176 pp, Quality PB, 978-1-58023-192-3 **$16.99**

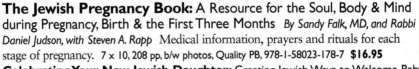

Making a Successful Jewish Interfaith Marriage: The Jewish Outreach Institute Guide to Opportunities, Challenges and Resources *By Rabbi Kerry M. Olitzky with Joan Peterson Littman*
6 x 9, 176 pp, Quality PB, 978-1-58023-170-1 **$16.95**

A Man's Responsibility: A Jewish Guide to Being a Son, a Partner in Marriage, a Father and a Community Leader *By Rabbi Joseph B. Meszler*
6 x 9, 192 pp, Quality PB, 978-1-58023-435-1 **$16.99**; HC, 978-1-58023-362-0 **$21.99**

So That Your Values Live On: Ethical Wills and How to Prepare Them
Edited by Rabbi Jack Riemer and Rabbi Nathaniel Stampfer
6 x 9, 272 pp, Quality PB, 978-1-879045-34-7 **$18.99**

Holidays/Holy Days

Who by Fire, Who by Water—Un'taneh Tokef
Edited by Rabbi Lawrence A. Hoffman, PhD
Examines the prayer's theology, authorship and poetry through a set of lively essays, all written in accessible language.
6 x 9, 272 pp, HC, 978-1-58023-424-5 **$24.99**

All These Vows—Kol Nidre
Edited by Rabbi Lawrence A. Hoffman, PhD
The most memorable prayer of the Jewish New Year—what it means, why we sing it, and the secret of its magical appeal.
6 x 9, 300 pp (est), HC, 978-1-58023-430-6 **$24.99**

Rosh Hashanah Readings: Inspiration, Information and Contemplation
Yom Kippur Readings: Inspiration, Information and Contemplation
Edited by Rabbi Dov Peretz Elkins; Section Introductions from Arthur Green's These Are the Words
Rosh Hashanah: 6 x 9, 400 pp, Quality PB, 978-1-58023-437-5 **$19.99**; HC, 978-1-58023-239-5 **$24.99**
Yom Kippur: 6 x 9, 368 pp, Quality PB, 978-1-58023-438-2 **$19.99**; HC, 978-1-58023-271-5 **$24.99**

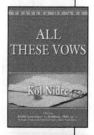

Jewish Holidays: A Brief Introduction for Christians
By Rabbi Kerry M. Olitzky and Rabbi Daniel Judson
5½ x 8½, 176 pp, Quality PB, 978-1-58023-302-6 **$16.99**

Reclaiming Judaism as a Spiritual Practice: Holy Days and Shabbat
By Rabbi Goldie Milgram 7 x 9, 272 pp, Quality PB, 978-1-58023-205-0 **$19.99**

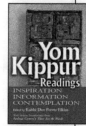

Shabbat, 2nd Edition: The Family Guide to Preparing for and Celebrating the Sabbath
By Dr. Ron Wolfson 7 x 9, 320 pp, Illus., Quality PB, 978-1-58023-164-0 **$19.99**

Hanukkah, 2nd Edition: The Family Guide to Spiritual Celebration
By Dr. Ron Wolfson 7 x 9, 240 pp, Illus., Quality PB, 978-1-58023-122-0 **$18.95**

The Jewish Family Fun Book, 2nd Edition
Holiday Projects, Everyday Activities, and Travel Ideas with Jewish Themes
By Danielle Dardashti and Roni Sarig; Illus. by Avi Katz
6 x 9, 304 pp, 70+ b/w illus. & diagrams, Quality PB, 978-1-58023-333-0 **$18.99**

Passover

My People's Passover Haggadah
Traditional Texts, Modern Commentaries
Edited by Rabbi Lawrence A. Hoffman, PhD, and David Arnow, PhD
A diverse and exciting collection of commentaries on the traditional Passover Haggadah—in two volumes!
Vol. 1: 7 x 10, 304 pp, HC, 978-1-58023-354-5 **$24.99**
Vol. 2: 7 x 10, 320 pp, HC, 978-1-58023-346-0 **$24.99**

Freedom Journeys: The Tale of Exodus and Wilderness across Millennia
By Rabbi Arthur O. Waskow and Rabbi Phyllis O. Berman
Explores how the story of Exodus echoes in our own time, calling us to relearn and rethink the Passover story through social-justice, ecological, feminist and interfaith perspectives. 6 x 9, 288 pp, HC, 978-1-58023-445-0 **$24.99**

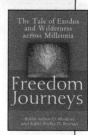

Leading the Passover Journey: The Seder's Meaning Revealed, the Haggadah's Story Retold *By Rabbi Nathan Laufer*
Uncovers the hidden meaning of the Seder's rituals and customs.
6 x 9, 224 pp, Quality PB, 978-1-58023-399-6 **$18.99**; HC, 978-1-58023-211-1 **$24.99**

Creating Lively Passover Seders, 2nd Edition: A Sourcebook of Engaging Tales, Texts & Activities *By David Arnow, PhD* 7 x 9, 464 pp, Quality PB, 978-1-58023-444-3 **$24.99**

Passover, 2nd Edition: The Family Guide to Spiritual Celebration
By Dr. Ron Wolfson with Joel Lurie Grishaver 7 x 9, 416 pp, Quality PB, 978-1-58023-174-9 **$19.95**

The Women's Passover Companion: Women's Reflections on the Festival of Freedom
Edited by Rabbi Sharon Cohen Anisfeld, Tara Mohr and Catherine Spector; Foreword by Paula E. Hyman
6 x 9, 352 pp, Quality PB, 978-1-58023-231-9 **$19.99**; HC, 978-1-58023-128-2 **$24.95**

The Women's Seder Sourcebook: Rituals & Readings for Use at the Passover Seder
Edited by Rabbi Sharon Cohen Anisfeld, Tara Mohr and Catherine Spector
6 x 9, 384 pp, Quality PB, 978-1-58023-232-6 **$19.99**

Inspiration

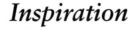

God of Me: Imagining God throughout Your Lifetime
By Rabbi David Lyon Helps you cut through preconceived ideas of God and dogmas that stifle your creativity when thinking about your personal relationship with God. 6 x 9, 176 pp, Quality PB, 978-1-58023-452-8 **$16.99**

The God Upgrade: Finding Your 21st-Century Spirituality in Judaism's 5,000-Year-Old Tradition *By Rabbi Jamie Korngold; Foreword by Rabbi Harold M. Schulweis* A provocative look at how our changing God concepts have shaped every aspect of Judaism. 6 x 9, 176 pp, Quality PB, 978-1-58023-443-6 **$15.99**

The Seven Questions You're Asked in Heaven: Reviewing and Renewing Your Life on Earth *By Dr. Ron Wolfson* An intriguing and entertaining resource for living a life that matters. 6 x 9, 176 pp, Quality PB, 978-1-58023-407-8 **$16.99**

Happiness and the Human Spirit: The Spirituality of Becoming the Best You Can Be *By Rabbi Abraham J. Twerski, MD* Shows you that true happiness is attainable once you stop looking outside yourself for the source. 6 x 9, 176 pp, Quality PB, 978-1-58023-404-7 **$16.99**; HC, 978-1-58023-343-9 **$19.99**

A Formula for Proper Living: Practical Lessons from Life and Torah *By Rabbi Abraham J. Twerski, MD* 6 x 9, 144 pp, HC, 978-1-58023-402-3 **$19.99**

The Bridge to Forgiveness: Stories and Prayers for Finding God and Restoring Wholeness *By Rabbi Karyn D. Kedar* 6 x 9, 176 pp, Quality PB, 978-1-58023-451-1 **$16.99**

The Empty Chair: Finding Hope and Joy—Timeless Wisdom from a Hasidic Master, Rebbe Nachman of Breslov *Adapted by Moshe Mykoff and the Breslov Research Institute* 4 x 6, 128 pp, Deluxe PB w/ flaps, 978-1-879045-67-5 **$9.99**

The Gentle Weapon: Prayers for Everyday and Not-So-Everyday Moments— Timeless Wisdom from the Teachings of the Hasidic Master, Rebbe Nachman of Breslov *Adapted by Moshe Mykoff and S. C. Mizrahi, together with the Breslov Research Institute* 4 x 6, 144 pp, Deluxe PB w/ flaps, 978-1-58023-022-3 **$9.99**

God Whispers: Stories of the Soul, Lessons of the Heart *By Rabbi Karyn D. Kedar* 6 x 9, 176 pp, Quality PB, 978-1-58023-088-9 **$15.95**

God's To-Do List: 103 Ways to Be an Angel and Do God's Work on Earth *By Dr. Ron Wolfson* 6 x 9, 144 pp, Quality PB, 978-1-58023-301-9 **$16.99**

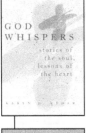

Jewish Stories from Heaven and Earth: Inspiring Tales to Nourish the Heart and Soul *Edited by Rabbi Dov Peretz Elkins* 6 x 9, 304 pp, Quality PB, 978-1-58023-363-7 **$16.99**

Life's Daily Blessings: Inspiring Reflections on Gratitude and Joy for Every Day, Based on Jewish Wisdom *By Rabbi Kerry M. Olitzky* 4½ x 6½, 368 pp, Quality PB, 978-1-58023-396-5 **$16.99**

Restful Reflections: Nighttime Inspiration to Calm the Soul, Based on Jewish Wisdom *By Rabbi Kerry M. Olitzky and Rabbi Lori Forman* 4½ x 6½, 448 pp, Quality PB, 978-1-58023-091-9 **$15.95**

Sacred Intentions: Morning Inspiration to Strengthen the Spirit, Based on Jewish Wisdom *By Rabbi Kerry M. Olitzky and Rabbi Lori Forman* 4½ x 6½, 448 pp, Quality PB, 978-1-58023-061-2 **$16.99**

Kabbalah/Mysticism

Jewish Mysticism and the Spiritual Life: Classical Texts, Contemporary Reflections *Edited by Dr. Lawrence Fine, Dr. Eitan Fishbane and Rabbi Or N. Rose* Inspirational and thought-provoking materials for contemplation, discussion and action. 6 x 9, 256 pp, HC, 978-1-58023-434-4 **$24.99**

Ehyeh: A Kabbalah for Tomorrow *By Rabbi Arthur Green, PhD* 6 x 9, 224 pp, Quality PB, 978-1-58023-213-5 **$18.99**

The Gift of Kabbalah: Discovering the Secrets of Heaven, Renewing Your Life on Earth *By Tamar Frankiel, PhD* 6 x 9, 256 pp, Quality PB, 978-1-58023-141-1 **$16.95**

Seek My Face: A Jewish Mystical Theology *By Rabbi Arthur Green, PhD* 6 x 9, 304 pp, Quality PB, 978-1-58023-130-5 **$19.95**

Zohar: Annotated & Explained *Translation & Annotation by Dr. Daniel C. Matt; Foreword by Andrew Harvey* 5½ x 8½, 176 pp, Quality PB, 978-1-893361-51-5 **$15.99** *(A book from SkyLight Paths, Jewish Lights' sister imprint)*

See also *The Way Into Jewish Mystical Tradition* in The Way Into... Series.

Meditation

Jewish Meditation Practices for Everyday Life
Awakening Your Heart, Connecting with God
By Rabbi Jeff Roth
Offers a fresh take on meditation that draws on life experience and living life with greater clarity as opposed to the traditional method of rigorous study.
6 x 9, 224 pp, Quality PB, 978-1-58023-397-2 **$18.99**

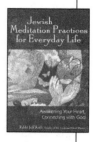

The Handbook of Jewish Meditation Practices
A Guide for Enriching the Sabbath and Other Days of Your Life
By Rabbi David A. Cooper Easy-to-learn meditation techniques.
6 x 9, 208 pp, Quality PB, 978-1-58023-102-2 **$16.95**

Discovering Jewish Meditation, 2nd Edition
Instruction & Guidance for Learning an Ancient Spiritual Practice
By Nan Fink Gefen, PhD 6 x 9, 208 pp, Quality PB, 978-1-58023-462-7 **$16.99**

Meditation from the Heart of Judaism: Today's Teachers Share Their Practices,
Techniques, and Faith *Edited by Avram Davis*
6 x 9, 256 pp, Quality PB, 978-1-58023-049-0 **$16.95**

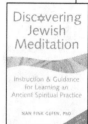

Ritual/Sacred Practices

The Jewish Dream Book: The Key to Opening the Inner Meaning of
Your Dreams *By Vanessa L. Ochs, PhD, with Elizabeth Ochs; Illus. by Kristina Swarner*
Instructions for how modern people can perform ancient Jewish dream practices and dream interpretations drawn from the Jewish wisdom tradition.
8 x 8, 128 pp, Full-color illus., Deluxe PB w/ flaps, 978-1-58023-132-9 **$16.95**

God in Your Body: Kabbalah, Mindfulness and Embodied Spiritual Practice
By Jay Michaelson
The first comprehensive treatment of the body in Jewish spiritual practice and an essential guide to the sacred.
6 x 9, 272 pp, Quality PB, 978-1-58023-304-0 **$18.99**

The Book of Jewish Sacred Practices: CLAL's Guide to Everyday &
Holiday Rituals & Blessings *Edited by Rabbi Irwin Kula and Vanessa L. Ochs, PhD*
6 x 9, 368 pp, Quality PB, 978-1-58023-152-7 **$18.95**

Jewish Ritual: A Brief Introduction for Christians
By Rabbi Kerry M. Olitzky and Rabbi Daniel Judson
5½ x 8½, 144 pp, Quality PB, 978-1-58023-210-4 **$14.99**

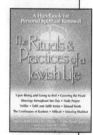

The Rituals & Practices of a Jewish Life: A Handbook for Personal Spiritual
Renewal *Edited by Rabbi Kerry M. Olitzky and Rabbi Daniel Judson*
6 x 9, 272 pp, Illus., Quality PB, 978-1-58023-169-5 **$18.95**

The Sacred Art of Lovingkindness: Preparing to Practice
By Rabbi Rami Shapiro 5½ x 8½, 176 pp, Quality PB, 978-1-59473-151-8 **$16.99**
(A book from SkyLight Paths, Jewish Lights' sister imprint)

Science Fiction/Mystery & Detective Fiction

Criminal Kabbalah: An Intriguing Anthology of Jewish Mystery &
Detective Fiction *Edited by Lawrence W. Raphael; Foreword by Laurie R. King*
All-new stories from twelve of today's masters of mystery and detective fiction—sure to delight mystery buffs of all faith traditions.
6 x 9, 256 pp, Quality PB, 978-1-58023-109-1 **$16.95**

Mystery Midrash: An Anthology of Jewish Mystery & Detective Fiction
Edited by Lawrence W. Raphael; Preface by Joel Siegel
6 x 9, 304 pp, Quality PB, 978-1-58023-055-1 **$16.95**

Wandering Stars: An Anthology of Jewish Fantasy & Science Fiction
Edited by Jack Dann; Introduction by Isaac Asimov
6 x 9, 272 pp, Quality PB, 978-1-58023-005-6 **$18.99**

More Wandering Stars: An Anthology of Outstanding Stories of Jewish Fantasy and
Science Fiction *Edited by Jack Dann; Introduction by Isaac Asimov*
6 x 9, 192 pp, Quality PB, 978-1-58023-063-6 **$16.95**

Spirituality

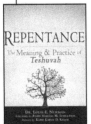

Repentance: The Meaning and Practice of *Teshuvah*
By Dr. Louis E. Newman; Foreword by Rabbi Harold M. Schulweis; Preface by Rabbi Karyn D. Kedar
Examines both the practical and philosophical dimensions of *teshuvah*, Judaism's core religious-moral teaching on repentance, and its value for us—Jews and non-Jews alike—today. 6 x 9, 256 pp, HC, 978-1-58023-426-9 **$24.99**

Tanya, the Masterpiece of Hasidic Wisdom
Selections Annotated & Explained
Translation & Annotation by Rabbi Rami Shapiro; Foreword by Rabbi Zalman M. Schachter-Shalomi
Brings the genius of *Tanya,* one of the most powerful books of Jewish wisdom, to anyone seeking to deepen their understanding of the soul.
5½ x 8½, 240 pp, Quality PB, 978-1-59473-275-1 **$16.99**
(A book from SkyLight Paths, Jewish Lights' sister imprint)

Aleph-Bet Yoga: Embodying the Hebrew Letters for Physical and Spiritual Well-Being
By Steven A. Rapp; Foreword by Tamar Frankiel, PhD, and Judy Greenfeld; Preface by Hart Lazer
7 x 10, 128 pp, b/w photos, Quality PB, Lay-flat binding, 978-1-58023-162-6 **$16.95**

A Book of Life: Embracing Judaism as a Spiritual Practice
By Rabbi Michael Strassfeld 6 x 9, 544 pp, Quality PB, 978-1-58023-247-0 **$19.99**

Bringing the Psalms to Life: How to Understand and Use the Book of Psalms
By Rabbi Daniel F. Polish, PhD 6 x 9, 208 pp, Quality PB, 978-1-58023-157-2 **$16.95**

Does the Soul Survive? A Jewish Journey to Belief in Afterlife, Past Lives &
Living with Purpose   By Rabbi Elie Kaplan Spitz; Foreword by Brian L. Weiss, MD
6 x 9, 288 pp, Quality PB, 978-1-58023-165-7 **$16.99**

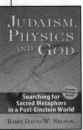

First Steps to a New Jewish Spirit: Reb Zalman's Guide to Recapturing the
Intimacy & Ecstasy in Your Relationship with God   By Rabbi Zalman M. Schachter-Shalomi
with Donald Gropman 6 x 9, 144 pp, Quality PB, 978-1-58023-182-4 **$16.95**

Foundations of Sephardic Spirituality: The Inner Life of Jews of the Ottoman
Empire
By Rabbi Marc D. Angel, PhD 6 x 9, 224 pp, Quality PB, 978-1-58023-341-5 **$18.99**

God & the Big Bang: Discovering Harmony between Science & Spirituality
By Dr. Daniel C. Matt 6 x 9, 216 pp, Quality PB, 978-1-879045-89-7 **$16.99**

God in Our Relationships: Spirituality between People from the Teachings of
Martin Buber   By Rabbi Dennis S. Ross 5½ x 8½, 160 pp, Quality PB, 978-1-58023-147-3 **$16.95**

The Jewish Lights Spirituality Handbook: A Guide to Understanding,
Exploring & Living a Spiritual Life   *Edited by Stuart M. Matlins*
What exactly is "Jewish" about spirituality? How do I make it a part of my life? Fifty of today's foremost spiritual leaders share their ideas and experience with us.
6 x 9, 456 pp, Quality PB, 978-1-58023-093-3 **$19.99**

Judaism, Physics and God: Searching for Sacred Metaphors in a Post-Einstein World
By Rabbi David W. Nelson 6 x 9, 352 pp, Quality PB, inc. reader's discussion guide,
978-1-58023-306-4 **$18.99**; HC, 352 pp, 978-1-58023-252-4 **$24.99**

Meaning & Mitzvah: Daily Practices for Reclaiming Judaism through Prayer, God,
Torah, Hebrew, Mitzvot and Peoplehood   By Rabbi Goldie Milgram
7 x 9, 336 pp, Quality PB, 978-1-58023-256-2 **$19.99**

Minding the Temple of the Soul: Balancing Body, Mind, and Spirit through Traditional
Jewish Prayer, Movement, and Meditation   By Tamar Frankiel, PhD, and Judy Greenfeld
7 x 10, 184 pp, Illus., Quality PB, 978-1-879045-64-4 **$18.99**

One God Clapping: The Spiritual Path of a Zen Rabbi   By Rabbi Alan Lew with Sherril Jaffe
5½ x 8½, 336 pp, Quality PB, 978-1-58023-115-2 **$16.95**

The Soul of the Story: Meetings with Remarkable People
By Rabbi David Zeller 6 x 9, 288 pp, HC, 978-1-58023-272-2 **$21.99**

There Is No Messiah ... and You're It: The Stunning Transformation of Judaism's
Most Provocative Idea   By Rabbi Robert N. Levine, DD
6 x 9, 192 pp, Quality PB, 978-1-58023-255-5 **$16.99**

These Are the Words: A Vocabulary of Jewish Spiritual Life
By Rabbi Arthur Green, PhD 6 x 9, 304 pp, Quality PB, 978-1-58023-107-7 **$18.95**

Spirituality/Prayer

Making Prayer Real: Leading Jewish Spiritual Voices on Why Prayer Is Difficult and What to Do about It *By Rabbi Mike Comins*
A new and different response to the challenges of Jewish prayer, with "best prayer practices" from Jewish spiritual leaders of all denominations.
6 x 9, 320 pp, Quality PB, 978-1-58023-417-7 **$18.99**

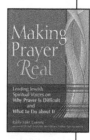

Witnesses to the One: The Spiritual History of the *Sh'ma*
By Rabbi Joseph B. Meszler; Foreword by Rabbi Elyse Goldstein
6 x 9, 176 pp, Quality PB, 978-1-58023-400-9 **$16.99**; HC, 978-1-58023-309-5 **$19.99**

My People's Prayer Book Series: Traditional Prayers, Modern Commentaries *Edited by Rabbi Lawrence A. Hoffman, PhD*
Provides diverse and exciting commentary to the traditional liturgy. Will help you find new wisdom in Jewish prayer, and bring liturgy into your life. Each book includes Hebrew text, modern translations and commentaries from all perspectives of the Jewish world.

Vol. 1—The *Sh'ma* and Its Blessings
  7 x 10, 168 pp, HC, 978-1-879045-79-8 **$29.99**
Vol. 2—The *Amidah* 7 x 10, 240 pp, HC, 978-1-879045-80-4 **$24.95**
Vol. 3—*P'sukei D'zimrah* (Morning Psalms)
  7 x 10, 240 pp, HC, 978-1-879045-81-1 **$29.99**
Vol. 4—*Seder K'riat Hatorah* (The Torah Service)
  7 x 10, 264 pp, HC, 978-1-879045-82-8 **$29.99**
Vol. 5—*Birkhot Hashachar* (Morning Blessings)
  7 x 10, 240 pp, HC, 978-1-879045-83-5 **$24.95**
Vol. 6—*Tachanun* and Concluding Prayers
  7 x 10, 240 pp, HC, 978-1-879045-84-2 **$24.95**
Vol. 7—Shabbat at Home 7 x 10, 240 pp, HC, 978-1-879045-85-9 **$24.95**
Vol. 8—*Kabbalat Shabbat* (Welcoming Shabbat in the Synagogue)
  7 x 10, 240 pp, HC, 978-1-58023-121-3 **$24.99**
Vol. 9—Welcoming the Night: *Minchah* and *Ma'ariv* (Afternoon and
  Evening Prayer) 7 x 10, 272 pp, HC, 978-1-58023-262-3 **$24.99**
Vol. 10—Shabbat Morning: *Shacharit* and *Musaf* (Morning and
  Additional Services) 7 x 10, 240 pp, HC, 978-1-58023-240-1 **$29.99**

Spirituality/Lawrence Kushner

I'm God; You're Not: Observations on Organized Religion & Other Disguises of the Ego
6 x 9, 256 pp, HC, 978-1-58023-441-2 **$21.99**

The Book of Letters: A Mystical Hebrew Alphabet
Popular HC Edition, 6 x 9, 80 pp, 2-color text, 978-1-879045-00-2 **$24.95**
Collector's Limited Edition, 9 x 12, 80 pp, gold-foil-embossed pages, w/ limited-edition silkscreened print, 978-1-879045-04-0 **$349.00**

The Book of Miracles: A Young Person's Guide to Jewish Spiritual Awareness
6 x 9, 96 pp, 2-color illus., HC, 978-1-879045-78-1 **$16.95** *For ages 9–13*

The Book of Words: Talking Spiritual Life, Living Spiritual Talk
6 x 9, 160 pp, Quality PB, 978-1-58023-020-9 **$18.99**

Eyes Remade for Wonder: A Lawrence Kushner Reader *Introduction by Thomas Moore*
6 x 9, 240 pp, Quality PB, 978-1-58023-042-1 **$18.95**

God Was in This Place & I, i Did Not Know: Finding Self, Spirituality and
Ultimate Meaning 6 x 9, 192 pp, Quality PB, 978-1-879045-33-0 **$16.95**

Honey from the Rock: An Introduction to Jewish Mysticism
6 x 9, 176 pp, Quality PB, 978-1-58023-073-5 **$16.95**

Invisible Lines of Connection: Sacred Stories of the Ordinary
5½ x 8½, 160 pp, Quality PB, 978-1-879045-98-9 **$15.95**

Jewish Spirituality: A Brief Introduction for Christians
5½ x 8½, 112 pp, Quality PB, 978-1-58023-150-3 **$12.95**

The River of Light: Jewish Mystical Awareness
6 x 9, 192 pp, Quality PB, 978-1-58023-096-4 **$16.95**

The Way Into Jewish Mystical Tradition
6 x 9, 224 pp, Quality PB, 978-1-58023-200-5 **$18.99**; HC, 978-1-58023-029-2 **$21.95**

Theology/Philosophy/The Way Into... Series

The Way Into... series offers an accessible and highly usable "guided tour" of the Jewish faith, people, history and beliefs—in total, an introduction to Judaism that will enable you to understand and interact with the sacred texts of the Jewish tradition. Each volume is written by a leading contemporary scholar and teacher, and explores one key aspect of Judaism. *The Way Into...* series enables all readers to achieve a real sense of Jewish cultural literacy through guided study.

The Way Into Encountering God in Judaism
By Neil Gillman
For everyone who wants to understand how Jews have encountered God throughout history and today.
6 x 9, 240 pp, Quality PB, 978-1-58023-199-2 **$18.99**; HC, 978-1-58023-025-4 **$21.95**
Also Available: **The Jewish Approach to God:** A Brief Introduction for Christians
By Neil Gillman
5½ x 8½, 192 pp, Quality PB, 978-1-58023-190-9 **$16.95**

The Way Into Jewish Mystical Tradition
By Lawrence Kushner
Allows readers to interact directly with the sacred mystical text of the Jewish tradition. An accessible introduction to the concepts of Jewish mysticism, their religious and spiritual significance and how they relate to life today.
6 x 9, 224 pp, Quality PB, 978-1-58023-200-5 **$18.99**; HC, 978-1-58023-029-2 **$21.95**

The Way Into Jewish Prayer
By Lawrence A. Hoffman
Opens the door to 3,000 years of Jewish prayer, making available all anyone needs to feel at home in the Jewish way of communicating with God.
6 x 9, 208 pp, Quality PB, 978-1-58023-201-2 **$18.99**

Also Available: **The Way Into Jewish Prayer Teacher's Guide**
By Rabbi Jennifer Ossakow Goldsmith
8½ x 11, 42 pp, PB, 978-1-58023-345-3 **$8.99**
Visit our website to download a free copy.

The Way Into Judaism and the Environment
By Jeremy Benstein
Explores the ways in which Judaism contributes to contemporary social-environmental issues, the extent to which Judaism is part of the problem and how it can be part of the solution.
6 x 9, 288 pp, HC, 978-1-58023-268-5 **$24.99**

The Way Into *Tikkun Olam* (Repairing the World)
By Elliot N. Dorff
An accessible introduction to the Jewish concept of the individual's responsibility to care for others and repair the world.
6 x 9, 320 pp, HC, 978-1-58023-269-2 **$24.99**; 304 pp, Quality PB, 978-1-58023-328-6 **$18.99**

The Way Into Torah
By Norman J. Cohen
Helps guide in the exploration of the origins and development of Torah, explains why it should be studied and how to do it.
6 x 9, 176 pp, Quality PB, 978-1-58023-198-5 **$16.99**

The Way Into the Varieties of Jewishness
By Sylvia Barack Fishman, PhD
Explores the religious and historical understanding of what it has meant to be Jewish from ancient times to the present controversy over "Who is a Jew?"
6 x 9, 288 pp, HC, 978-1-58023-030-8 **$24.99**

Theology/Philosophy

The God Who Hates Lies: Confronting and Rethinking Jewish Tradition
By Dr. David Hartman with Charlie Buckholtz
The world's leading Modern Orthodox Jewish theologian probes the deepest questions at the heart of what it means to be a human being and a Jew.
6 x 9, 208 pp, HC, 978-1-58023-455-9 **$24.99**

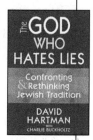

Jewish Theology in Our Time: A New Generation Explores the Foundations and Future of Jewish Belief *Edited by Rabbi Elliot J. Cosgrove, PhD; Foreword by Rabbi David J. Wolpe; Preface by Rabbi Carole B. Balin, PhD*
A powerful and challenging examination of what Jews can believe—by a new generation's most dynamic and innovative thinkers.
6 x 9, 240 pp, HC, 978-1-58023-413-9 **$24.99**

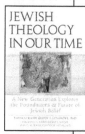

Maimonides, Spinoza and Us: Toward an Intellectually Vibrant Judaism
By Rabbi Marc D. Angel, PhD A challenging look at two great Jewish philosophers and what their thinking means to our understanding of God, truth, revelation and reason. 6 x 9, 224 pp, HC, 978-1-58023-411-5 **$24.99**

The Death of Death: Resurrection and Immortality in Jewish Thought
By Rabbi Neil Gillman, PhD 6 x 9, 336 pp, Quality PB, 978-1-58023-081-0 **$18.95**

Doing Jewish Theology: God, Torah & Israel in Modern Judaism *By Rabbi Neil Gillman, PhD*
6 x 9, 304 pp, Quality PB, 978-1-58023-439-9 **$18.99**

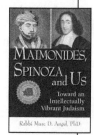

Hasidic Tales: Annotated & Explained *Translation & Annotation by Rabbi Rami Shapiro*
5½ x 8½, 240 pp, Quality PB, 978-1-893361-86-7 **$16.95***

A Heart of Many Rooms: Celebrating the Many Voices within Judaism
By Dr. David Hartman 6 x 9, 352 pp, Quality PB, 978-1-58023-156-5 **$19.95**

The Hebrew Prophets: Selections Annotated & Explained
Translation & Annotation by Rabbi Rami Shapiro; Foreword by Rabbi Zalman M. Schachter-Shalomi
5½ x 8½, 224 pp, Quality PB, 978-1-59473-037-5 **$16.99***

A Jewish Understanding of the New Testament *By Rabbi Samuel Sandmel;*
Preface by Rabbi David Sandmel 5½ x 8¼, 368 pp, Quality PB, 978-1-59473-048-1 **$19.99***

Jews and Judaism in the 21st Century: Human Responsibility, the Presence of God
and the Future of the Covenant *Edited by Rabbi Edward Feinstein; Foreword by Paula E. Hyman*
6 x 9, 192 pp, Quality PB, 978-1-58023-374-3 **$19.99**

A Living Covenant: The Innovative Spirit in Traditional Judaism
By Dr. David Hartman 6 x 9, 368 pp, Quality PB, 978-1-58023-011-7 **$25.00**

Love and Terror in the God Encounter: The Theological Legacy of Rabbi Joseph
B. Soloveitchik *By Dr. David Hartman* 6 x 9, 240 pp, Quality PB, 978-1-58023-176-3 **$19.95**

A Touch of the Sacred: A Theologian's Informal Guide to Jewish Belief
By Dr. Eugene B. Borowitz and Frances W. Schwartz
6 x 9, 256 pp, Quality PB, 978-1-58023-416-0 **$16.99**; HC, 978-1-58023-337-8 **$21.99**

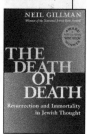

Traces of God: Seeing God in Torah, History and Everyday Life *By Rabbi Neil Gillman, PhD*
6 x 9, 240 pp, Quality PB, 978-1-58023-369-9 **$16.99**

Your Word Is Fire: The Hasidic Masters on Contemplative Prayer
Edited and translated by Rabbi Arthur Green, PhD, and Barry W. Holtz
6 x 9, 160 pp, Quality PB, 978-1-879045-25-5 **$15.95**

I Am Jewish
Personal Reflections Inspired by the Last Words of Daniel Pearl
Almost 150 Jews—both famous and not—from all walks of life, from all around the world, write about many aspects of their Judaism.
Edited by Judea and Ruth Pearl 6 x 9, 304 pp, Deluxe PB w/ flaps, 978-1-58023-259-3 **$18.99**
Download a free copy of the *I Am Jewish Teacher's Guide* at www.jewishlights.com.

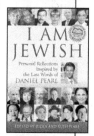

Hannah Senesh: Her Life and Diary, The First Complete Edition
By Hannah Senesh; Foreword by Marge Piercy; Preface by Eitan Senesh; Afterword by Roberta Grossman
6 x 9, 368 pp, b/w photos, Quality PB, 978-1-58023-342-2 **$19.99**

---

*A book from SkyLight Paths, Jewish Lights' sister imprint

About Jewish Lights

People of all faiths and backgrounds yearn for books that attract, engage, educate, and spiritually inspire.

Our principal goal is to stimulate thought and help all people learn about who the Jewish People are, where they come from, and what the future can be made to hold. While people of our diverse Jewish heritage are the primary audience, our books speak to people in the Christian world as well and will broaden their understanding of Judaism and the roots of their own faith.

We bring to you authors who are at the forefront of spiritual thought and experience. While each has something different to say, they all say it in a voice that you can hear.

Our books are designed to welcome you and then to engage, stimulate, and inspire. We judge our success not only by whether or not our books are beautiful and commercially successful, but by whether or not they make a difference in your life.

For your information and convenience, at the back of this book we have provided a list of other Jewish Lights books you might find interesting and useful. They cover all the categories of your life:

Bar/Bat Mitzvah	Life Cycle
Bible Study / Midrash	Meditation
Children's Books	Men's Interest
Congregation Resources	Parenting
Current Events / History	Prayer / Ritual / Sacred Practice
Ecology / Environment	Social Justice
Fiction: Mystery, Science Fiction	Spirituality
Grief / Healing	Theology / Philosophy
Holidays / Holy Days	Travel
Inspiration	Twelve Steps
Kabbalah / Mysticism / Enneagram	Women's Interest

Stuart M. Matlins, Publisher

Or phone, fax, mail or e-mail to: **JEWISH LIGHTS Publishing**
An imprint of Turner Publishing Company
4507 Charlotte Ave. • Suite 100 • Nashville, Tennessee 37209
Tel: (615) 255-2665 • www.jewishlights.com
Prices subject to change.

**For more information about each book,
visit our website at www.jewishlights.com**